British Diplomacy in Oman and Bahrain

This book marks the first comprehensive examination of contemporary British influence in Oman and Bahrain, analysing Britain's legacy since the official withdrawal from the Gulf in 1971.

Using theories of power as a framework, the book examines the development of British economic, strategic, and political influence in the two countries post-withdrawal, a topic overlooked by academics and political observers. The author argues that a divergence has developed between Britain's influence in Oman (a site of strategic power) and Bahrain (a site of economic power). Focusing on the British Government, private corporations, and individuals, topics range from the development of British Foreign Direct Investments and the presence of British oil and gas companies in the region to joint defence training exercises and the presence of Omani and Bahraini military cadets in British military academies. The book also crucially assesses the increasing influence that the Gulf states are gaining over Britain as the legacy of the Residency gradually fades.

British Diplomacy in Oman and Bahrain will be useful to students and scholars studying politics and economics in the Gulf and Britain, as well as policy analysts, international relations experts, and historians interested in the legacy of colonialism.

Joe Worthington is currently a senior policy practitioner. He completed his doctoral studies in Middle Eastern Politics in the University of Exeter's Institute of Arab and Islamic Studies whilst working as a policy consultant. His main research interests are Gulf politics, trade, and British imperialism.

Routledge Studies in Middle Eastern Politics

114 **Egyptian Foreign Relations Under al-Sisi**
External Alignments Since 2013
Christian Achrainer

115 **The New Silk Road Grand Strategy and the Maghreb**
China and North Africa
Mordechai Chaziza

116 **British Diplomacy in Oman and Bahrain**
50 Years of Change
Joe Worthington

117 **Islamic Perspectives on International Conflict Resolution**
Theological Debates on the Israel-Palestinian Peace Process
Shameer Modongal

118 **Conflict and Peace in Western Sahara**
The Role of the UN's Peacekeeping Mission (MINURSO)
Edited by János Besenyő, Joseph Huddleston and Yahia H. Zoubir

119 **Western Democracy and the AKP**
A Dialogical Analysis of Turkey's Democratic Crisis
Mehmet Celil Çelebi

120 **Islamic Identity and Development after the Ottomans**
The Arab Middle East
Ozay Mehmet

For a full list of titles in the series: https://www.routledge.com/middleeaststudies/series/SE0823

British Diplomacy in Oman and Bahrain
50 Years of Change

Joe Worthington

LONDON AND NEW YORK

First published 2023
by Routledge
4 Park Square, Milton Park, Abingdon, Oxon OX14 4RN

and by Routledge
605 Third Avenue, New York, NY 10158

Routledge is an imprint of the Taylor & Francis Group, an informa business

© 2023 Joe Worthington

The right of Joe Worthington to be identified as author of this work has been asserted in accordance with sections 77 and 78 of the Copyright, Designs and Patents Act 1988.

All rights reserved. No part of this book may be reprinted or reproduced or utilised in any form or by any electronic, mechanical, or other means, now known or hereafter invented, including photocopying and recording, or in any information storage or retrieval system, without permission in writing from the publishers.

Trademark notice: Product or corporate names may be trademarks or registered trademarks, and are used only for identification and explanation without intent to infringe.

British Library Cataloguing-in-Publication Data
A catalogue record for this book is available from the British Library

Library of Congress Cataloging-in-Publication Data
Names: Worthington, Joe (Policy advisor), author.
Title: British diplomacy in Oman and Bahrain : 50 years of change / Joe Worthington.
Description: Abingdon, Oxon ; New York, NY : Routledge, 2023. | Series: Routledge studies in Middle Eastern politics | Includes bibliographical references and index.
Identifiers: LCCN 2022023917 (print) | LCCN 2022023918 (ebook) | ISBN 9781032295268 (hardback) | ISBN 9781032295282 (paperback) | ISBN 9781003302001 (ebook)
Subjects: LCSH: Great Britain—Foreign relations—Oman. | Oman—Foreign relations—Great Britain. | Great Britain—Foreign relations—Bahrain. | Bahrain—Foreign relations—Great Britain.
Classification: LCC DA47.9.O43 W67 2023 (print) | LCC DA47.9.O43 (ebook) | DDC 327.41053—dc23/eng/20220909
LC record available at https://lccn.loc.gov/2022023917
LC ebook record available at https://lccn.loc.gov/2022023918

ISBN: 978-1-032-29526-8 (hbk)
ISBN: 978-1-032-29528-2 (pbk)
ISBN: 978-1-003-30200-1 (ebk)

DOI: 10.4324/9781003302001

Typeset in Times New Roman
by codeMantra

Contents

List of tables   xi
Acknowledgements   xiii
List of abbreviations   xv

1 Introduction   1
   1.1 Historiography – legacy and power in Britain's bilateral relations with Oman and Bahrain 1
      1.1.1 Britain's historic experience in Oman 2
      1.1.2 Establishing the foundations of Britain's contemporary influence in Oman 5
      1.1.3 Britain's historic experience in Bahrain 7
   1.2 Theory: Themes in British power and influence 8
      1.2.1 What is soft power? 9
      1.2.2 Bases of power 9
      1.2.3 Power used by states 10
      1.2.4 Soft power through influence 11
      1.2.5 Power as capability 12
      1.2.6 Power as balance 12
      1.2.7 Power as security 12
      1.2.8 Smart power 13

2 The foundations of British power in Oman: past and present   18
   2.1 British involvement in the Dhofar War 18
      2.1.1 Turning the tide of the war 21
      2.1.2 Beginning of the end of the rebellion 22
      2.1.3 Effect of Dhofar on British influence in Oman 23
   2.2 The Arab Spring in Oman and its impact on Britain's influence 24
      2.2.1 Protests after the Arab Spring in Oman 25
      2.2.2 Effect of Oman's protests on Anglo-Omani relations 25

PART I
Strategic power, defence and security · 29

3 Britain's strategic engagement with Oman and the development of a new power dynamic · 31
  3.1 Introduction 31
    3.1.1 Legacy in action 33
  3.2 How has Britain utilised its privileged strategic education capabilities to secure influence in Oman? 34
    3.2.1 Oman's presence in British military academies 36
    3.2.2 Oman's wider security educational presence 39
  3.3 How do joint security exercises contribute to the development of the UK–Omani relationship? 41
    3.3.1 Shared defence exercises in Oman 43
  3.4 How does the loan service personnel relationship influence British power in Oman? 45
    3.4.1 Continued reliance on British expertise 47
    3.4.2 Loan service personnel and British arms sales 50
    3.4.3 A relationship shift 52
  3.5 What influence do arms sales to Oman have on Britain's influence? 52
    3.5.1 Defence contracts after the end of hegemony 54
    3.5.2 Continued preference to buy British 56
  3.6 Britain's strategic influence in Oman and future engagement with the Sultanate 57
    3.6.1 Britain's power transition in Oman 58
    3.6.2 A relationship built on its legacy 59
  3.7 What impact will the succession from Qaboos to Haitham have on Britain's strategic influence in Oman? 61
  3.8 Policy implications arising from Britain's strategic influence in Oman 62

4 Britain's shifting strategic power in Bahrain since 1971 · 70
  4.1 Introduction 70
    4.1.1 A continued power legacy or loss of influence? 71
  4.2 How have Britain's military and security education capabilities affected influence in Bahrain? 71
    4.2.1 The effects of political divisions in Britain 73
    4.2.2 British commitment and re-engagement in Bahrain 75
    4.2.3 Education as an attempt to retain influence 78
  4.3 To what extent does bilateral military cooperation between Britain and Bahrain contribute to the power discourse? 81
    4.3.1 How should Bahraini requests for British assistance be understood in terms of power? 82

4.3.2 The financial element of UK–Bahraini strategic cooperation 86
4.3.3 Limitations of bilateral cooperation 88
4.3.4 Bahrain's perception of risk and the resulting degree of cooperation with Britain 90
4.4 *How have British arms sales contributed to the retention of British power in Bahrain?* 91
4.4.1 An emerging British dependence on arms sales to Bahrain? 94
4.4.2 Convergence between defence economics and strategic priorities 95
4.5 *How do British public relations companies employed by Bahrain's Government affect Britain's power in the Kingdom?* 97
4.5.1 The financial aspect of advising 98
4.6 *Shifting power balances and the future of UK–Bahraini strategic affairs* 99
4.6.1 The internationalisation of Britain's security presence in Bahrain 100
4.6.2 A contemporary relationship and a power shift 102
4.6.3 A model for future international cooperation 103

PART II
Trade and the power of money 111

5 Omani prosperity and the British power dimension 113
5.1 Introduction 113
5.1.1 Economic diversification in Oman and the British connection 114
5.2 *Arms for influence. What impact does export financing have on British power in Oman?* 116
5.2.1 The British commitment to arming Oman 117
5.2.2 British export financing and the resulting influence 119
5.2.3 The power dimension to export finance 121
5.3 *What impact does the legacy of British exclusivity have on Oman's oil and gas sector?* 122
5.3.1 The start of Omani nationalisation 123
5.3.2 The British role in Oman's energy market development 126
5.3.3 Competition to Britain's influence in Oman's energy markets 127
5.4 *How has the Omani diversification agenda affected Britain's economic influence?* 129
5.4.1 Britain's necessary shift from hard to soft power 129
5.4.2 Malaysian involvement in Omani diversification 130
5.4.3 Sectoral diversification and the British footprint 131

viii   Contents

    5.5 The future development of economic bilateralism
        and the role of FDI 132
        5.5.1 The multi-faceted nature of bilateral business
            representation 133
        5.5.2 The British Business Forum 134
        5.5.3 Representation of British interests in Oman 135
        5.5.4 The impact of British FDI into Oman on the power
            dynamics 136
        5.5.5 FDI as one element of the wider bilateral relationship 138
        5.5.6 External factors affecting Britain's economic influence 139
        5.5.7 Domestic factors affecting Britain's economic influence 140
    5.6 The power of British money in Oman 141
        5.6.1 Implications of the continued British economic
            influence in Oman 143

**6 The development of UK–Bahraini economic influence since
withdrawal**   **150**
    6.1 Introduction 150
    6.2 British economic influence in the years after withdrawal 151
        6.2.1 Bilateralism and a shift in the relationship 152
    6.3 The arms trade since withdrawal 154
        6.3.1 The power dimension of arms sales 155
        6.3.2 The impact of marketing British arms to Bahraini
            decision makers 156
        6.3.3 Competition to Britain's retained hegemony 157
        6.3.4 The emergence of a competitive arms sales process 159
        6.3.5 British attempts to retain influence in Bahrain 161
        6.3.6 Re-engagement and arms sales since withdrawal 162
    6.4 British power retention within Bahrain's economic
        diversification 163
        6.4.1 Britain and Bahrain's oil and gas industry 164
        6.4.2 Britain's contribution to Bahraini diversification 165
        6.4.3 Economic shifts in Bahrain 167
    6.5 Why has Britain remained an influential partner in
        financial market cooperation with Bahrain? 167
        6.5.1 Islamic finance cooperation 168
        6.5.2 British assistance with Bahrain's financial modernisation 170
        6.5.3 Financial education and the power of learning 172
    6.6 Bahraini financial reforms and the resulting
        British influence 174
        6.6.1 British governmental support for reforms 175
        6.6.2 Limitations of British assistance 177
        6.6.3 Public–private cooperation 178
        6.6.4 Governmental funding for Bahraini development 179
    6.7 An economic legacy under strain? 181
        6.7.1 The relevance of this research – UK–Bahraini economics 183

7 British power in review 191
  7.1 *Historical foundations 191*
  7.2 *Contributing factors to the power legacy 193*
  7.3 *Legacy of arms sales 196*
  7.4 *Convergence of Britain's strategic and economic priorities 198*
  7.5 *Economic priorities 200*
  7.6 *British re-engagement in the Gulf 203*
  7.7 *The commercialisation of influence and privatisation of bilateral affairs 204*
  7.8 *What effect will the death of Sultan Qaboos have on British influence in Oman? 207*
  7.9 *Policy implications of this research and future research opportunities 208*
     7.9.1 Implications of cross-governmental working on the British position in the Gulf 209

Index 213

Tables

3.1	Number of Omanis seconded to Sandhurst, 2005–06 to 2015–16	37
3.2	Number of Omanis seconded to RAF College Cranwell, 2005–06 to 2015–16	37
3.3	Number of Omanis seconded to Britannia Royal Naval College, 2005–06 to 2015–16	37
3.4	Total number of foreign cadets seconded to the UK, 2012–16	38
4.1	Number of Bahrainis seconded to Sandhurst, 2005–06 to 2016–16	79
4.2	Number of Bahrainis seconded to Britannia Royal Naval College, 2005–06 to 2015–16	79
4.3	Number of Bahrainis seconded to RAF Cranwell, 2005–06 to 2015–16	79
4.4	Number of approved arms export licences from the UK to Bahrain	94
5.1	Oil production and exports data between 1967 and 2017	125
5.2	The value of foreign direct investments into Oman, 2012–16	137
6.1	International financial commitments made to Bahrain, 1981–82	176

Acknowledgements

The research and writing of this thesis has been equally the most challenging and enjoyable project in my life so far, and there are many who have contributed along this journey that I would like to thank.

I wish to thank Professors Marc Valeri at the University of Exeter, who first ignited my passion for Oman, and Gareth Stansfield and Timothy Insoll, who shared with me their knowledge of the Gulf and supported my deep dive into this fascinating part of the world.

I owe a special debt of gratitude to Maggie Jeans OBE, who shared with me her sage advice on life in Oman and gave me much-needed encouragement, opened her home and life in Muscat to me on several occasions, and introduced me to people across all areas of Omani society.

Finally, I want to thank my grandma, Linda, for her emotional support, understanding, and her listening ear throughout the research and writing of this book.

Abbreviations

AIT	Army Information Team
BAPCO	Bahrain Petroleum Company
BBF	British Business Forum (Oman)
BDF	Bahrain Defence Force
BIDEC	Bahrain International Defence Exhibition and Conference
CSOAF	Commander of the Sultan of Oman's Armed Forces
CSSF	Conflict, Stability and Security Fund (FCO)
CTF	Combined Task Force
DAF	Defence Assistance Fund
DFID	Department for International Development
DIPTEL	Diplomatic Telegram
DIT	Department for International Trade
DMAF	Defence Military Assistance Fund
DSO	Defence and Security Organisation
ECGD	Export Credits Guarantee Department
EIC	East India Company
FCO	Foreign and Commonwealth Office
FDI	Foreign Direct Investment
GCC	Gulf Cooperation Council
GCHQ	Government Communications Headquarters
GDP	Gross Domestic Product
HMG	His/Her Majesty's Government
HMS	His/Her Majesty's Ship
HOC	House of Commons
HOL	House of Lords
IR	International Relations
ISS	Internal Security Service
LSP	Loan Service Personnel
MOD	Ministry of Defence
NATO	North Atlantic Treaty Organisation
NCO	Non-Commissioned Officer
NI-CO	Northern Ireland Cooperation Overseas

NSF	Naval Support Facility
OBFA	Omani British Friendship Association
OOCEP	Oman Oil Company Exploration and Production
PDO	Petroleum Development Oman
PM	Prime Minister
PR	Public Relations
PSNI	Police Service of Northern Ireland
RAF	Royal Air Force (UK)
RAFO	Royal Airforce of Oman
RD	Regional Directorate
RMA	Royal Military Academy
RMTT	Royal Marines Training Team
RNC	Royal Naval College
ROP	Royal Oman Police
SAF	Sultan's Armed Forces
SAS	Special Air Service (UK)
SIPRI	Stockholm International Peace Research Institute
SOAF	Sultan of Oman's Armed Forces
SOLF	Sultan of Oman's Land Forces
SON	Sultan of Oman's Navy
SWF	Sovereign Wealth Fund
TOS	Trucial Oman Scouts
UAE	United Arab Emirates
UK	United Kingdom of Great Britain and Northern Ireland
UKEF	United Kingdom Export Finance
UKTI	United Kingdom Trade and Investment
US	United States of America

1 Introduction

1.1 Historiography – legacy and power in Britain's bilateral relations with Oman and Bahrain

This study explores a topic that has been largely overlooked by academics studying both Arabian Gulf politics and postcolonialism – the legacy power that arises from the historic British position in the Gulf, transitioning power, and the influence that arises from this. The study aims to assess the types of power that Britain[1] holds in Oman and Bahrain, the transition from hard to softer types of power because of the *official* political, strategic, and economic withdrawal from the region in the 1970s, and the contributing factors to the retained influence. In this research, rooted in a combination of political history, foreign policy analysis, and theory, three major statements will be examined. Firstly, what impact the dissolution of the Persian Gulf Residency has had on British economic and strategic influence in Oman and Bahrain, secondly, how British power in the two states has developed since 1971 as a result of this major diplomatic shift, and thirdly, why Britain's contemporary relations with Oman and Bahrain have diverged despite both being established with similar hard power foundations.

The legacy of British imperialism and its effects on global politics has long attracted the attention of scholars and analysts, but the Gulf has largely remained overlooked in this context. After 1971, when Harold Wilson's desire to withdraw the British presence from East of the Suez came to fruition and the *official* British footprint was withdrawn, the bureaucratic levers that had secured the British influence in the Gulf states since 1820 also became weaker. After withdrawal, bilateral relationships that had depended on treaties for so long to secure the British hegemony and influence over local decision-making became increasingly reliant on the power legacy that had developed across the region. The local rulers in Oman and Bahrain had unrestricted opportunities to choose which states to cooperate with on economic and strategic affairs, necessitating changes in the methods used by both the British Government and private sector companies to secure their influence in light of unprecedented international competition. The extent to which Britain was able to retain power in Oman and Bahrain has become

DOI: 10.4324/9781003302001-1

conditional on the willingness of the local rulers to uphold the various levels of cooperation since withdrawal and their individual attraction to the skills and capabilities offered by Britain. Whether in relation to large-scale joint military programmes in Oman and not Bahrain, BAE Systems remaining the preferred supplier to the Omani military but not Bahrain, or the strong relations between the City of London and Bahrain's Islamic banks, the relational variations are indicative of power shifts that have occurred.

British officials who have worked in the Gulf as diplomats, in military posts, or in trade representative organisations, and representatives of British private companies have never been fully aware of their ability to enhance the post-withdrawal British influence in Gulf affairs by utilising the power that they hold. Britons in Oman have retained influence because of the expert power that they are able to impart upon locals, especially within the oil and gas sectors, but in Bahrain, Americans have largely dominated the sphere of expertise. Nonetheless, governmental policymakers and decision makers in Britain have emerged as important contributors to British power in the Gulf, responsible for courting the local rulers in Oman and Bahrain to entice them to continue cooperating closely with Britain. This study assesses power capabilities that are perhaps unknown to the wielders of this influence but correlates with an aspect of British foreign policy that is becoming increasingly important to successive governments, particularly Conservative-led – soft power policy making and smart power implementation. The focus of this study is largely on the activities of major multi-national British corporations and bilateral government initiatives that indicate the strength of British power in both Gulf states, as these are the main wielders of diplomatic influence, whilst recognising that smaller-scale commercial relationships do exist and also affect the transition of British power in Oman and Bahrain.

1.1.1 Britain's historic experience in Oman

Existing literature in relation to the British historic influence in Oman concentrates largely on the formal development of the Sultanate and the maintenance of influence in the state. As Oman was neither a colony nor an official protectorate, it is perhaps surprising that the British and British–Indian Governments put so much effort into building the structures of a functioning state on behalf of subsequent Sultans. Britain's experience in Oman before withdrawal in 1971 was underpinned by a joint strategic and economic approach, both of which contributed to the securing of Britain as the unrivalled hegemonic power in the Sultanate for over 150 years. This historic influence was largely manifested through hard power means, specifically through the use of military treaties that restricted which states Oman could deal with and the permission of British companies to develop and maintain control over the economic levers of the state. After 1970, when Sultan Qaboos acceded to the Omani throne and began to exert a level of independence from Britain that was always guaranteed but never exercised by previous rulers, British power gradually shifted to a softer style of influence. The British Government increasingly became reliant on Qaboos' willingness to continue Oman's cooperation with Britain, courting the Sultan with favourable export financing and advanced military training cooperation.

The authority text on UK–Omani relations, albeit largely focusing on the 320 years until the accession of Qaboos to the throne, has been written by Robert Alston and Stuart Laing, both of whom are former British Ambassadors to Oman – *Unshook till the End of Time: A History of Relations between Britain & Oman 1650–1970*. Their book seemingly compares Oman's desires for the Gulf and the wider Indian Ocean in the 18th and early 19th centuries as similar to those of the British several decades later; to exert influence over the region and expand Omani culture and rule. The title of the book offers an insight into the recurring theme, that of a bilateral relationship between Britain and Oman that has remained strong. The Omani experience in the Gulf is influenced by the Anglo-French struggle for control in the Gulf, the Ottoman and Saudi threats, and the eventual hegemony that Britain was able to develop in Oman despite the Sultanate never officially becoming a Residency protectorate.[2]

Jeremy Jones and Nicholas Ridout, in *Oman, Culture and Diplomacy*, recognised that Britain's first intervention into Omani affairs came in 1820 to end the slave trade which was rife in the Sultanate, much like in neighbouring Trucial states. The two historians also discussed the naval influence that Britain had in Omani affairs, intercepting slave trips travelling between Oman and its semi-autonomous Zanzibar territory. Trying to get Sultan Sayyid to abolish slavery divided British diplomats in the Indian Ocean, with Captain Fairfax Moresby pushing for abolition, but the British Governor of Mauritius, Sir Robert Townsend Farquhar, arguing that this violated the sovereignty and independence of Oman.[3] This book also documents the important influential British individuals who were key in securing the unrivalled British influence in Oman before withdrawal.

In *Trade and Empire in Muscat and Zanzibar: Roots of British Domination*, M. Reda Bhacker dissected the Franco–Omani relationship, which arguably prevented Britain from signing exclusivity agreements with Omani Sultans similar to those implemented in neighbouring Gulf states, and both Britain and France agreed to uphold Omani independence through the *Franco-British Declaration of 1862*. This book suggests that in Oman, as a result of the individual voluntary defence agreements signed between Omani Sultans and the British–Indian Government, Sultans had to request military assistance from Britain, but no Sultans until Sa'id in the second half of the 20th century did request this assistance.[4] The research in this text highlights how British trade with the Gulf was predicated on the strength of the bilateral relationship with Oman, possibly offering the foundations of an explanation for why the post-withdrawal trade relationship with Oman was so strong. It is notable from this book that no literature suggests the Sultans ever requested military assistance from France, which they were entitled to do as a result of the Franco-British Declaration.

Although few analysts have assessed the British impact on the formation of the contemporary Omani state structure, Joseph A. Kechichian, in *Oman and the World: The Emergence of an Independent Foreign Policy*, argued that the British division of power between mainland Oman and Zanzibar caused more issues in the future than it resolved.[5] Whether this is the case or not is open to dispute, but Kechichian does argue that it strengthened and secured the power of future Sultans in Muscat and weakened Oman's hold over Zanzibar. As one of few examples, this book also links the rule of Sultan Qaboos to the history of his country. He explains that Qaboos has 'adopted foreign policy measures that [are] pragmatic and noticeably consistent.'[6] The internal tribal divisions within Oman are highlighted as one of the most important determinants of Oman's foreign policy, particularly as a result of the Ibadi Imam claiming independence from Oman and the resulting Dhofar War. This links back to the British experience in Oman shortly before and after 1971 and is demonstrable of the British military involvement in Oman. An aspect of UK–Omani relations that has received a limited amount of focus amongst analysts is the British involvement in the Dhofar War, and historic direct involvement in wider military relations in the Sultanate.

More research exists on the influence of British expatriates on domestic Omani affairs, particularly at the intersection between economics and security. John Townsend undertook the first comprehensive study on British–Omani military relations in the immediate years after withdrawal in his book *Oman: The Making of the Modern State*. In this book, written in 1976 by a former economic advisor to Sultan Sa'id and published shortly after British withdrawal from the Sultanate, Townsend highlights the important and prestigious role held by British expatriates working in Oman, advising both Sultans Sa'id and Qaboos on military affairs, and holding governmental positions that contributed to the development of a peaceful Omani state. Townsend detailed how Sa'id had:

> a Personal Adviser (British) and a Military Secretary (British). He appointed a Development Secretary in 1958, but this man's salary was paid by the British Government, as was the cost of the staff of the Development Department set up at the time. When oil revenues began in 1967, he appointed an expatriate Secretary for Financial Affairs and Secretary for Petroleum Affairs, both British.[7]

Accurately, Townsend detailed the special interest that Qaboos had in military issues and the continued reliance on Britain for security.

J.E. Peterson, in *Oman in the Twentieth Century, Political Foundations of an Emerging State*, similarly wrote that Sultan Sa'id realised that he was reliant on British military officers, and although he wanted to develop his own independent army, he knew from an early stage that he had to embrace the assistance offered to him by Britain.[8] Peterson's book also highlights the important positions of power held by British expatriates, and as it was published in 1978, the study was based on primary interviews and accounts of the British advisors profiled throughout. The study discusses the first Commandant of the Muscat Levy Corps, Captain McCarthy, who tried to 'Arabise' the army that he established but was unsuccessful in doing so because few Omanis were skilled enough to fill vacant positions in the army; British and British–Indian soldiers were recruited to fill these vacancies.[9] Evidence of the British influence on Omani military affairs is present throughout this text and Britain and Oman have had historically close military ties that, according to analysts, continued largely unabated after withdrawal in 1971.

John Beasant, in *Oman: The True-Life Drama and Intrigue of an Arab State*, developed on this notion of Omani reliance on British military officers both prior to and after 1971, albeit from a very critical perspective on the British expatriates. He wrote about how Jim McClean, Sultan Sa'id's Private Secretary and a former British Naval Officer, chose to follow his employer into exile when Qaboos took power. Beasant also detailed Qaboos' continued reliance on British officers, which was evident in his appointment of a British soldier to redesign the Omani flag upon his accession to the throne. When Qaboos rose to power, his close confidant, British expatriate Timothy Landon, was recruited in an intelligence position, and David Bayley, another former British Army officer, was employed as a private Defence Resource Advisor.[10] The book focuses on the palace coup that brought Qaboos to power in 1970, with Beasant arguing that Britons were crucial for its planning and success.

1.1.2 Establishing the foundations of Britain's contemporary influence in Oman

In *Oman: Politics and Development*, Ian Skeet analysed the work of Sultan Qaboos' team of advisors, most of whom were British, despite his repeated attempts to 'Omanise' his close team in the early years of his reign. Skeet detailed how, in 1973, Qaboos relied heavily on his close advisory team to bring plans for his state into fruition, comprising General Creasey as Commander of the Sultan's Armed Forces, John Townsend as Economic Advisor, Colonel Dennison in the role of Director of Intelligence, Felix D'Silva (a British-trained Sri Lankan national) as Commissioner of Police, and British Colonel Timothy Landon as Qaboos' Private Secretary.[11] The continued presence of British advisors who remained after British withdrawal suggests that Britain was a trusted and reliable partner in Oman, and that Qaboos did not want to make too many changes to a team that had served Oman so effectively. In Skeet's book, there is evidence that Qaboos wanted to demonstrate his independence and he was not afraid to reject and refuse the advice given to him by his advisors, most of whom were now in his private employ as opposed to on secondment from HMG in London, as was the case before 1971.

However, Calvin Allen and W. Lynn Rigsbee, in *Oman Under Qaboos: From Coup to Constitution, 1970–1996*, suggests that upon coming to power, Qaboos was eager to diversify his advisory team, and that British expatriates did not, in fact, have a monopoly on advice, which directly contradicts most research on this topic. Allen and Rigsbee listed the closest advisors to Qaboos, including Colonel Tim Landon, a Briton, alongside Robert Anderson, an American, Libyans named Omer Barouni and Yahya Omar, and a Saudi national named Ghassan Shakir, amongst other non-British expatriates.[12] This book brings the role of Qaboos into the relatively modern era and it claims that Qaboos remained grateful to the British for supporting his coup, demonstrable by the favourable position that Britons continued to hold in Oman until recently.

Jeremy Jones is one of a small number of academics to focus on the modern Omani state. In *Oman's Quiet Diplomacy*, he focuses on the contemporary status of Oman on the international stage, as a neutral actor trying to bring together states that have historically been enemies. Crucially for this research, the effect of Britain's withdrawal from the Gulf is considered to be one of the key reasons for Oman's newfound neutral diplomacy. Jones argues that 'when Britain left the Gulf there was a need to look elsewhere for security guarantees,'[13] evidence of the pragmatism of Oman since the 1970s. Although this research does not specifically focus on Britain's influence, it does document the extent to which Oman has diverged from the position when Britain withdrew and the loss of Britain's ability to directly influence domestic and international Omani policies.

Perhaps the most indicative research on how the Omani state has developed in the contemporary era, approached from a wide-ranging political, economic, and societal perspective, has been undertaken by Marc Valeri in his book *Oman: Politics and Society in the Qaboos State*. Valeri balances the contemporary power of Sultan Qaboos with the historic position that secured his family's power, primarily focusing on Britain's influence in the state. Where this book particularly shines is in its focus on the future of Oman, a state with a young population that is eager for change, evident through protests and social movements. This is arguably evidence of a shift away from the British presence that dominated Omani politics and society for centuries and an important study for understanding how Oman has developed since British withdrawal. Valeri's book also links back to the historic protection that was offered to Oman by the British and the opposition by France to this,[14] an issue that dictated Britain's relations with the Sultanate until withdrawal.

There has been a small but informative supply of published literature relating to the British experience in Oman. The literature that does exist offers, to differing extents, an important summation and analysis of

Britain's historic relations with Oman. Most literature does not, however, bring UK–Omani relations to the present day, nor does it contextualise the historic British influence with the contemporary experience or attempt to understand the fundamentals of the relationship using political theories as a basis.

1.1.3 Britain's historic experience in Bahrain

For a significant amount of the 20th century, Bahrain was at the centre of the British Gulf, and thus the foundations were laid for a strong future relationship. As with much of the literature focusing on the history of the region, James Onley has undertaken the most comprehensive research on historic UK–Bahraini relations. In *The Arabian Frontier*, he detailed how Britain and India, originally through the East India Company, employed a local agent in the state between 1819 and 1900. These agents were responsible for organising EIC trade with Bahraini tribes, gathering intelligence on local affairs, sending news back to the Governments of Bombay and Bengal, and eventually coordinating relations between the Residency in Bushire and the local rulers of Bahrain.[15] Bahrain, with Manama at its centre, was the most developed and thus perhaps also the most important of the Persian Gulf states during Britain's tenure in the region. The first schools were built in Manama, oil was first extracted in Bahrain, and under Sir Charles Belgrave, Bahrain's security and customs infrastructure developed more than in any of the other Gulf states.

Nelida Fuccaro, in *Histories of Cities and State in the Persian Gulf: Manama Since 1800*, assesses the British creation of a functioning bureaucracy and civil service in Bahrain from 1919. A municipality was established in Manama, the Bahraini capital, under the Government of British India, which held dual responsibilities as the centre of the Bahraini state and the municipal centre of the capital city. Fuccaro also argues that the municipal council, which was overseen by British Agents and Residents, created alliances between the rulers of the state and merchants who traded through Manama port.[16] This study suggests that British diplomats in Bahrain were genuinely interested in trying to develop the state, albeit based on a British model, and wanted to enhance age-old ruler-merchant communications. The development of a functioning bureaucratic system, with the ruling Al Khalifa family at its heart, was also potentially an attempt by the British to secure the power and authority of Bahrain's Sunni rulers because it created a system of accountability for the largely Shia merchant families and withheld some of the power that they once had when they oversaw the governance of lands and fisheries through former Bahraini fiefdoms.

In *Gulf Security Policy after the Arab Spring: Considering Changing Security Dynamics*, Andreas Krieg wrote that with British support since the early 20th century, the ruling Al Khalifa family has been able to successfully monopolise control of the domestic political and economic landscape across Bahrain, marginalising many Shia communities.[17] Several pieces of literature suggest that through the political and administrative systems developed by British diplomats, the ruling Sunni Al Khalifa family has become comparatively more powerful and wealthy than they were before British intervention.

The most significant studies on UK–Bahraini relations focus on the British involvement in the development of the state's domestic security infrastructure. In the Bahrain chapter of Miriam Joyce's *Ruling Shaikhs and Her Majesty's Government: 1960–1969*, Joyce analyses the strong and close relations between HMG in London and the ruling shaikhs of Bahrain since the reign of the first Emir, Shaikh Isa. This chapter suggests that Shaikh Isa greatly respected the British and was grateful for the expertise that they brought to Bahrain, particularly their ability to quell demonstrations by disillusioned locals since the 1956 demonstrations. Joyce wrote that 'since the demonstrations that had erupted in 1956, Bahrain had remained peaceful. Nevertheless, the police force had been strengthened and a competent special branch established under the direction of a British Commandant.'[18] Joyce also remarked that the king of Jordan offered Isa several Jordanian teachers and police officers, but he initially refused because he only wanted British police officers whom he trusted to protect his state.[19] Joyce highlights the important influence that British individuals had on the domestic affairs of Bahrain. In *Bahrain's Uprising*, Zoe Holman also highlighted the close UK–Bahraini security relationship, claiming that it was Colonel Ian Henderson, a British former manager of the Bahraini General Directorate for State Security Investigations who safeguarded Bahraini security. Holman's research, similar to findings by James Onley and Jeffrey Macris, concluded that it was the Treaty of Friendship signed between Britain and Bahrain that allowed this strong security relationship to develop.[20]

1.2 Theory: Themes in British power and influence

Power is a wide-ranging realist theory that is both complex and multifaceted, but there are several elements that are useful for understanding Britain's legacy in the Gulf. There is widespread disagreement about what exactly 'power' is, the impact and influence that different variations of power have on relations between states, the ways to measure the extent of power held by states, and the methods that can be used to interpret power.

In 1950, Harold Lasswell and Abraham Kaplan described the concept of power as 'the most fundamental in the whole of political science'[21] and the innate disagreements between analysts on how to define power has been best surmised by Robert Dahl and Bruce Stinebrickner who concluded that 'in neither ordinary language nor political analysis is there agreement on the definition and usage of what might be called 'influence terms.'[22] In 1960, Hans Morgenthau advocated that all aspects of politics are determined by a struggle for power and a desire to become the most powerful politician or

Introduction 9

state.²³ Similarly, Kenneth Waltz defined his idea of power as depending on *all* of the following: 'size of population and territory, resource endowment, economic capability, military strength, political stability and competence.'²⁴ Power has traditionally been approached from a *hard* perspective, neglecting the personal and voluntary nature of influence. This is why Nye's soft power is so significant.

1.2.1 What is soft power?

The foundations of this study are framed by Joseph Nye's original theory of *Soft Power*, in which he attempted to explain how states try to gain influence in other states without resorting to force or coercion. To understand soft power, it is necessary to assess how this type of power fits into the wider power discourse. The soft vs hard debate fits into a wider analysis of power, which Nye defines as being divided between 'threats of coercion ('sticks'), inducements and payments ('carrots'), and attraction that makes others want what you want.'²⁵ Power is a type of currency used by states to achieve their aims within the international system. Soft power is the more contemporary manifestation of power, emerging in a world that is increasingly averse to military interventions and enforced action. As the global economy becomes increasingly inter-connected, and as states are having to compete more to preserve their influence, enacting change without the use of overt force has become a key tenet of foreign policy. The British Government is also responsible for advancing British soft power tools to develop power abroad, including through the annual £60 million GREAT campaign fund,²⁶ operational in 144 countries, trying to ensure that Britain remains at the forefront of the minds of decision makers, is able to attract internal investment, and to boost exports.

Soft power is a constructivist theory of international relations predicated on 'the ability to get what you want through attraction rather than coercion or payments. ... the attraction of a country's culture, political ideals and policies.'²⁷ Soft power can be understood as the result of attraction by one state to the actions and beliefs of another.

Building upon Nye's theory, David Kearn argued that soft power can be successful 'if a state shares the underlying interests or goals of a leading state but its preferences or strategies for achieving vital goals are ambivalent, or underdeveloped.'²⁸ A strong soft power state can provide a positive example that policy makers in other states choose to adopt in the hope that it will be successful in their own states.²⁹

1.2.2 Bases of power

An agreed aspect of power in IR is that there are several bases on which state power is established. The first base of power is believed to be 'referent power' or the ability of an individual or country to attract others to do as they desire and achieve particular outcomes. John French and Bertram Raven argued that if O is a person toward whom P is highly attracted, then P will have a desire to become closely associated with O, and if O is an attractive group, P will have a feeling of a desire to join.[30] Kenneth Waltz argued that 'the more productive and the more technologically advanced countries have more ways of influencing international outcomes than do the laggards'[31] and Britain would fall into the category of the world's most advanced countries.

Similarly, proponents of 'expert power' consider actions by individuals and states in the international system the result of attraction to the expertise and skills offered by others. Just as Britain would be considered a technologically attractive country (particularly in the area of military technology), Britain could be considered the expert within the bilateral relationships with the Gulf states. Donelson Forsyth claimed that the perception of expertise, whether actual or not, awards power to that individual or group and thus enhances their power base.[32] On the international level, the perception that the British Government and British private companies possess the economic and strategic expertise needed within the Gulf states, provides Britain with an element of attractive power on the world stage.

The third base of power, referred to as 'reward power,' is dependent on rewarding actions as opposed to relying on decision makers to choose to do something because of attraction. Proponents of this theory suggest that the ability of the power wielder to confer rewards on another individual or group is important in the power dynamic; if there are tangible rewards from an action, it is likely that the action will be undertaken.

The final type of power, 'coercive power,' is the closest representation of hard power and the purest example of realist power analysis. Coercive power is predicated on the desire for rewards by political actors, such as states and rulers, and the threat to withhold or withdraw these benefits by the power holder. Power in this case is the ability to exercise military or economic domination over others, even if the holder of this power is not aware that they have the power to utilise.

1.2.3 Power used by states

The basic differentiating factors in the understanding of power are power as *actions* and power as the *result* of actions. In Classical Realism, Morgenthau claims that powerful states attempt to maximise their power in relation to other states, with the ultimate result being a so-called 'balance of power.' The power resources, or the capabilities that states have to utilise their power for their own benefit, could then be used to assess the power and influence that a state had within the international community.[33]

From the perspective of foreign policy, the realist theory of politics equates sensible foreign policy to the minimisation of risks (such as conflict), and the maximisation of benefits to the foreign policy actor.[34] Conversely, proponents of neorealism claim that states essentially seek self-preservation and security over everything else.

A third concept, referred to as 'capability,' is the resources that a state has in relation to other states. The natural resources available, national wealth, population, technological, and military might each individually contribute to the capability of states, with more powerful states often being the ones that have a greater capability. This constant push to develop greater capability ultimately leads to a power struggle between states. State Y does what a more powerful state X wants it to do partly because of the physical security benefits that will arise from this action (such as Oman agreeing to cooperate in military training), but also because of the appearance that state Y will gain as a trusted partner of state X, and thus the resulting reputational benefits that state Y will gain within the bilateral relationship.

1.2.4 Soft power through influence

One of the most important tenets of the theory of power is that of 'power as influence,' or the ability of a state or international actor to exert influence upon other states. Viotti and Kauppi defined power as influence as

> the means by which a state or other actor wields or can assert actual or potential influence or coercion relative to other states and non-state actors because of the political, geographic, economic and financial, technological, military, social, cultural, or other capabilities it possesses.[35]

Rather than overt power forced upon another state, power as influence is the covert power that a state enjoys in another.

The various forms of power that contribute to a state's influence fall into several categories: military, which includes physical warfare, arms sales, defence cooperation, security bases, and defence pacts; economics, through trade relationships, financial cooperation, and the impact of national companies in the state; and symbolism, including educational and cultural influence,[36] which could be defined as 'diplomatic capital.'[37] According to Nye, the military aspect of power is diminishing in favour of economics. Norman Angell, in his book *The Great Illusion*, attested to the importance of economic interdependence as 'the real guarantor of the good behaviour of one state to another.'[38]

There is a more recent addition to the study of influential power in IR, referred to as *Relational Power*. This approach to power contends that states prefer to continue relationships as they are rather than try to force change that could jeopardise and end the relationship.

1.2.5 Power as capability

Power as capability is closely aligned with the theory of hard power, as the theory focuses on the volume of weapons and military assets available to a state, the measurable assets available for sale and export, and the sought-after resources produced in a state. American diplomat Charles Freeman, Jr. described *power as capability* as the capacity to direct the decisions and actions of others, deriving from the strength and will of a state, and from the utilisation of resources to achieve capabilities. Statecraft in the international system seeks to utilise the mass of resources available and attractiveness of this power to gain strength.[39]

The means that a state can generate when required would generally be considered as armaments, troop numbers, objects to export, or otherwise, and Waltz argues that all states are self-reliant and must use their capabilities to 'enhance their own power within the international system.' According to Waltz, power can also arise from the multi-polar balancing effect of the international system. States adapt their foreign and military strategies to appeal to partners and change their behaviour to attract allies; states are willing to ally with any other state to preserve their own power; competition between superpowers will force weaker states to choose partners.[40]

1.2.6 Power as balance

John Mearsheimer argued that the international system is predicated on the balance of power between states and the main aim of individual states is to maximise power, even if this is at the expense of other states. As a so-called offensive realist, Mearsheimer, like Morgenthau, believes that power is the currency of great powers. He claimed that great powers actively pursue power-building activities when interacting with other states, establishing a hegemony where possible, and utilising this power to ensure their own survival within an unpredictable international system. Mearsheimer inferred that 'states soon realise that the most efficient way to guarantee survival … is to maximise their relative power with the ultimate aim of becoming the strongest power – that is, a hegemon.'[41] He also suggests that only a small number of the most powerful states can compete to maximise their own power at the same time, so other states have to choose to ally and partner with these stronger countries to ensure the survival of their states.[42]

1.2.7 Power as security

Power as security corresponds with Morgenthau's realist theory contending that states ultimately strive to protect themselves and their own interests over all else, but neorealism also posits that national security is the primary motivation of states. There are inevitable crossovers with the other theories of power; strong security, whether directly or indirectly, leads to increased influence of states on the world stage, increased capability through the expansion of armaments, and the inevitable formation of alliances led by great powers to balance the system.

John Herz suggested that the constant and competitive pursuit of security by states, referred to as the 'security dilemma' or the 'spiral model,' is tied to the constant pursuit of power. The security dimension of international politics, and the power dynamics that arise from the actions of states, ultimately results in competition for power between all states.

1.2.8 Smart power

In an attempt to define the changing global power dynamics, the *Center for Strategic and International Studies* described the more contemporary understanding of power, *smart power*, as 'an approach that underscores the necessity of a strong military, but also invests heavily in alliances, partnerships, and institutions of all levels to expand one's influence and establish legitimacy of one's action.'[43]

Ernest Wilson argued that smart power is the only theory of power that can be used to analyse state actions because hard power is facing increased domestic and international opposition and thus is less likely to achieve the desired outcomes, and soft power cannot be considered in a vacuum because there is no tangible way to measure the impact of attractiveness between countries.[44]

Smart power is considered a tool of foreign policy that is more aligned with liberal internationalist states. Liberal countries tend to 'see trade, diplomacy, foreign aid, and the spread of ... values as equally important [as military influence].' These states must also develop a 'stable grid of allies, institutions, and norms'[45] that can be utilised to enhance power around the world.

Notes

1 The terms *Britain* and *United Kingdom* are used interchangeably throughout this book, referring to England, Scotland, Wales and Northern Ireland. Any activities involving individual constituent nations are clearly stated.
2 Alston, R. and Laing, S., *Unshook till the End of Time: A History of Relations between Britain & Oman 1650–1970*, (London, Gilgamesh Publishing, 2012).
3 Jones, J. and Ridout, N., *Oman, Culture and Diplomacy*, (Edinburgh, Edinburgh University Press, 2012), pp.124–125.
4 Bhacker, M.R., *Trade and Empire in Muscat and Zanzibar: Roots of British Domination*, (London, Routledge, 1994), esp. pp.31–44 and 45–64.
5 Kechichian, J.A., *Oman and the World: The Emergence of an Independent Foreign Policy*, (Santa Monica, CA, Rand, 1995), p.136.
6 Ibid., p.3.
7 Townsend, J., *Oman: The Making of the Modern State*, (London, Croom Helm Ltd, 1977), p.57.
8 Peterson, J.E., *Oman in the Twentieth Century: Political Foundations of an Emerging State*, (London, Croom Helm, 1978), esp. pp.76–92.

9 Ibid., p.92.
10 Beasant, J., *Oman: The True-Life Drama and Intrigue of an Arab State*, (Edinburgh, Mainstream Publishing Company Ltd, 2002), esp. pp.97–160.
11 Skeet, I., *Oman: Politics and Development*, (New York, St. Martin's Press, 1992), esp. p.47.
12 Allen, C.H. and Rigsbee II, W.L., *Oman under Qaboos: From Coup to Constitution, 1970–1996*, (Oxford, Routledge, 2013), p.36.
13 Jones, J., 'Oman's Quiet Diplomacy', *NUPI Paper*, 6 (2014), p.2.
14 Valeri, M., *Oman: Politics and Society in the Qaboos State*, (New York, Columbia University Press, 2009).
15 Onley, J., *The Arabian Frontier of the British Raj: Merchants, Rulers, and the British in the Nineteenth-Century Gulf*, (Oxford, Oxford University Press, 2007), esp. pp.136–187.
16 Fuccaro, N., *Histories of City and State in the Persian Gulf: Manama Since 1800*, (Cambridge, Cambridge University Press, 2009), esp. pp.112–150.
17 Krieg, A., 'Gulf security policy after the Arab Spring: considering changing security dynamics', in *The Small Gulf States: Foreign and Security Policies Before and After the Arab Spring*, Khalid S. Almezaini and Jean-Marc Rickli (eds.), (Oxford, Routledge, 2017), pp.47–63.
18 Joyce, M., *Ruling Shaikhs and Her Majesty's Government: 1960–1969*, (London, Frank Cass Publishers, 2003), p.62.
19 Ibid., p.63.
20 Holman, Z., 'On the side of decency and democracy: The history of British-Bahraini relations and transnational contestation' in *Bahrain's Uprising*, Ala'a Shehabi and Marc Owen Jones (eds.), (London, Zed Publishing, 2015), pp.175–206.
21 Lasswell, H. and Kaplan, A., *Power and Society: A Framework for Political Inquiry*, (New Haven, CT, Yale University Press, 1950), p.75.
22 Dahl, R.A. and Stinebrickner, B., *Modern Political Analysis (6th ed.)*, (Hoboken, NJ, Prentice Hall, 2003), p.12.
23 See: Morgenthau, H.J., *Politics among Nations: The Struggle for Power and Peace*, (New York, Knopf, 1960); Kalijarvi, T.V. and Associates, *Modern World Politics*, (New York, Thomas Y. Cromwell Co., 1953).
24 Waltz, K.N., *Theory of International Politics*, (Reading: MA, Addison-Wesley Publishing Company, 1979), p.131.
25 Nye, Jr., J.S., 'Public Diplomacy and Soft Power', *The Annals of the American Academy of Political and Social Science*, 616 (2008), p.94.
26 Cabinet Office, 'Refreshed GREAT campaign launched in 145 countries'. Available at: <https://www.gov.uk/government/news/refreshed-great-campaign-launched-in-145-countries>.
27 Nye, Jr., J.S., *Soft Power: The Means to Success in World Politics*, (New York, PublicAffairs, 2004), p.11.
28 Kearn, Jr., D.W., 'The Hard Truths about Soft Power', *Journal of Political Power*, 4:1 (2011), p.69.
29 Ruggie, J.G., 'International Regimes, Transactions, and Change: Embedded Liberalism in the Postwar Economic Order', *International Organization*, 36:2 (1982), pp.379–415.
30 French, J.R.P. and Raven, B., 'The bases of social power' in D. Cartwright (ed.), *Studies in Social Power*, (Ann Arbor, University of Michigan, 1959), pp.150–167.
31 Waltz, K., 'The Emerging Structure of International Politics', *International Security*, 18:2 (1993), p.60.
32 See: Forsyth, D.R., *Group Dynamics (6th ed.)*, (Belmont, CA, Wadsworth Cengage Learning, 2014).

33 Morgenthau, H.J., *Politics among Nations: The Struggle for Power and Peace (5th ed.)*, (New York, Alfred A. Knopf, 1978).
34 Ibid., esp. p.12.
35 Viotti, P.R. and Kauppi, M.V., *International Relations and World Politics (5th ed.)*, (New York, Pearson, 2013), p.202.
36 Goddard, S.E. and Nexon, D.H., 'The Dynamics of Global Power Politics: A Framework for Analysis', *Journal of Global Security Studies*, 1:1 (2016), p.11.
37 Adler-Nissen, R., 'The Diplomacy of Opting Out: A Bourdieudian Approach to National Integration Strategies', *Journal of Common Market Studies*, 46:3 (2008), p.670.
38 Ferguson, N., *The Pity of War*, (New York, Basic Books, 1999), p.21.
39 Gabriel, M., 'National security and the interagency process', in J. Boone Bartholomees, Jr. (ed.), *U.S. Army War College Guide to National Security Policy and Strategy* (Carlisle, PA, United States Army War College, 2004), esp. pp. 239–260.
40 Waltz, *Theory of International Politics*, pp.161–193.
41 Toft, P. and John J., 'Mearsheimer: An Offensive Realist between Geopolitics and Power', *Journal of International Relations and Development*, 8 (2005), p.383.
42 Mearsheimer, J.J., *The Tragedy of Great Power Politics*, (New York, W.W. Norton & Company, 2001), pp.29–54.
43 Center for Strategic and International Studies (2007), *CSIS Commission on Smart Power: A Smarter, More Secure America*, p.7. Available at: <https://csis-prod.s3.amazonaws.com/s3fs-public/legacy_files/files/media/csis/pubs/071106_csissmartpowerreport.pdf> [accessed 16 September 2019].
44 Wilson, E.J. III, 'Hard Power, Soft Power, Smart Power', *The ANNALS of the American Academy of Political and Social Science*, 616:1 (2008), pp.111; 112; 117; 121.
45 Nossel, S., 'Smart Power', *Foreign Affairs*, 83:2 (2004), p.132.

Bibliography

Adler-Nissen, R., 'The Diplomacy of Opting Out: A Bourdieudian Approach to National Integration Strategies', *Journal of Common Market Studies*, 46:3 (2008), pp.663–684.

Allen, C.H. and Rigsbee II, W.L., *Oman under Qaboos: From Coup to Constitution, 1970–1996*, (Oxford, Routledge, 2013).

Alston, R. and Laing, S., *Unshook till the End of Time: A History of Relations between Britain & Oman 1650–1970*, (London, Gilgamesh Publishing, 2012).

Beasant, J., *Oman: The True-Life Drama and Intrigue of an Arab State*, (Edinburgh, Mainstream Publishing Company Ltd, 2002).

Bhacker, M.R., *Trade and Empire in Muscat and Zanzibar: Roots of British Domination*, (London, Routledge, 1994).

Cabinet Office, 'Refreshed GREAT Campaign Launched in 145 Countries'. Available at: <https://www.gov.uk/government/news/refreshed-great-campaign-launched-in-145-countries>.

Center for Strategic and International Studies (2007), CSIS Commission on Smart Power: A Smarter, More Secure America, p.7. Available at: <https://csis-prod.s3.amazonaws.com/s3fs-public/legacy_files/files/media/csis/pubs/071106_csissmartpowerreport.pdf> [accessed 16 September 2019].

Dahl, R.A. and Stinebrickner, B., *Modern Political Analysis (6th ed.)*, (Hoboken, NJ, Prentice Hall, 2003).

Ferguson, N., *The Pity of War*, (New York, Basic Books, 1999).

Forsyth, D.R., *Group Dynamics (6th ed.)*, (Belmont: CA, Wadsworth Cengage Learning, 2014).

French, J.R.P. and Raven, B., 'The bases of social power' in D. Cartwright (ed.), *Studies in Social Power*, (Ann Arbor, University of Michigan, 1959), pp.150–167.

Fuccaro, N., *Histories of City and State in the Persian Gulf: Manama Since 1800*, (Cambridge, Cambridge University Press, 2009).

Gabriel, M., 'National Security and the Interagency Process'. In J. Boone Bartholomees, Jr. (ed.). *U.S. Army War College Guide to National Security Policy and Strategy*, (Carlisle, PA, United States Army War College, 2004).

Goddard, S.E. and Nexon, D.H., 'The Dynamics of Global Power Politics: A Framework for Analysis', *Journal of Global Security Studies*, 1:1 (2016), pp.4–18.

Holman, Z., 'On the side of decency and democracy: The history of British-Bahraini relations and transnational contestation' in A. Shehabi and M.O. Jones (eds.), *Bahrain's Uprising*, (London, Zed Publishing, 2015), pp.175–206.

Jones, J., 'Oman's Quiet Diplomacy', NUPI Paper, 6 (2014).

Jones, J. and Ridout, N., *Oman, Culture and Diplomacy*, (Edinburgh, Edinburgh University Press, 2012).

Joyce, M., *Ruling Shaikhs and Her Majesty's Government: 1960–1969*, (London, Frank Cass Publishers, 2003).

Kalijarvi, T.V. and Associates, *Modern World Politics*, (New York, Thomas Y. Cromwell Co., 1953).

Kearn, Jr., D.W., 'The Hard Truths about Soft Power', *Journal of Political Power*, 4:1 (2011), pp.65–85.

Kechichian, J.A., *Oman and the World: The Emergence of an Independent Foreign Policy*, (Santa Monica, CA, Rand, 1995).

Krieg, A., 'Gulf security policy after the Arab Spring: considering changing security dynamics', in K.S. Almezaini and J.-M. Rickli (eds.), *The Small Gulf States: Foreign and Security Policies Before and After the Arab Spring*, (Oxford, Routledge, 2017), pp.47–63.

Lasswell, H. and Kaplan, A., *Power and Society: A Framework for Political Inquiry*, (New Haven, CT, Yale University Press, 1950).

Mearsheimer, J.J., *The Tragedy of Great Power Politics*, (New York, W.W. Norton & Company, 2001).

Morgenthau, H.J., *Politics among Nations: The Struggle for Power and Peace*, (New York, Knopf, 1960).

Morgenthau, H.J., *Politics among Nations: The Struggle for Power and Peace (5th ed.)*, (New York, Alfred A. Knopf, 1978).

Nossel, S., 'Smart Power', *Foreign Affairs*, 83:2 (2004), pp.131–142.

Nye, Jr., J.S., 'Public Diplomacy and Soft Power', *The Annals of the American Academy of Political and Social Science*, 616 (2008), pp.94–109.

Nye, Jr., J.S., *Soft Power: The Means to Success in World Politics*, (New York, PublicAffairs, 2004).

Onley, J., *The Arabian Frontier of the British Raj: Merchants, Rulers, and the British in the Nineteenth-Century Gulf*, (Oxford, Oxford University Press, 2007).

Peterson, J.E., *Oman in the Twentieth Century: Political Foundations of an Emerging State*, (London, Croom Helm, 1978).

Ruggie, J.G., 'International Regimes, Transactions, and Change: Embedded Liberalism in the Postwar Economic Order', *International Organization*, 36:2 (1982), pp.379–415.

Skeet, I., *Oman: Politics and Development*, (New York, St. Martin's Press, 1992).
Toft, P. and John J., 'Mearsheimer: An Offensive Realist between Geopolitics and Power', *Journal of International Relations and Development*, 8 (2005), pp.381–408.
Townsend, J., *Oman: The Making of the Modern State*, (London, Croom Helm Ltd, 1977).
Valeri, M., *Oman: Politics and Society in the Qaboos State*, (New York, Columbia University Press, 2009).
Viotti, P.R. and Kauppi, M.V., *International Relations and World Politics (5th ed.)*, (New York, Pearson, 2013).
Waltz, K., 'The Emerging Structure of International Politics', *International Security*, 18:2 (1993), pp.44–79.
Waltz, K.N., *Theory of International Politics*, (Reading, MA, Addison-Wesley Publishing Company, 1979).
Wilson, E.J. III, 'Hard Power, Soft Power, Smart Power', *The ANNALS of the American Academy of Political and Social Science*, 616:1 (2008), pp.110–124.

2 The foundations of British power in Oman
Past and present

2.1 British involvement in the Dhofar War

Britain's privileged position in Omani affairs cannot be understood without acknowledging the role that British forces played in the restoration of order in Oman during the oft-forgotten Dhofar War, the biggest threat to Oman in modern times. The influence that Britain gained, particularly on a strategic level, from its commanding role in the counter-insurgency operations undoubtedly instilled a mindset of gratitude and trust by the new Sultan Qaboos in the British Government and ensured that the historic British influence continued when Qaboos replaced his father, Sa'id bin Taimur, as Sultan of a reunified Oman.

In 1962, tribal leader Musallam bin Nufi, who had been involved in previous Saudi-led rebellions against Muscat's rule in the Jebel Akhdar between 1957 and 1959, corralled a number of tribes from across the southern province of Dhofar. Most tribes were either dissatisfied with Sultan Sa'id's refusal to finance health and economic developments across the region or were followers of the exiled Imam Ghalib bin Ali, the last elected ruler of the Imamate of Oman. Armed with weapons and vehicles supplied by Saudi sympathisers, the guerrillas of the Dhofar Liberation Front (DLF) started ambushing oil tankers operating in Dhofar and attacking the British military air base at Salalah. It is these small-scale attacks that brought the DLF to the attention of British decision makers, and as many of the guerrillas were former soldiers of the Sultan of Oman's Armed Forces and the Trucial Oman Scouts, they understood British military tactics and used these against British and Omani security personnel to undermine domestic security. These direct attacks on key British economic and strategic assets changed a relatively minor domestic civil disobedience issue into a looming war that would eventually involve over 1,000 elite British troops, 4,000 Imperial Iranian Armed troops, a small troop unit from the Trucial Oman Scouts, and a squadron of Royal Jordanian Army engineers supporting some 10,000 Omani and 2,000 Firqat militiamen to quash the rebellion.

In April 1966, the Dhofar Rebellion took a turn that would result in significant power being handed to British officials in Oman, leading to opponents of the British in the Sultanate labelling their role as that of a shadow government controlling a 'phantom Sultan.' Sultan Sa'id had relied on a small 60-man unit, the Dhofar Force, to guarantee peace in Dhofar, but when they attempted to assassinate him, the Sultan hid away in his palace in Salalah never to be seen again in public. A subsequent full-scale military offensive was ordered by Sa'id, using heavy-handed tactics, including search and destroy, concreting over wells, and burning houses belonging to rebels. Although the British Government opposed these tactics, opponents of British imperialism across the Middle East, including Nasserites, the Palestine Liberation Organisation, and left-wing rebels in Aden, conflated these attacks on the DLF in Oman with the wider British presence in the Gulf. The DLF soon developed into a Marxist-Leninist armed political movement, akin to the uprising in neighbouring Aden, which ultimately proved successful when the British Protectorate of South Arabia was dismantled in 1967, spurring on their Dhofari counterparts.

In May 1968, the DLF guerrillas emerged as a more cohesive and well-trained military force, supported, armed, and trained by the Soviet Union and China, when they defeated a battalion of the SAF in the Jebel Qamar. Four months later, at the second congress of the DLF, the armed political movement was renamed the *Popular Front for the Liberation of the Occupied Arabian Gulf* (PFLOAG). It is this increased politicisation of the rebellion that could actually be understood as the start of the slow decline of the uprising. The early tribal rebels who had joined Mussallam bin Nufi were fighting largely for increased regional autonomy and development funding in Dhofar, whereas the politicised wing of the new PFLOAG wanted a complete overthrow of the monarchy and the implementation of a Republican Marxist administration across the whole Gulf. Senior supporters of bin Nufi began holding unofficial peace talks with British and Omani government officials before defecting to the allies. Northern rebels soon established the breakaway *National Democratic Front for the Liberation of Oman and the Arabian Gulf* (NDFLOAG), further eroding the unity of the rebellion.

Despite the divisions, by 1969, rebels had taken control of the only road connecting Salalah to Thumrait in the northern deserts of the region, they were heavily armed with Soviet AK-47 and SKS carbine rifles, DShK heavy machine guns, and Katyusha rockets, and younger fighters were sent to train in unconventional warfare tactics in China and the Soviet Union. In contrast, the SAF was under-manned, with only 1,000 troops in Dhofar by 1968, they were armed with inadequate Second World War-era bolt-action rifles, inappropriate clothing for the environment, and they were untrained to fight a guerrilla war. This led to many senior British political and military officials calling for regime change in Oman and unavoidable short-term deployments of British and allied troops to Salalah to protect the strategically important airfield. On several occasions, the No.2 Paras, 15th Field and 51st Field squadrons of the RAF, a Royal Artillery group and a Royal Jordanian artillery unit had to intervene. The necessary support that British and allied militaries gave to the Sultan, ensuring that he did not lose control of all of Dhofar, arguably marked a point of no return for the British Government. Britain had to provide significant military support to the new Sultan Qaboos after he came to power on 23 July 1970.

Qaboos' father had fought the war with the PFLOAG using terror tactics, but Qaboos, with significant assistance from expert British special forces, 'adopted a more effective COIN (counter-insurgency) strategy that combined conventional operations with civil development and political reform.'[1] This reformed strategy, led by British advisors who had used similar tactics during the Malayan Emergency between 1948 and 1960, eroded much of the discontent that many of the original rebels held against the former Sultan. Upon his accession to the throne, Qaboos implemented a five-point plan to bring the war to a swift end. The plan involved: granting an amnesty to rebels, the formalisation of Dhofar as Oman's southern province rather than the Sultan's personal fiefdom, military operations against rebels that refuse the amnesty, widespread development measures, and diplomatic initiatives to gain international recognition of Oman as an Arab state and block rebel support from other Arab states.

In August 1970, SAS Commander Brigadier Ferguson Semple proposed to Qaboos that small numbers of SAS troop teams should be distributed across Dhofar in an 'advise and assist' capacity. The *British Army Training Teams* (BATT) recruited rebels who had defected from the cause to develop insider knowledge and worked with Omani bureaucrats to implement Qaboos' reforms, including opening hospitals, offering veterinary care for goats and sheep, and teaching tribesmen basic skills to aid employment capabilities.[2] The British Government and SAS commanders ensured that the British presence was as covert as possible. This ensured that Omani troops were viewed as competent actors by the Dhofaris. Locals subsequently became convinced that the Sultan's government was capable of ending the prolonged rebellion. When the SAS arrived, they identified four strategies to undermine the PFLOAG:

1. implementation of a 'hearts and minds' campaign to win over locals;
2. development of a comprehensive intelligence gathering strategy based on British intelligence principles;
3. veterinary assistance and medical assistance for locals and their livestock;
4. a psychological campaign to pressure rebels to defect to the government.[3]

In 1971, the first Firqat Salahadin, a locally raised force of Dhofaris and Jebalis who had remained loyal to Muscat, was established. More Firqats were subsequently raised, each led by four to six SAS soldiers. Although the SAS troops were officially acting in a purely advisory capacity, it was clear that these Britons would fight if attacked by rebels. This confirmed to local fighters that the British military was committed to bringing peace to Oman.

Alongside the SAS, practical British support was provided by a team of 20 Royal Engineers to construct buildings and dig wells, and medics from the Royal Army Medical Corps and RAF medical teams operated new hospitals. The British Government also provided funding for these developments through the *Dhofar Development Programme* in 1972 worth several million pounds. By 1975, some eight Firqats had been created, over 155 miles of roads had been laid between the central and eastern parts of Dhofar, 17 freshwater wells had been dug, and around 200 rebels had surrendered and shared intelligence with the allies.[4] Involving local fighters via Firqats was an important tactic transferred by the SAS from their experiences in Malaya, but the close connections between the Firqat fighters and Dhofar was not without its complications. Many had relatives in the PFLOAG, refused to fight in other tribal areas across Dhofar, and laid down arms during Ramadan. This annoyed the British, northern Omanis and Baluchi soldiers, but the SAS ensured that these divisions did not affect the cohesive nature of the Firqat system.

The BATT teams often became relied upon by remote tribes who had, until this time, received little financial, medical, or development support from subsequent Sultans. A veterinarian who served in one of the BATT teams remarked of his time in Dhofar that the Dhofaris viewed BATT support akin to a welfare state. They were repeatedly asked by locals for ammunition and weapons, human and animal medicines, better shelters and food.[5]

Although British strategic assistance was a defining factor in turning the war for the Sultan, the collaboration between the SAS and Omani civil and military personnel was arguably the first case of large-scale collaboration between Britain and Oman on a relatively equal basis. Until this point, Britain had made most of the decisions in Oman and Sultans had followed; now Qaboos used his extensive knowledge of social and political tactics that he learned at Sandhurst and from serving with the British Army and the British to create a cohesive plan to end the war and the British implemented it.

2.1.1 *Turning the tide of the war*

The impact of both SAS leadership and Qaboos' 'hearts and minds' strategy, and the eventual turn of the war, started on 2 October 1971 when *Operation Jaguar* was launched. An SAS/Firqat group, using newly introduced rapid FN MAG and Browning M2 heavy machine guns, replacing less powerful Bren guns, established a permanent position north of the key coastal town of Mirbat in Medinat Al Haq, taking Jibjat and Wadi Darbat along the way. When allied troops and civilian support stayed during the monsoon, local tribesmen began to spread the word that the Sultan was indeed committed to the region.[6] Offensives were launched named *Operation Leopard* in the remote mountains around Mughsayl in west Dhofar and *Operation Panther* in Tawi Attair. These simultaneous attacks weakened PFLOAG resolve, destroyed rebel infrastructure, and resulted in rebel surrenders across the region. On 19 July 1972, the PFLOAG launched an artillery bombardment on a 30-man defensive position led by Captain Mike Kealy of the 22nd SAS, followed by a 200-man rebel attack on Mirbat in the east. The BATT group, with close air support from SOAF BAC 167 Strikemaster attack aircraft were able to hold Mirbat. Heroic acts by Sergeant Talaisi Labalaba, who ran through rebel fire to operate a 25-pounder artillery gun to fend off oncoming attacks, and Trooper Sekonaia Takavesi, who ran 800 metres across open land covered by Omani Special Forces firepower[7], resulted in an allied victory in the Battle of Mirbat and demonstrated the strength of a combined British-Omani force. 'The battle was a major blow to the PFLOAG, forcing them to recognise their weakness in conventional operations against [the] Dhofar Brigade – it was, in fact, the last time the insurgents attempted open warfare'[8] against the Anglo-Omani force.

From late 1972, the British Government provided the Omani military with advanced weapons, larger numbers of specialist British Army and Royal Marines (along with some Pakistani officers) were seconded to Oman, and more Omani officer cadets were accepted into officer training colleges across the UK. This demonstrated the British Government's willingness to expand its support for the new Sultan, but also the desire for Britain to gradually cede more control to Omanis by offering advanced training and modern arms. Fortified advanced transportation routes, surrounded by barbed wire and heavily armed platoons, named the 'Hornbeam Line,'

ran from Mughsayl on the coast to the north of Dhofar. This was a marked change since the start of the war when supply lines were easily disrupted by rebels and overall strategy was incoherent. At this time, the SOAF underwent its largest expansion in its history at the time, with BAC Strikemasters, Shorts Skyvans, Agusta Bell 205 transport helicopters, and Westland Wessex helicopters supplied by the UK to Oman to support the cause.

2.1.2 Beginning of the end of the rebellion

The combined strategy and arms of the SAS and Omani forces arguably had a significant impact on the gradual defeat of the PFLOAG, but it cannot be understood in isolation as a purely domestic issue. As much of the PFLOAG's support came from foreign governments, China's decision to establish diplomatic relations with Iran, who supported the Sultan's government in Dhofar, as part of its attempted containment of the Soviet Union, led to an almost immediate closure of rebel supply and training lines from China. 'Chinese arms aid was cut off, and the Chinese media stopped endorsing the Dhofar rebels and covering their activities. Similar indifference was soon accorded to other anti-government rebel movements in the Persian Gulf.'[9]

In 1973, the Shah of Iran sent a brigade of 1,200 Iranian Army troops and attack helicopters to contribute to the Sultan's increasingly international fightback against the rebels. The Iranian contingent, in collaboration with the British, took control of the strategic Salalah to Thumrait road and the remote settlement of Sarfait. The Imperial Iranian Taskforce, comprising over 4,000 men, spent much of 1974 fighting to capture the *Damavand Line* between Manston base and the coast, eventually capturing the self-declared rebel capital of Rakhyut. The PFLOAG suffered increasing numbers of defections and divisions in 1974, renaming itself the *Popular Front for the Liberation of Oman* (PFLO), reflecting the lack of international support and diminished aims of the remaining rebels. The Firqats took control of Jebel Qara, the eastern half of Jebel Qamar and Jebel Samhan with little sustained opposition.

In the final months of 1974, the Firqats captured the important PFLO airstrip at Deefa, and as the SAF had received 31 Hawker Hunter aircraft from the Royal Jordanian Air Force, the PFLO's attacks using SA-7 anti-aircraft missiles were ineffective. Throughout, the SAS remained in control of the overall planning but received approval from the Sultan before undertaking major activities. This signalled the shift that was taking place in wider Anglo-Omani affairs, whereby Britain offered Oman critical strategic and economic support but Sultan Qaboos gave his approval for any activity.

The final offensive started in October 1975, with the Firqats, SAF, Iranian brigades, and Jordanians undertaking simultaneous operations. An attack on Simba and Dalqhut successfully cut off the rebels from their bases, Iranians attacked Shershitti Caves from the south, the SAF advanced from Deefa into Jebel Qamar, and sustained SOAF air attacks destroyed most remaining rebel hideouts in the mountains. On 11 March 1976, the Dhofar War was declared at an end, but small-scale attacks on SAF personnel continued until 1979, including an attack on an Omani military officer in the Pakistani port city of Gwadar, where many Baloch troops were recruited into the Firqats.

2.1.3 *Effect of Dhofar on British influence in Oman*

The British intervention in the Dhofar War had a profound impact on the relations between the British Government and military and the new Sultan Qaboos and his armed forces. Until Qaboos' accession to the throne, hastened because of his father's failure to contain the rebellion, British military activities were determined with little input from Sultans. When Qaboos took power, his experience serving with the British Army and proven capabilities to lead led to British authorities relinquishing strategic control to him, offering planning and assistance when required. The power shift that took place, from hard power governance of Omani affairs, to a smarter type of power, where British hard power was predicated on assisting Qaboos with his long-term development goals alongside military support.

2.2 The Arab Spring in Oman and its impact on Britain's influence

When the Arab Spring erupted across the Middle East and North Africa in 2011, much of the focus was on states with long-term Republican dictatorships; the effect on the established Arab monarchies in the Gulf has been largely overlooked. The protests and sit-ins that occurred across Oman were described as James Worrall as the forgotten corner of the Arab Spring. The first small demonstrations in Oman took place on 17 January 2011, not long after the downfall of President Zine bin Ali in Tunisia. Some 200 Omanis started protesting outside of the Housing Ministry offices to draw attention to rising food prices and corruption.[10] Over subsequent months, the protests became significantly larger and violent, with teachers and educated professionals demanding lower pension contributions, better promotion opportunities, and wage increases. Green Marches, which emphasised peaceful demonstration, took place across the country. On 18 February 2011, the second Green March was held in Muscat, with protestors demanding 'educational and economic reforms … some intellectual groups filed a petition calling for the powers of the Shura Council to be expanded and the removal of specific ministers. … [Media personnel] wanted loosened restrictions on the press….'[11] Qaboos received a petition outlining the protestor's demands through the Diwan of the Royal Court on 23 February. When over 10,000 people took to the streets and organised mass sit-ins in Salalah, the capital of Dhofar, delivering a petition to the Sultan via the regional governor, Omani and British officials and other Gulf governments watched on hoping that a new Dhofar Rebellion would not erupt. The protests escalated on 26 February 2011, when a large number of young Omanis congregated in Salalah and Sohar, issuing a statement to Sultan Qaboos demanding change. The next day, these young protestors set fire to the governor's office, a LuLu hypermarket and a police station in Sohar. The protests culminated with a gathering at Globe roundabout, nicknamed 'Reform Square,' where they were fired upon by the police with rubber bullets.[12] Mass protest followed in Muscat and Sur, with up to 10,000 gathering outside of the Shura Council building in Muscat.

Qaboos' response to the more violent protests was unusual when viewed through the prism of the wider Arab Spring. At the end of February 2011, the Sultan replaced a number of government ministers, created 50,000 public sector jobs for locals, and increased private sector wages by 43% to the equivalent of $520 a month.[13]

On 1 March, the army was deployed to clear Globe Roundabout in Sohar. The violence in this port city was unusual, with most protests taking the form of general strikes and sit-ins, most of which demanded policy reforms rather than the overthrow of the government as was seen in other MENA states. In fact, some protestors in Sohar released a statement declaring their support for Sultan Qaboos and regret for the violence that occurred.[14] The initial protests in Oman tied to the wider Arab Spring gradually ceased.

2.2.1 Protests after the Arab Spring in Oman

Sporadic protests have broken out across Oman since 2011, the most significant happening in 2019 and 2021, when protestors demanded an end to rising unemployment. In May 2021, the first protests since Haitham became Sultan erupted in Sohar and Salalah. The 2021 protests were in response to the new Sultan's Covid austerity measures, including the introduction of a VAT tax, public sector wage cuts, utility subsidy cuts, and borrowing from Qatar. Sit-ins in front of government buildings and criticism of the government on social media were met with the police firing CS tear gas canisters and arrests.

In an attempt to quell the protests, the Sultan created hundreds of temporary civil service and military jobs, at a reduced pay rate, and permanently deployed riot police across the capital region as a precaution. Again, the protests gradually dissipated.

2.2.2 Effect of Oman's protests on Anglo-Omani relations

As the most important ally to Oman and the ruling Sultan, any protests in the state ultimately impact Britain and British interests. When workers at the PDO oil refineries joined the general strikes in 2011, this had an effect on Shell's productivity and short-term profits in Oman. British advisors and intelligence agencies are ingrained in the domestic security agencies, so British input, however small, would have been present in identifying key agitators within the protest movements. The strategic importance of the UK Joint Logistics Support Base at Duqm undoubtedly caused nerves within the British Government. There was never an expectation or preparation amongst British policymakers for the downfall of the Omani Government. British economic and strategic activities in Oman continued unabated, despite the protests. This undoubtedly reinforced the signal to the Sultan and his ministers that Britain stood with Oman during peace or strife.

Britain committed to guarantee peace in Oman in 1820, at the start of the protection era in the Gulf, and even after 1971 subsequent British administrations have recommitted to this pledge. This contribution to Omani peace is manifested in many forms, the most prominent during the sporadic protests being the British training of Omani police personnel. PSNI training of Omani police officers, dating back to 2014, focused on public order training, including crowd control. Throughout the Arab Spring protests, this crowd control training was likely put into action on many occasions. Although the British authorities no longer have any direct influence over the actions of the Omani security services, nor the directions of government ministers, the lessons learned in British policing colleges have undoubtedly contributed to the suppression of any major threats to the ruling order in Oman. This, combined with unique local issues that were more about airing frustration rather than forcing regime change, has ensured that Britain's most reliable and historically in the Middle East has remained largely intact.

Notes

1. Paul, C., Clarke, C.P., Grill, B. and Dunigan, M., 'Oman (Dhofar Rebellion), 1965–1975: Case Outcome: COIN Win' in *Paths to Victory: Detailed Insurgency Case Studies*, (Santa Monica, CA, RAND Corporation, 2013), p.274.
2. Orderman, T., *Strategic Lessons from the Dhofar Rebellion*, (Aberdeen, University of Aberdeen, 2011), p.17.
3. UK forces in Oman, 26 July 1971, DEFE 25/186 (1971), TNA.
4. Mockaitis, T.R., *British Counterinsurgency in the Post-imperial Era*, (Manchester, Manchester University Press, 1995), esp. pp.73–80.
5. Higgins, A., *With the S.A.S. and Other Animals: A Vet's Experiences During the Dhofar War, 1974*, (Barnsley, Pen & Sword Military, 2011).
6. Pimlott, J., 'The British Army: The Dhofar Campaign, 1970–1975' in I.F.W. Beckett and J. Pimlott (eds.), *Counter-Insurgency: Lessons from History*, (Barnsley, Pen & Sword Military, 2011).
7. Scholey, P., *SAS Heroes: Remarkable Soldiers, Extraordinary Men*, (London, Bloomsbury Publishing, 2011), pp.217–224.
8. Pimlott, *Counter-Insurgency: Lessons from History*, 2011.
9. Garver, J.W., *China and Iran: Ancient Partners in a Post-Imperial World*, (Seattle, University of Washington Press, 2006).
10. Worrall, J., 'Oman: The "Forgotten" Corner of the Arab Spring', *Middle East Policy*, 19:3 (2012), p.98.
11. Al-Rawahi, M.A.S., *The Sultanate of Silence: A Critical Analysis of the Omani Newspapers' Coverage of the 2011 Protests*, (Doctoral Thesis: Cardiff University, October 2019), pp.88–89.
12. Al-Abri, O., (2011), The Middle East in crisis: Looters take control of Oman's streets, *The Telegraph*, 25 April.
13. Valeri, M., 'Simmering Unrest and Succession Challenges in Oman', (Carnegie Endowment for International Peace, 2015). Available at: <https://carnegieendowment.org/2015/01/28/simmering-unrest-and-succession-challenges-in-oman-pub-58843>.
14. Worrall, 'Oman: The "Forgotten" Corner of the Arab Spring', pp.106–107.

Bibliography

Al-Abri, O., (2011), 'The Middle East in Crisis: Looters Take Control of Oman's Streets', *The Telegraph*, 25 April.

Al-Rawahi, M.A.S., 'The Sultanate of Silence: A Critical Analysis of the Omani Newspapers' coverage of the 2011 protests', (Doctoral Thesis: Cardiff University, October 2019).

Garver, J.W., *China and Iran: Ancient Partners in a Post-Imperial World*, (Seattle, University of Washington Press, 2006).

Higgins, A., *With the S.A.S. and Other Animals: A Vet's Experiences During the Dhofar War, 1974*, (Barnsley, Pen & Sword Military, 2011).

Mockaitis, T.R., *British Counterinsurgency in the Post-imperial Era*, (Manchester, Manchester University Press, 1995).

Orderman, T., *Strategic Lessons from the Dhofar Rebellion*, (Aberdeen, University of Aberdeen, 2011).

Paul, C., Clarke, C.P., Grill, B. and Dunigan, M., *'Oman (Dhofar Rebellion), 1965– 1975: Case Outcome: COIN Win' in Paths to Victory: Detailed Insurgency Case Studies*, (Santa Monica, CA, RAND Corporation, 2013).

Pimlott, J., 'The British Army: The Dhofar Campaign, 1970–1975', in I.F.W. Beckett and J. Pimlott (eds.), *Counter-Insurgency: Lessons from History*, (Barnsley, Pen & Sword Military, 2011).

Scholey, P., *SAS Heroes: Remarkable Soldiers, Extraordinary Men*, (London, Bloomsbury Publishing, 2011).

UK forces in Oman, 26 July 1971, DEFE 25/186 (1971), TNA.

Valeri, M., 'Simmering unrest and succession challenges in Oman', (Carnegie Endowment for International Peace, 2015). Available at: <https://carnegieendowment.org/2015/01/28/simmering-unrest-and-succession-challenges-in-oman-pub-58843>.

Worrall, J., 'Oman: The "Forgotten" Corner of the Arab Spring', *Middle East Policy*, 19:3 (2012), pp.98–115.

Part I
Strategic power, defence, and security

3 Britain's strategic engagement with Oman and the development of a new power dynamic

3.1 Introduction

Set against the backdrop of regional colonial expansion and rivalry between the British and Napoleonic French empires, Britain has been interested in the military affairs of Oman, formerly known as Muscat and Oman, since as early as 1798 when the two states signed a *Treaty of Friendship*, or the *Anglo–Omani Qawl-nama (agreement)*. In 1800, the treaty was amended so that a British Agent could base himself in Muscat and oversee British military activities in Omani ports, but as both Britain and Oman were equally powerful naval powers at the time, the treaties were based on a shared desire to build a long-lasting friendship. The treaty even stated that the UK–Omani relationship would 'remain unshook till the end of time, and till the sun and moon have finished their revolving career.'[1] It was not until 1895, however, that the British Political Resident in the Persian Gulf directly involved Britain in the domestic military affairs of the Sultanate. Shaikh Abdullah bin Salih launched an attack on Muscat and the Political Resident at the time, Colonel Frederick Alexander Wilson, wrote to the Secretary to the Government of India's Foreign Department declaring his support for British military protection for future Sultans of Muscat and Oman. He wrote:

> the best safeguard would be a clear intimation to the leading Sheikhs of Oman that, whatever differences they may have with their Sultan, we will not permit an attack on Mutrah and Muscat. … In return for this support we might demand from the Sultan a closer reliance on us, an earnestness on his part to be willing to be guided by our advice, the right to inspect his fortifications and advise him in the matter of his defences for which we might supply him with a moderate amount of newer arms and ammunition.[2]

Oman never became an official protectorate of British India, in contrast to other Gulf states including Bahrain, and Britain's military relations with the Sultanate were arguably based on a more equal footing from the early days of Britain's active involvement in the Arabian Gulf. Sultans of Muscat

DOI: 10.4324/9781003302001-4

and Oman since Sayyid Faisal bin Turki in 1895 and his successors have enjoyed varying levels of respect and voluntary cooperation with the British military. There was a desire from the early days of British involvement in Omani affairs, however, to establish a reliance by Oman on British protection using hard power means. Since 1895, Oman has supported all British military actions in the Middle East, but more significantly when assessing the strength of UK–Omani military relations and the presence of a British legacy in the Sultanate, there is significant evidence of continued Omani support for British military activity post-1971, albeit with British troops being invited to Oman rather than being based there as a self-appointed right; a shift from historic hard power to contemporary soft power. During Operation Desert Shield, a period from August 1990 to February 1991 when allied militaries were building up their forces in preparation for the expulsion of Iraqi troops from Kuwait (First Gulf War), the first big task of the new British Ambassador in Oman at the time was to 'manage the British element using Omani naval and air bases in preparation to push Iraq out of Kuwait. Oman's government gave the British Government its full support.'[3] A significant shift in defence policy by Sultan Qaboos, however, was allowing US troops to use facilities and supplies in Oman throughout the First Gulf War. The *Facilities Access Agreement*, signed in 1980 by both the Omani and US administrations, arguably signalled the end of Britain's military hegemony in the Sultanate; a precedent established in 1829 when British India nominally granted the Sultan military protection by the British Gulf Squadron, the Bombay Marine.[4]

Although the British Government lost its ability to prevent foreign states from basing troops in Oman when Harold Wilson decided to withdraw from East of the Suez, the ability of Britain to influence Omani defence policy was not lost entirely. In 1971, Britain announced its intention to cut its formal defence ties with Oman on a governmental level, but this did not come into fruition until the end of the Dhofar War in 1975 when the bulk of British troops left the country. Nevertheless, the informal and more covert ability of the British Government to influence aspects of Omani defence policy, indirectly through the numerous British expatriate military advisors and loan service personnel who have been based in Oman for over four decades, was retained. This was evidenced by a defence review produced by the Defence Attaché at the British Embassy in Oman in 1984 in which Colonel Lea wrote:

> The three (Omani) services have prospered under the continuance in command of the three UK Loan Service Commanders, Major General Watts, Air Vice Marshal Bennett and Rear Admiral Gunning. ... UK Loan Service Commanders continued to be in command.[5]

This small but influential cohort of British military personnel kept the British presence in Oman at the forefront of the minds of decision makers within the Omani government. Although at the end of the Dhofar War Britain lost the privilege of openly making security decisions on behalf of the Sultan and the trade hegemony that Britain had enjoyed for more than a century, a small number of British expatriates and loaned personnel ensured that the British Government still retained a presence at the frontier of the Gulf and that British defence manufacturers still had a number of influential Britons continuing to promote the benefits of buying British to Omani decision makers.

3.1.1 Legacy in action

In December 2016, Prime Minister Theresa May told attendees at the GCC's 17th summit that

> Gulf security is our security ... We in the UK are determined to continue to be your partner of choice as you embed international norms ... based on true partnership and an enduring commitment between our countries and our peoples.[6]

This security commitment to Oman is demonstrated by Britain's establishment of the 'regional land training hub in Oman'[7] in 2017, the only all-year-round permanent training base for British troops in the world and a joint base where British and Omani troops can share skills and experiences. This is a significant commitment both by the British Government to the continued protection of Oman, but also by the government in Oman to supporting close military relations with Britain progressing in the future. In 2018, the British influence in Oman was still evidently on as strong a footing as it has ever been, albeit without the overt presence that had dominated the relationship since the 1800s. This is arguably evidence of the contemporary soft power position in which Britain finds itself, one based on cooperative relations with Oman. On one of several visits to the Gulf in April 2018, British Secretary of State for Defence, Gavin Williamson, told an audience of reporters that Britain's defence interests are inextricably linked to the security of the region, which seemingly offers one explanation as to why the British Government has remained committed to close cooperation with Oman despite withdrawal from the military infrastructure of the Gulf states being one of the main elements of Harold Wilson's withdrawal from East of the Suez policy. Williamson declared that:

> Our long-standing and deep relationship with our Gulf partners epitomises Britain's global outlook. Be it through our involvement in the Duqm Port project in Oman or the opening of the Naval Support Facility in Bahrain, we are committed to regional security and stability.[8]

34 *Strategic power, defence, and security*

Williamson also proclaimed that 'Gulf security is our security and what happens in the Gulf has a direct impact on the security of the British public at home.'[9] This was quite an apt comment for a serving Defence Secretary to make, as in the case of Oman, there are a number of British nationals still serving with the Omani military. The preservation of the British strategic presence in Oman after withdrawal was as much determined by the willingness of the Government of Oman to permitting the continued presence of British troops in the country as the commitment by the government in London. Unlike before withdrawal, Oman was now able to exert influence over Britain and the relationship balance began to gradually shift. The British and Omani militaries are to some extent inextricably linked, and as British officers and military advisors have been an integral part of the Omani military since before Qaboos' accession to power, and these British military personnel are jointly responsible for securing the domestic affairs of the Sultanate, following British military procedures and protocols that were learned in British military academies, whatever happens to Oman also affects British nationals and therefore Britain. The UK–Omani defence relationship is multifaceted and arguably more complex than any other that Britain has. The relationship has also undergone a power balance shift, from one where Britain was the protector of Oman to a relationship based on trust and cooperation as allies who need each other equally. After 1975, Britain's power in the Gulf became almost instantly dependent on Sultan Qaboos' willingness to retain the partnership – soft power – rather than treaties and a physical presence that guaranteed British hegemony – hard power.

3.2 How has Britain utilised its privileged strategic education capabilities to secure influence in Oman?

At a time when Britain was drawing down its commitments in the Gulf in the final years of the 1960s, there seemed to be no will amongst ruling Gulf families to terminate their military education in British military academies. Even five decades after withdrawal from East of the Suez, the UK is still the main go-to country for the ruling families of the former Residency states to send future kings, emirs, and sheikhs for military training. There seems to be a continued political will by both the sending states (the Gulf countries) and the receiving partner (the UK Ministry of Defence who is responsible for allocating places to foreign students in military schools) to preserving the long-standing defence education relationship. Britain's willingness to continue educating future Gulf rulers should not be misunderstood purely as an act of kindness on the part of the British Government. There are numerous benefits to Britain's soft power capabilities, none more important than the ability of the British armed forces to continue influencing the military tactics and ideology of future rulers of the Gulf, a key component of 'defence diplomacy.'[10] Sultan Qaboos, as the longest-serving ruler in the region and the first of the regional rulers to receive military education in the UK, was certainly the most prominent example of how British military training continued to influence the military affairs of a Gulf state post-withdrawal and the defence-purchasing decisions of Oman six decades after Qaboos' graduation from the Royal Military Academy Sandhurst. Qaboos' successor, Haitham bin Tariq, did not receive any military training but did graduate from the Foreign Service Programme at the University of Oxford in 1979. However, his half-brother and Deputy Prime Minister for International Cooperation Affairs, Asa'ad bin Tariq, is a graduate of Sandhurst and thus the influential British strategic mindset has continued at the highest levels of power in Oman.

This aspect of the legacy could be referred to as 'expert power.' Oman's rulers have retained an attraction to the expertise offered by British military training academies, and the necessary skills required by the Omani military grants the British Government an amount of leverage over Oman's future security.

Sultan Qaboos was accepted into Sandhurst in Berkshire, England in 1960 at the age of 20, and at the time he was the heir to the throne of Oman. Although many former and current rulers of Gulf states were also trained at the same academy, it is these two years, and subsequent year serving in the 1st Battalion The Cameronians (Scottish Rifles) as a *de facto* member of the British Army, that are often considered the key reasons for the close relations that endured after Qaboos' accession to the Omani throne in 1970. The British military mindset and tactics that were instilled into Qaboos at Sandhurst are referred to as the 'Sandhurst connection,'[11] and it is this connection that is often cited as the main reason why the British and Omani militaries came to cooperate so closely after 1971. A senior British diplomat in Oman reiterated that

> Qaboos and a number of senior Omani commanders trained in the UK and this was a powerful binder that brought the UK and Oman together at the time of his accession, and the many sentiments that are now shared between the two allies were developed in the academic surroundings at Sandhurst.[12]

The military and security educational links do undoubtedly underpin the UK–Omani military relationship, but it is a multidimensional relationship.

Many senior Omani officials have continued to undertake their education in the UK despite an ending of the exclusivity of the relationship after withdrawal, which is arguably testament to the respect that Omanis still continue to have for the skills and tactics that British educational establishments instil within them. Although Oman has had its own university, Sultan Qaboos University, since 1986, and its own command and staff college since 30th September 1987, which relocated to Bait Al-Falaj Camp in March 1988, trainee officers are regularly still seconded to RMA Sandhurst (army), RAF College Cranwell (air force), and the Britannia Royal Naval College Dartmouth (navy). Generally, the sending country pays the course fees for military education in the UK, and according to the UK MOD's *International Defence Engagement Strategy* from 2017, military training of foreign officers in the UK provides

> the UK with enduring influence and cementing our bilateral relations with partners. Both training and education also increase understanding of UK and international norms on priority areas such as human rights, transparency and the rules-based international order, while also helping to develop enabling capabilities and institutions.[13]

3.2.1 Oman's presence in British military academies

According to a written answer by the Minister of State for Defence in 2016, Earl Howe stated that officer training courses at UK military academies 'expose international partners to UK policy, and promote concepts of accountability, human rights and transparency. They are important in building skills which enable other countries to deal appropriately with their own internal problems, thereby contributing to regional security.'[14] A document entitled *Nations trained at RMA Sandhurst*, produced by Earl Howe, stated that the number of Omanis seconded to Sandhurst between 2005–06 and 2015–16 were as follows (see Table 3.1):

A freedom of information request submitted to the UK MOD to request numbers of Omanis seconded for training to RAF College Cranwell and Britannia Royal Naval College found that although the numbers are small, which may suggest that Britain is losing its influence as a training destination in comparison to the large numbers of secondees historically, the numbers are demonstrably holding steady year-on-year, as the figures show (see Tables 3.2 and 3.3):

In every year except 2008–09, there has been a small Omani presence at RAF Cranwell but not a consistent Bahraini one, suggesting that the Omani defence ministry is still reliant on British training to some extent and willing to keep this important soft power dynamic in place. The case could also be made, however, that these academies have also become dependent on the Government of Oman's soft power and their choice to continue sending cadets to the UK. As the table below demonstrates, there has been a steady number of Omanis seconded to Britannia Royal Naval College since at least 2005–06, and again, less Bahrainis who have proved more likely to train in the US rather than Britain, perhaps further evidence of a loss of British military training influence in Bahrain but not in Oman. The reasons behind the differentiation in numbers of seconded officers from both states could be attributed to costs and other factors rather than solely the strength of a British legacy, but Oman is openly more accepting of military cooperation

Table 3.1 Number of Omanis seconded to Sandhurst, 2005–06 to 2015–16

Number of Omanis seconded to RMA Sandhurst for officer training[15]											
2005–06	2006–07	2007–08	2008–09	2009–10	2010–11	2011–12	2012–13	2013–14	2014–15	2015–16
5	4	6	10	5	9	7	5	6	6	9

Table 3.2 Number of Omanis seconded to RAF College Cranwell, 2005–06 to 2015–16

Number of Omanis seconded to RAF College Cranwell for officer training[16]											
2005–06	2006–07	2007–08	2008–09	2009–10	2010–11	2011–12	2012–13	2013–14	2014–15	2015–16
10	≤5	≤5	0	≤5	≤5	≤5	≤5	≤5	≤5	≤5

Table 3.3 Number of Omanis seconded to Britannia Royal Naval College, 2005–06 to 2015–16

Number of Omanis seconded to Britannia Royal Naval College for officer training[17]											
2005–06	2006–07	2007–08	2008–09	2009–10	2010–11	2011–12	2012–13	2013–14	2014–15	2015–16
10	10	10	10	10	10	10	10	10	10	10

38 *Strategic power, defence, and security*

with Britain than Bahrain (as demonstrated by the continued joint UK–Omani *Saif Saarea* exercises).

Although the number of Omanis seconded to Sandhurst, Cranwell and RNC Britannia between 2005 and 2016 have not been particularly large in comparison to the number of Omanis accepted to study in mainstream British universities, Oman does not currently second officers for training to any country other than the UK, so despite the small numbers, Britain is unrivalled in its ability to influence officers at the start of their military careers. This instils British security values into the future development of the Omani armed forces. The consistent number of cadets seconded to RNC Britannia suggests that British expert power in naval tactics has remained more constant than army or air force expertise.

It is important to contextualise the number of Omani cadets at each military academy with the total number of international students each year. The following table highlights the strong presence of Omani cadets in each year where data was available in comparison to the total international presence, particularly at RNC Britannia where Omanis formed the largest single nationality each year[18] (see Table 3.4).

A former British Ambassador to Oman claimed that Sultan Qaboos was emotionally invested in the Sandhurst system, he adored the way that British military academies teach British-specific tactics of warfare, and the generations of Omani officers trained in British military institutions keeps the ties between the two countries alive. There is an impression that Oman remains British-oriented for defence training, and there is no sign that this will change in the near future because the government in Oman feels comfortable with the interdependence between the British and Omani militaries.[20]

Table 3.4 Total number of foreign cadets seconded to the UK, 2012–16

Academy	Year	Number of foreign cadets	Total number of nationalities[19]
RMA Sandhurst	2012	70	59
	2013	70	
	2014	80	
	2015	80	
	2016	80	
RNC Britannia	2012	60	41
	2013	60	
	2014	60	
	2015	60	
	2016	40	
RAF Cranwell	2012	30	40
	2013	30	
	2014	70	
	2015	50	
	2016	60	

In the case of Qaboos, the military education in the UK that he received is a major contributing factor to the continued influence and presence of British defence companies and individuals in the contemporary Omani state. This influence has continued in Sultan Haitham's government, but it would be difficult to contend that the attraction to British education is as strong as under Qaboos because the new Sultan has not received defence training in Britain and thus has not developed the same mindset.

The importance of the relationships that developed between Qaboos and his fellow students is also of note as this proved to be a long-lasting personal channel through which a sense of Britishness was instilled into Omani defence affairs. Many of the defence advisors in Qaboos' first government after his accession to power in 1970 were friends that he had met during his time in education in the UK, all of whom stayed in post past 1971 and many past 1975, after the majority of British troops were withdrawn at the end of the Dhofar War. The closest relationship that Qaboos developed at Sandhurst was with Timothy Landon, a British Brigadier who would come to be the closest confidante of the Sultan after his rise to power and the main advisor on the development of the economy and government of the modern Omani state. Often referred to as one of the 'coterie of expatriate advisers known as the Muscat mafia,'[21] Landon was a former loan officer in Oman at the time of the coup that brought Qaboos to power and a friend that would outlast many of the other advisors that he appointed. Although Landon was undoubtedly influential in the military affairs of Oman, with evidence in the countless archival documents suggesting that he was one of the key proponents of purchasing British-manufactured weapons and defence equipment throughout the 1980s and 1990s, it was another influential British expatriate that Qaboos had come into contact with during his time serving with the British forces in Germany, General Timothy Creasey, that proved more influential on defence decisions in Oman.

The military educational links between Oman and Britain were visibly one-sided for several decades, with Omani officers training in Britain but not the reverse. In what could be described as a sign of the gradual shift of balance in the bilateral relationship and evidence of Oman's recent divergence away from its reliance on Britain, in 2018, a British officer graduated from Oman's own equivalent of Sandhurst. British attraction to the skills and expertise of Oman's officer training academy now plays a part in the decision-making processes of British military officials. This attraction grants Oman unrivalled levels of persuasion that has never been present before.

3.2.2 *Oman's wider security educational presence*

Security training of Omanis in the UK does not end at military training, there is also close cooperation between the Royal Oman Police (ROP) and various police forces in Britain. This highlights the relevance of British expert power on wider contemporary security affairs in the minds of Omani decision makers. A security and justice project, in force between March 2014 and March 2017, which is reported to have been worth £900,000, resulted in at least two[22] senior ROP officers spending ten days training alongside PSNI officers[23] – although the number is almost certainly much higher than this. The police training at the Garnerville Police College in Belfast, Northern Ireland was organised by a not-for-profit public body owned by Northern Ireland's investment agency, Invest NI, called *Northern Ireland Cooperation Overseas*, and received an undisclosed amount of money from the FCO's *Conflict, Stability and Security Fund* (CSSF).[24] Oman is not in the UK Government's list of aid countries, which the CSSF is intended to support, so it is notable that British funds are being used to support security development there. Previously, British advisors would lead the training on the ground in Oman, but it is perhaps a sign of the shift in the relationship that ROP officers are now being funded to spend time in the UK for training rather than Britons being seconded to Oman. The *CSSF Annual Report 2016/17* defines its aims as:

> investing in reforms to the police, military, justice and prisons, as well as engaging with community providers of security and safety, the CSSF supports the ability of countries emerging from fragility to respond effectively to local security issues, thereby reducing the risk to the UK and our interests overseas.[25]

Omani police and justice reforms are a continuation of the post-1971 cooperation efforts by the British Government, and in this case also the devolved administrations within the UK. Oman is not considered to be a fragile or emerging state by the UK Government's own standards, so funds have been allocated to assist the Sultanate outside of the remit of the CSSF guidelines. It could be argued that offering financial inducements to cooperate with Britain is a form of 'reward power.' This form of power is one of the purest types of soft power; influence that does not require any force.

As seems to be the case across the wider security realm, the British legacy in Oman is likely the reason for the ROP choosing to request and accept training in the UK rather than elsewhere. British advisors cemented their influence in Oman's domestic security services when the foundations of a police force were laid prior to withdrawal and it is this influence that has seemingly given the Omani government the assurance that the British police forces are best placed to teach the ROP the skills necessary to deal with security issues that may arise, possibly linked to the threat of an uprising by opposition groups as was seen in other Middle Eastern states during the Arab Spring. A senior official in the ROP clearly stated that

> we would only consider training in the UK. The UK and Oman have cooperated closely historically, and the UK police have skills that we

Britain's strategic engagement with Oman 41

need here in Oman. We send officers to Northern Ireland to train with a police force that shares things in common with the ROP.[26]

There is strong evidence of a British presence and influence in every area of Omani security education and training young Omanis at the beginning of their careers is one way to secure the future of British influence in Omani security affairs. The key observation that can be made about the UK–Omani security training relationship is a commonality that has become ever-present across the wider bilateral relationship. As the years since withdrawal have progressed, Britain's influence has arguably become dependent on the continued willingness and acceptance of the Omani authorities to train in Britain; an immediate transition in 1975 from Omani officers having no other options but to train in the British academies, as the Residency barred foreign states from cooperating with Oman, to Omani security officials opting to retain the educational links.

3.3 How do joint security exercises contribute to the development of the UK–Omani relationship?

On a similar theme to security training, the British and Omani militaries cooperated closely prior to and during the transition from Sultan Sa'id to Qaboos, largely as a result of the Dhofar War and the commitments that the British Government had made to ruling Sultans since the early 19th century. It was arguably after Qaboos' rise to power that the military relationship shifted from one based on Omani reliance on British protection to a relationship built on equality and shared values; a transition from unrivalled hard power to voluntarily cooperative soft power. The extent to which Britain cooperates with Oman (and the wider Gulf) ultimately depends on the political party in power in the UK. Conservative governments since 1971 have demonstrated a willingness to cooperate more closely on military matters with the Gulf governments than Labour administrations. This could explain why joint military training exercises between the British and Omani militaries, known as *Saif Saarea* (swift sword), first took place during the Thatcher government in 1986. In a statement to Parliament, Minister of State for the Armed Forces at the time of the first *Saif Saarea*, John Stanley, described the exercise:

> Exercise Saif Sareea (Swift Sword), a combined United Kingdom–Omani exercise took place in Oman between 15 November and 8 December and was most successful. The exercise, involving nearly 5,000 British service men, achieved its aim of demonstrating our capability for rapid strategic deployment outside the NATO area. It also enabled the three services to practice combined operations with a host nation.[27]

At the time of this first UK–Omani joint training exercise, the UK was not undertaking any other training on the same scale with any other foreign state, and it is this factor that arguably demonstrates a special relationship between the UK and Oman that endured withdrawal in 1975. Although it is not clear exactly why Sultan Qaboos accepted the invitation to host a 5,000-strong training mission from Michael Heseltine, British Secretary of State for Defence in 1985 when plans were being laid, the bonds between the two militaries cemented during the Dhofar War is a plausible explanation. The fact that 'there is a shared military heritage between the UK and Oman, visible through joint regiments and regimental history that has come about as officers have returned back to their regiments after training and serving with the British military and imparted what they had learned onto their service personnel'[28] could also explain why the two militaries are so able and willing to cooperate to the extent of *Saif Saarea*. The practical military element of the bilateral relationship is seemingly the last remaining vestige of British hard power in Oman. Joint military exercises are an overt way to prove to would-be enemy states that Oman has the protection of one of the most powerful military powers in the world and that Britain still has a security presence at the entrance to the Gulf and the Indian Ocean.

Proponents of Nye's power theory would describe this cooperative military exercise as a combination of hard and soft power, termed as 'smart power.' Nye claimed that military prowess can be used to both coerce and attract, so in the case of *Saif Saarea*, British policymakers have used Britain's hard power military assets to demonstrate that British values include protecting historic allies, and attractive values are considered a key element of soft power.[29] The military legacy also comes into play, as the grounds for British troops to train alongside Omanis were most likely laid during the Dhofar War. John Stanley told parliament of the operations that:

> The aim of the exercise will be to practise our ability to respond rapidly to a crisis outside the NATO area. The exercise will involve some 5,000 service men from all three services. The units taking part will include elements of 5 Airborne Brigade and 3 Commando Brigade. It will also involve ships from the Royal Navy task group, which will be on its way back from its planned deployment to the Pacific. In addition, the RAF will make a major contribution in the form of a detachment of Tornado aircraft and substantial air transport resources. Exercise Saif Sareea will be the largest out-of-area exercise we have undertaken for many years.[30]

The repeated requests by Omani decision makers for these training exercises implies that, even in the contemporary era, the British military has retained expert power that appeals to Oman. It could also be argued that the acceptance of training requests results in another type of power for Britain – reward power, as British arms manufacturers gain a larger number of orders for weapons shortly after these exercises have taken place. The Omani military is also rewarded for their cooperation with Britain through the extension of generous export credit guarantees to buy from British arms manufacturers.

3.3.1 Shared defence exercises in Oman

The first joint military exercise since withdrawal included elements of each of the three armed forces, both British and Omani, demonstrating the widespread determination on both sides to undertake an operation that would be seen by the rulers of the other Gulf states as a commitment by Britain to regional security and a demonstration of the close military bond between Britain and her oldest ally in the Middle East.

The second *Saif* Saarea exercise took place between September and October 2001 and at the time was the largest deployment of British troops since the First Gulf War, and the third in 2018, was the largest deployment of the three. It has been estimated by the UK MOD that the third exercise cost approximately £100 million to stage and involved 5,500 British troops and 2% of the whole Omani population (over 92,700 people) at every stage of organising and undertaking the training exercise.[31] The cost was shared between the two states, and this undoubtedly demonstrates a willingness to cooperate on defence and contribute significant resources to the cause. It also demonstrates that Britain has been able to retain significant respect and influence within Oman's defence ministry and the wider Omani leadership for the SAF to commit so many resources to training with an ally, albeit one that decided to abandon the Sultanate in 1975 after more than a century of hegemony. The army of Oman has traditionally, and remains, the most 'Omani' of the three main armed forces as a result of the tribal roots in the history of the establishment of the army.[32] This makes the third *Saif Saarea* exercise more interesting from an analytical perspective as the joint training operation largely focused on the British and Omani armies, evidence that the government in Oman is still willing to practice tactics with the British. The third exercise, as with the previous two, should not be considered just as a commitment by the UK MOD to assisting Oman with the development and enhancement of its military tactics, there is an element of pragmatism involved with Britain taking part in the exercise. At the heart of the military exercise is the ability for Britain's forces to

> test their capability to deploy at scale in terrain (i.e. the arid deserts of Oman) unfamiliar to many of the British troops taking part in *Saif Saarea*. The exercise in 2018 was also an attempt to test the interoperability skills of the British Army that could be replicated with other countries in future conflicts.[33]

As was the case in the previous exercises, Britain demonstrating its continued influence in Oman and the securing of a British military footprint in the Sultanate arguably also sent a message to other states looking to gain a foothold in Oman, such as France or the US, that Oman was still firmly within Britain's sphere of influence. The latest joint exercise was one method through which the British Government has been able to utilise historic ties to protect UK interests – both economic and strategic – in perhaps one of the most overt ways possible. As Britain no longer enjoys guaranteed access to Oman for training in desert warfare, the British Government is unquestionably reliant on the Sultan of Oman to continue inviting Britain to take part in training exercises in an increasingly important part of the world.

Joint security exercises do not solely relate to military training. Indeed, non-military security cooperation between the UK and Oman is more covert than the *Saif Saarea* exercise, which ultimately aimed to be a visible sign to the international community of the shared military commitments of Britain to Oman. Another tenet of the UK and Oman's special relationship is the covert cooperation in intelligence gathering,[34] with Oman home to the largest GCHQ base outside of the UK. Although it is not known exactly how many intelligence bases GCHQ has in Oman, security analyst Anthony Cordesman mentioned three in his 1997 book *Bahrain, Oman, Qatar, and the UAE: Challenges of Security*; 'an intelligence post near Muscat and [use] the Omani base at Goat Island in the Strait of Hormuz and a new intelligence post at Qabl in the Musandam Peninsula.'[35] A retired diplomat in the Gulf confirmed that 'former SAS and intelligence officers are currently running "research offices" in obscure regions of Oman.'[36] Oman, and the Strait of Hormuz, form one of the most important meeting points of trade and digital communications in the world, and as the Omani ISS (*Jahaz al Amn al Dakhly*) was established by the British, it arguably makes sense for the British Government to utilise its influence in the Sultanate to intercept communications from Iran and Middle Eastern non-state actors that could pose a threat to British interests both in the Gulf and the UK. It is believed that Oman also cooperates with the US on intelligence gathering too, which would not have been allowed to happen prior to 1971. GCHQ and the ISS are in many ways intertwined in Oman, with the British Government putting great trust in the ISS to keep the site locations and intercepted data secret, and the Omani government respecting Britain's security services so much that they have allowed them to retain a significant presence in, it appears, many regions within the Sultanate. As is the case on every level of the post-1971 UK–Omani relationship, there is undoubtedly a benefit to Oman for agreeing to host numerous GCHQ sites, namely Britain wanting to protect its intelligence-gathering capabilities in Oman and thus indirectly also protecting Oman so that these capabilities are not threatened by hostile states or groups in the region. Oman's intelligence cooperation with GCHQ could also be understood as another example of how Sultan Qaboos leaned towards countries that he understood and was comfortable working with, and as he grew up and was trained in the British security tradition and British intelligence officials established the ISS on the basis of Britain's intelligence services, there is undoubtedly no country that he felt comfortable cooperating with to the same extent as the UK. In what is becoming a common theme, Britain has become increasingly dependent on various aspects of the Omani relationship to secure its position in the world. This Omani strategic power over Britain has emerged as one of the strongest assets that Oman has, in contrast to the economic power that most other Gulf states have as a result of their extensive oil reserves.

Since Sultan Haitham's accession to the Omani throne, intelligence cooperation with Britain has remained strong. Qaboos permitted the ISS and GCHQ to work so closely together that it would be difficult to end this partnership. In the first year of his reign, Haitham has remained committed to retaining the security links to Britain as these contribute to domestic security, but future GCC integration or the development of deeper relations between Oman and China or India could persuade Haitham to abandon security cooperation with Britain. In the post-Qaboos era, Omani decision makers are more pragmatic, prioritising state interests over a historic relationship.

The joint security exercises between Britain and Oman, whether military or non-military, are inextricably linked to a political will on the part of both states to continue the expansion of cooperation despite the ending of the treaties that bound Britain to protecting Oman after withdrawal. There is also an obvious attraction for the Omani authorities to continue cooperating with their oldest security ally, to learn in-field British tactics, and assist Britain with intelligence gathering; evidence of British soft power attraction manifesting as physical hard power military and security activities, albeit with a reduced ability to influence decision-making.

3.4 How does the loan service personnel relationship influence British power in Oman?

Security cooperation between Britain and Oman is not limited to in-field training: the privileged British position is also demonstrated by the number of British loan service personnel serving in the Sultan's Armed Forces and the roles that these personnel hold, both the number who stayed behind in 1971 at the point of withdrawal and those who are still seconded from the British military over five decades after 1971. The secondment of British personnel to Oman is often overlooked by contemporary analysts, with focus largely on the reverse, the number of Omanis seconded to military academies in the UK, this despite LSPs holding key positions in Oman's military since at least the turn of the 20th century. Britain's expert power is yet again demonstrated at the highest levels of the Omani military and the presence

46 *Strategic power, defence, and security*

of British secondees secures a British voice in the senior ranks of Omani strategic decision-making.

The number of LSPs serving in the Omani military fluctuates every year, and although the number has fallen significantly since the 1970s and the roles of the loaned personnel have changed since that time, the presence of British service personnel in the independent military force of the Sultanate arguably suggests that there exists an underlying willingness by both countries to retain the close ties that bind the UK and Oman together. There are a number of reasons why both sides may want to retain the loan service system as it currently exists: comfort with the relationship and an unwillingness to change what has proven beneficial for both the UK as the sender state and Oman as the receiver state, the British Government wanting to reduce costs arising as officers retire from the British services, Britain wanting to retain influence in the military affairs of a strategically important state in the Middle East, historical links dating back to the Dhofar War, and the presence of British advisors in the government of Oman and their preference for recruiting British personnel.

According to a retired Omani Brigadier General, loaned British LSPs are directly answerable to the Chief of Staff of the Sultan's Armed Forces,[37] so all seconded military officers and Senior NCOs are effectively serving in the interests of Oman as *de facto* Omanis throughout the period of their secondment. A former Colonel in the Trucial Oman Scouts who also trained Omani forces to use battle tanks in the 1980s, suggested that

> British and Omani troops always saw themselves as equal as they came from similar circumstances, and thus British LSPs since the 1970s actually wanted to serve alongside Omanis as there was a close bond and affinity between them; they were not serving in Oman because they had to be there on the orders of the UK MOD.[38]

Only British LSPs are permitted by the Omani government to serve in Oman despite requests from other GCC states to Oman's defence officials to permit the placement of their troops and trainers into the SAF,[39] so although Oman has been in effective control of its own military and security affairs since 1971, there is a reluctance on the Omani side to sever the personnel ties with the UK. It also appears that Omani officials are also guarding the independence of their military from interference by other GCC governments. This could be explained as evidence of a continuation of Britain's ability to influence Omani military affairs, a sentiment that was never actually lost after withdrawal, but it could also be a sign of pragmatism by the late Sultan Qaboos.

Throughout most of his time in power, Qaboos was reluctant to change tactics from those that have proven to work in Oman's interests, and in the case of allowing LSPs from Britain to serve and train the SAF, which has contributed to Oman's military becoming the largest and best trained in the Gulf. There is arguably no reason why Qaboos would have permitted other countries to second personnel to the SAF as this could have altered the balance that exists between the UK and Oman. Lord Dear, a crossbench member of the House of Lords, spoke about a visit to Oman on the invitation of his son-in-law, a senior British Army officer stationed in the country, where he highlighted 'the tremendous warmth that exists towards this country (UK) and the value that they (Omanis) place on our military support,'[40] this, despite no formal treaty being in place until 2018 pertaining specifically to LSPs. As the LSP relationship was not formalised by a treaty until very recently, the sharing of personnel can only be described as based on the will of both states to share expertise and the presence of a lasting legacy of Britain's historic military role in the Sultanate.

One of the key factors of soft power is the ability to attract support rather than coerce a state to do something. Although since withdrawal, the role of LSPs has changed from an overt position of serving with the Omani forces to one of just training Omani troops, a shift from a hard position to a soft one, Britain is still the only state permitted by the Omani Government to send trainers to the Sultanate. This is undoubtedly soft power in action, where Britons have retained influence largely as a result of the attractiveness of their military style and joint trust in each other's abilities. Nye argued that as states have become more interconnected globally, the use of hard power coercion has become less acceptable.[41] This corresponds to the situation between Britain and Oman, where the relationship has developed towards one based on a shared desire to share skills rather than have it forced upon Oman by the British Government. If British soft power is as strong as this research suggests, then the succession in Oman should have no bearing on the attraction or willingness of Omani decision makers to continue the LSP relationship.

3.4.1 Continued reliance on British expertise

Military affairs is the main area of the UK–Omani relationship where expert power is the most important asset for the British Government. The Omani government did not end its reliance on British LSPs or contract personnel immediately after the majority of British troops left at the end of the Dhofar War in 1975, so this was a major asset left behind by the British after withdrawal, even if not necessarily intentionally on the part of London. When the British Government informed Qaboos that British troops would be fully withdrawn from the RAF base at Salalah in 1975, 'he much hoped that HMG would be prepared to leave "one or two" seconded RAF officers behind to assist SOAF.'[42] The Sultan personally requested that the British Government retain some military influence in the SOAF, which is arguably testament to the respect that he had for the British personnel that had seen serving in his country, and perhaps also as a result of his wariness of a resurgence by the tribes in the country's southern provinces after the visible

48 *Strategic power, defence, and security*

British military presence had left. Britain's personnel influence is one aspect of the bilateral relationship that seemingly weathered withdrawal from East of the Suez, it just changed form.

By 1980, the British Government had agreed with Qaboos that a process of Omanisation, whereby Omanis would take over all of the roles previously held by British LSPs in the SOAF, would be undertaken at pace.[43] This transfer of senior roles to Omanis did not go to plan, and thus a major obstacle to British military withdrawal was that the Omani lieutenants[44] who were to take control from British commanders in the SON 'lacked the skills necessary to replace loan service or contract personnel.'[45] The Defence Attaché similarly reported of Omanis in the SOLF that 'a significant problem is the lack of experience on the part of formation and unit commanders in the handling of Battle Groups and Combat Teams.'[46] So, although the Omanisation of the military was an accepted policy of both the British and Omani governments, it was not practically possible, at least to the timetable put forward by Qaboos in 1980. Thus in 1984, the Omani military was still actively recruiting British personnel to serve in senior ranks, in some cases to shift the balance away from other nationalities. In the British Embassy's defence review of 1984, it is mentioned that 'SON is recruiting 20 contract British Senior Ratings to shift the balance of Senior Rates away from Pakistanis.'[47] The same defence review also mentions that:

> 78 Loan Service posts are now agreed for SOAF ... Air Works LLC, now with over 1,000 employees in Oman, British Aerospace and Marconi provide technical support and training under contract. The Loan Service Personnel, led by CSOAF himself, and contract civilian staff do a most commendable job educating and encouraging young Omanis towards British procedures and equipment in the face of intensifying American competition ... for influence.[48]

The political will on both sides to retain a British presence in Oman, albeit on a smaller and less overt scale than previously, resulted in the transition of the roles held by loaned personnel from openly serving in the SOAF alongside and in command of Omani troops, to a relationship based on the recruitment of 'British "Training Teams" to assist and advise the new (Omani) Commanding Officers.'[49] A wide-ranging report produced by the Directors of Defence Policy in MOD, entitled *British Military Assistance to Oman – 1976*, stated:

> in present circumstances the security of Oman remains highly dependent on the continuation of British military support. ... When the RAF Detachment hands over to the Omanis at the end of March 1977, the direct assistance commitment will be reduced by over 100 servicemen. ... We support the plan for the retention of 3 liaison teams (which

would reduce the total SAS strength in Oman from 55 to 15) ... it has been proposed to replace the existing 4 members of the AIT (a team dealing with psychological operations) with LSP in September 1976. ... the Royal Engineers should remain in Dhofar for as long as possible and has requested an increase of 9 men ... the Royal Engineer Squadron will be augmented by 6 Army administrative personnel ... by the beginning of April 1977, the numbers of direct assistance personnel remaining in Oman can be reduced from the current figure of 268 to 120.[50]

In 1976, one year after the conclusion of the Dhofar War and after the bulk of British combat troops had been withdrawn from Oman, the MOD was evidently trying to reduce the numbers of military personnel in the country, but the excerpts from the defence report suggests that British military officials were trying to find ways to either keep Britons in their roles for an extended period or reassign them to similar roles with different titles, such as 'liaison teams' or 'administrative personnel.' Although the British Government had committed to withdrawing a majority of personnel from Oman, it could be assumed that the military high command were not as willing to do this. The shift from overt to covert influence, at least in the area of LSPs in the SOAF, demonstrated the continued influence that Britain was able to retain over domestic defence affairs after the realities of withdrawal had become evident in Oman in the early 1980s and Omani nationals were being put forward to take over senior military and security roles across the Sultanate. In 1982, PM Margaret Thatcher confirmed in a letter to Sultan Qaboos:

I can confirm that we agree to an increase in numbers of British Loan Service Personnel until Omani replacements are available. We hope to be able to meet the current bid for an increase of 82 posts in 1982/83 ... On the question of the position of British Loan Service Personnel in time of either internal or regional conflict ... we would be content that British personnel should play their full part in Oman's defence.[51]

Although the Omanisation policy began in 1980, fully signed up to by the Thatcher administration, and at this point, the British Government demonstrated its commitment to reduce the overt image of Britons in Oman, this letter sent directly from the Conservative Prime Minister to the Sultan suggested otherwise. It also demonstrated that the British Government was not ready at that time to fully submit to its new soft power status, where Britons were no longer in direct command of the Omani military, and perhaps evidence of Thatcher's reluctance to accept the outright withdrawal from the Gulf on the terms set out by Harold Wilson, a former Labour PM.

3.4.2 Loan service personnel and British arms sales

The withdrawal, or lack of, by the British of their personnel from Oman was also linked to the rapid modernisation efforts that Qaboos was determined to undertake through the purchase of advanced weaponry from British defence companies that only British personnel were trained to use at the time; British LSPs were therefore required to teach the Omanis how to use this new machinery effectively. As has become the norm in bilateral defence relationships around the world, and also in the UK–Omani relationship, the personal aspects of defence – the British officers and trainers in Oman – are inextricably linked to defence sales and the development of trading partnerships between British arms manufacturers and the SAF. Senior officials in the British Government were already well aware of this fact by 1981 when John Gamp, a representative of the MOD, told his government that it is recognised 'that additional LSP posts will be necessary as a result of the equipment expansion programme being undertaken by SOAF.'[52] The self-reliance that was supposed to arise in Oman after the withdrawal of British personnel and the Omanisation policies implemented by the government were apparently setback by the determination to modernise the SOAF with equipment and weaponry purchased from British defence manufacturers. Although it was undoubtedly in Britain's interests to retain a small number of military personnel in Oman as trainers, who taught and continue to teach British tactics to the Omani military, it was arguably a result of the positions that British officers and LSPs had held in the Sultanate's forces for over a century that resulted in this continuation of Omani requests for British personnel to accompany the new equipment purchases and develop Omani tactics for the future. It also makes sense that purchasing from British defence companies, where the weapons have been developed by British engineers, inevitably required British contract personnel, at least in the short term.

One key element of British soft power is the ability to persuade the Omanis to purchase the majority of their defence equipment from British manufacturers; non-defence manufactured exports from Britain to Oman are negligible. Although weapons and machinery are considered hard power assets, the political will is evident on the Omani side to willingly choose to buy British, despite offers of sometimes better priced and higher-quality equipment from the US, France, Italy, and others, so Britain retained the ability to co-opt Oman to modernise their military with British hardware.

Throughout the 1980s, senior figures within the Omani military, many who had been elevated to senior ranks as a result of Omanisation targets, opted to contract British military personnel with whom they had served alongside either during the Dhofar War or in the Trucial Oman Scouts prior to 1971, to train Omani troops in the use of advanced military technology. This could be referred to as 'personal power' from the perspective of Britain, as the connections between individuals is often a key reason for governments agreeing to training requests.

In the 1980s, a former British Colonel who had served with the Trucial Oman Scouts tank regiment in the Trucial States and Oman in the 1960s was asked by senior Omani military officials to return to Oman on contract to train Omanis in the use of British tanks. Prior to the 1980s, Oman had no tanks of its own, but Sultan Qaboos and his senior leadership team had seen them in use on television and let it be known that they wanted the SOLF to purchase tanks and have them operational, with Omani drivers, within six months in time for the National Day celebrations. The Colonel recounted how, as a result of Oman being open to non-British companies by the 1980s,

> the US sent a number of American-made tanks to Oman, but the Sultan said that he wanted tanks from Britain instead. A senior Omani royal visited the office where I was working and asked to see my Commanding Officer to ask him to go to Oman to teach Omanis how to use tanks. My CO was out, so I volunteered, got permission from my seniors, and travelled to Oman to teach a small number of Omanis in tank warfare in time for the National Day six months later.[53]

In this example, but also in many areas of defence procurement since, Oman has been offered rival equipment to that available from British manufacturers and other countries have offered their military trainers to the Omanis, but senior figures in the SOAF have on many occasions opted to choose the British options instead. It would not be amiss to suggest that the reason for this is a combination of the British military support for the Omanis in times of need throughout modern history and the fact that the Sultan was educated at Sandhurst in Britain. Although these are important factors, the more practical reason for senior Omani defence officials choosing to purchase weaponry from Britain and request training by seconded British officers in light of offers from other countries is because of the accompanying service offered by British companies supplying the weapons and machinery.

Along with the tanks that were sold to Oman in the 1980s, and the many military aircraft and artillery, 'Airwork Limited sent lots of British engineers to Oman to maintain the military equipment sold to the country's armed forces. Sultan Qaboos was reassured that Britons were looking after them,'[54] and this reliable after service undoubtedly contributed to the continuation by the Omani government's offering to British companies first refusal until recently. The contractors working for Airwork in Oman, many of which were retired British servicemen, was also arguably evidence of the necessity to retain a British presence in the Sultanate as a result of modernisation of the military hardware. Airwork seconded over 3,000 engineers and support staff to Oman, some maintaining British weapons in use by the SOAF and others undertaking pilot training of Omani cadets.

3.4.3 A relationship shift

The UK–Omani defence relationship entered a new stage under the Conservative administrations of PMs David Cameron and Theresa May, one seemingly built on the basis of equality between the two states once again. Plans for the third *Saif Saarea* joint exercise likely hastened the strengthening of this relationship. A Memorandum of Understanding was signed by the British Secretary of Defence at the time, Gavin Williamson, and Oman's Minister of Defence Affairs, Sayyid Badr bin Saud Al Busaidi, to strengthen the loaning of service personnel between the two countries and, for the first time in history, permit Omani officers to serve in the British armed forces[55] on equal terms with British and Commonwealth personnel. Oman is the only country with a reverse LSP scheme in place with the MOD. Other countries do second troops to serve in the UK military, but British troops are not seconded back to the sending force.[56] Not only does this new-found equality in sharing military personnel further symbolise the close political ties between the British and Omani militaries, ties that are evidently stronger than with any other Middle Eastern state, it also suggests that Oman has developed its own modern military capabilities in such a way as to be very similar to those used by the British military that the MOD feels comfortable allowing Omani troops to serve and train alongside British counterparts in the UK.

The MOD has sent hundreds of LSPs to Oman since withdrawal to train the Omanis, so there is little to separate the two militaries. Similarly, a strong British LSP legacy binds the two together. There is also a very evident soft power element at play here, as the Omanis have been free to choose who trains their troops and supplies defence equipment since Britain's withdrawal, but the Omani military leaders are still openly committed to keeping alive their strong personnel ties with Britain. Oman is arguably still attracted to what British LSPs can offer to their forces, and 'referent power' is demonstrated in action by the ability of Britain to attract Oman because of the admiration and respect that Omani decision makers have for British technology and leadership.

3.5 What influence do arms sales to Oman have on Britain's influence?

Oman is a major purchaser of defence equipment from UK-based defence manufacturers, the largest and most high-profile being BAE Systems plc, but the likes of Airwork, Vickers Defence Systems, and AgustaWestland have also been awarded important contracts to supply modern weaponry to the Omani military since 1971. The economics of defence should not be underestimated, as supplying defence equipment to Oman is seemingly one way that Britain has been able to retain its privileged position in the country and a strong soft power asset. This type of power could also be defined as referent power, as Oman remains attracted to the technology offered by British arms manufacturers because of the training opportunities with British tanks and aircraft. Prior to 1971, Omani defence purchases were restricted to British companies or those approved by the Consul-General in Muscat or the Residency in Bahrain, so it should come as no surprise that British defence companies are present and influential in the Sultanate. After British withdrawal in 1975, Oman was able to open up to non-British defence suppliers, so it is important to assess the reasons why British defence companies have remained so important in Oman, with BAE sometimes being referred to as a shadow government in Oman because of its almost unrivalled position as the go-to supplier for the SAF and the non-defence activities that the company undertakes domestically, including investing in youth development and leadership training through *Outward Bound Oman*[57] and financing Chevening study scholarships for a number of Omani students to study at UK universities[58] in 2018.

Retired Brigadier General A claimed that when the Omani government embarks on an upgrade process of its military equipment and weaponry, the government is sensible with the prices that it is willing to pay for new equipment, but price is not the most important factor taken into account when considering which companies to buy from. He suggested that the political stability of the seller country is more important, as is the knowledge that the government of the seller state will stand beside Oman in times of need.[59] This claim corresponds to Oman's tendency to buy from British defence manufacturers, particularly from BAE Systems. Weapons produced by BAE are not always the cheapest on the market (partial BAE-manufactured Eurofighter Typhoons cost between $65 and $136 million each; French Dassault Rafale cost approximately $84–91 million each; American General Dynamics F-16 Fighting Falcon cost between $30 and $75 million each),[60] nor are they always the most advanced, but BAE is backed by the British Government, and this is undoubtedly an influential contributing factor to Oman's preference for buying British. BAE was formerly a majority British Government-owned Public Limited Company until 1981, after the merger of British Aircraft Corporation, Hawker Siddeley Dynamics and Scottish Aviation. Although British institutional investors owned only 9.71% of the company compared with 22.92% US ownership at the time of writing,[61] the fact is that the manufacturer is still headquartered in the City of London and receives significant policy and financial support from the UK Government.

From the point of Sultan Qaboos' accession to power until 1985, major Omani military procurement decisions were determined by a chain of command consisting of just two British expatriates close to the Sultan, Air Vice Marshal Erik Bennett, former Commander of the Sultan of Oman's Air Force and General Sir Timothy Creasey, former Chief of the Defence Staff, and Sultan Qaboos himself.[62] It is understandable, and therefore arguably inevitable, that British defence companies were given priority for the first two decades of Sultan Qaboos' reign. From 1983, it was decided that SOAF

54 *Strategic power, defence, and security*

needed to modernise its air fleet, and according to the British Ambassador in Oman at the time, 'Bennett [was] firmly convinced that the ADF Tornado [was] the air-defence fighter he need(ed) to replace his ageing Hunters and so [has] convinced Creasey and the Sultan.'[63] It took until early 1984 for Qaboos to commit to purchasing replacement aircraft, but he did choose the ADF Tornado (also known as the Panavia Tornado), which was partially manufactured by BAE. 'When General Creasey called on Mr Luce yesterday, he confirmed that the Omanis had indeed decided to buy 8 Tornados (he added that they had also decided to buy FH70 guns).'[64] The FH70 gun is majority-manufactured in Barrow-in-Furness, UK by Vickers Shipbuilding and Engineering Ltd. This was perhaps the first occasion that British defence companies faced competition to supply military aircraft to Oman in history, but also the first major procurement decision that Qaboos had to make since his accession to the throne; he eventually chose to buy from two of the largest suppliers in the UK. The British legacy of supplying reliable defence equipment to Oman does come into play here, and Qaboos likely felt comfortable purchasing equipment from a manufacturer that he was personally familiar with, but it is also possible that British soft power dynamics and strong contract law that would reassure Qaboos that he would receive all of the equipment that he purchased and a strong diplomatic presence in Oman lobbying on behalf of BAE also proved influential in this decision.

3.5.1 *Defence contracts after the end of hegemony*

Defence sales is perhaps the most striking example of how withdrawal impacted the monopoly that Britain once had on equipment sales to Oman. This is also the aspect of the strategic relationship that overlaps with economic priorities. After the belated withdrawal in 1975, the former British treaty right to choose which companies (and countries) could supply weaponry and machinery to Oman ended. The highest levels of the British Government committed to continuing to supply Oman with the weapons that it needed in 1976 and work to overcome financial issues, as demonstrated in a briefing paper produced for James Callaghan prior to his first meeting with Sultan Qaboos.

> Particular difficulties have arisen over payment for the expensive (approximately £300m) air defence system (Jaguar/Rapier) being supplied by the British Aircraft Corporation. The Omanis recently approached HMG for help through ECGD in staggering payments … We are the leading (defence) exporter to Oman and must try to stay in that position.[65]

As was also the case in Bahrain, major French and US companies, with the support of their respective governments and embassies, were quick to move in to seize the new opportunity to sell defence equipment to the SOAF.

Although other countries attempted to sell equipment to Oman throughout the 1980s, documents suggest that the significant British influence at the top of the decision-making chain ensured that British companies were either given first refusal or their bids were accepted over those from non-British companies. Creasey, former Commander of the SOAF, was the most active of the senior British officials in Oman pushing for British companies to be awarded defence contracts.

In 1983, the SOAF was searching for a tri-service fixed communications system, which 'looked to be in the pocket of Lytton (US) operating under Saudi influences, has now been pushed firmly our way by General Creasey ... we can expect to achieve very substantial equipment sales (estimated at up to £200m).'[66] Also in the same year, Bennett, former Commander of SOAF, actively persuaded the Sultan to opt for British weapons after a French ministerial visits to Oman in an attempt to sell French equipment.

> The French Minister of Defence, M. Charles Hernu, visited Oman from 8–10 January ... Yesterday Erik Bennett confirmed my assumption that the main object of the visit was to press the sale of the Mirage 2000 ... Bennett remains firmly committed to Tornado and his view is supported by Creasey and the Sultan.[67]

Despite the firm commitments by the US and French governments and high-profile visits by senior ministers to support their bids, the contracts were awarded to British companies.

British advisors to the Sultan were usually seen as an asset by the British Government and British defence companies, as a way to persuade the Sultan to buy British, but sometimes the advisors put Omani interests before British ones. In 1981, Creasey notified negotiators from the MOD of the necessity to renegotiate the supply of Chieftain tanks to the SOAF. Creasey, with less money to spend as a result of Omani financial difficulties at the time, told British negotiators that:

> he intended to buy only 15 tanks (1 squadron of 12 plus 3 WMR), that he wished to buy the 12 Chieftains on lease, and that he would consider a further buy of 12 more 'surplus' Chieftains in 1985/90. He was reminded that the agreement to lease 12 tanks to Oman at a greatly reduced rental (50k per tank per year) for 2 years had been clearly linked with the purchase of 35 new tanks.[68]

The initial agreement was to buy three times more tanks several years later but knowing that the British Government was no longer the only supplier to Oman, Creasey told negotiators that 'if he was being "threatened" he would revert to the American L60 tanks.'[69] The opening of Oman to non-British suppliers as a result of withdrawal ultimately did weaken the British negotiating hand, as did the UK MoD's shift from British to European manufactured vehicles and the subsequent collapse of British manufacturing. British advisors close to Qaboos did not necessarily always have Britain's commercial interests in mind. Despite the occasional setbacks to Britain's supplying of armaments to Oman throughout the years since withdrawal, British manufacturers have been able to retain the position as the main supplier for the past five decades and have benefitted from several modernisation programmes initiated by Qaboos and the strong presence of these British companies already in the country at the time of the opening of the bidding processes. This could be interpreted as a type of reward power, where the action of retaining a British presence within the Omani chain of command was rewarded by the extension of favourable offers of weapon sales.

3.5.2 Continued preference to buy British

The preference to buy British weaponry until recently is likely based on two factors. Firstly, Sultan Qaboos undertook his military training in the UK, served with the Cameronian Highlanders in the UK and Germany, and inevitably learned his own military tactics using equipment produced by British defence manufacturers. The presence of British equipment throughout his training inevitably had an impact on his purchasing decisions in later life. Qaboos knew how the weapons worked, he could trust that they would be reliable during use, and as is the case with many of the decisions made by the Sultan, he likely decided to stick to what he felt comfortable with instead of taking a risk with weapons from other countries that he was unfamiliar with. The second dimension is the presence of influential British advisors and confidantes who helped Qaboos to make decisions about which weaponry to purchase. Numerous archival sources suggest that throughout the 1980s, which is when Qaboos was undertaking a major modernisation of his armed forces, Britons Erik Bennett and Tim Creasey were consulted by the Sultan prior to placing firm orders, and as they both came from a similar military background to Qaboos, it is likely that they often lobbied in favour of British equipment.

Military sales and politics are inextricably linked, and the political legacy of Britain in Oman is undoubtedly a major reason for British defence manufacturers retaining their position as first port of call when the Omani government embarks on modernisation programmes. During the Residency era in the Gulf, British defence suppliers were firmly ingrained into the security infrastructure of Oman – senior Omanis were trained both in the UK and Oman using British equipment, British suppliers established bases in Oman and Qaboos developed close relations with senior figures at the top of defence manufacturing companies – all of which could only come into fruition with the political support of both British and Omani governments, regardless of which party was in power in the UK. However, the largest bilateral defence supply contracts with Oman have largely been signed by Conservative administrations.

The British soft power influence in Oman is a key contributor to the retention of Britain's role as the go-to supplier of defence equipment. Two important soft power qualities are linked to the strength of British enterprise and engagement. Britain has been seen as business-friendly and an easy partner to trade with by the Omanis since the early 19th century, starting when Omani ports were used as refuelling bases and transitioning to unrivalled trading partner and eventual first choice supplier of defence equipment. Since the 18th century, Britain has also engaged with the Omani Government on a personal level, with British agents and residents communicating directly with ruling Sultans and the governments having direct channels of communication, and it is this historic close engagement that laid the ground for Britain's position as Qaboos' defence supplier of choice. It is unclear whether Sultan Haitham will retain this mindset, so the three types of strategic power – referent, expert, and reward will be tested.

3.6 Britain's strategic influence in Oman and future engagement with the Sultanate

Despite Harold Wilson's declaration that Britain would be withdrawing from all of the military structures of the Gulf by 1971, which would not come into effect in Oman until 1975, the British security presence in Oman has certainly not disappeared. The British military presence in Oman has become noticeably less overt since the early 1970s, but it cannot be said that Britain did actually withdraw militarily at the conclusion of the Dhofar War. The shift from an overt presence where British soldiers were openly serving in the Omani forces to one that is more covert and less obvious to outside observers likely became a necessity because of the sentiment in the UK parliament at the conclusion of the war, particularly within the ruling Labour Party. In a 1975 letter to London, the British Ambassador in Oman at the time wrote that 'ministers (in the British Government) were under strong pressure from a significant number of Parliamentarians who disliked the idea of any British military involvement in Oman.'[70] The British Labour Party has had an uncomfortable relationship with the Gulf for decades, at least amongst the backbenchers, and it was the Labour Party that ultimately decided that Britain would withdraw from East of the Suez. One retired British Ambassador to Oman suggested that the main reason for this is because 'Labour Governments struggle with Gulf-style rulers, however, at the working level under Tony Blair, Omani bases were widely used during the second Iraq War.'[71] During Thatcher's tenure, she 'reversed Labour's decisions pertaining to Oman which were undermining the relationship, and she met with Qaboos in London every summer.'[72] Again, the personal relationship between senior British and Omani officials is influential as this is an important commitment by the British Government to preserving the historic relationship and retaining the British presence in the Sultanate.

3.6.1 Britain's power transition in Oman

Britain has inevitably had to transition from a hard power in Oman to a soft power, from a position of making decisions within the state with British expatriates serving in the military and security apparatus to one of relying on the Sultan to continue choosing to cooperate closely with Britain. This voluntary cooperation is present in all areas of the security relationship, particularly in the future developments of joint military bases in Oman. Along with the opening of HMS Juffair in Bahrain, Britain's commitment to Duqm Port in Oman is arguably evidence of a re-pivot by the British Government back to Oman and the wider Gulf. Duqm is the future of the British presence in Oman and physical evidence of how the British legacy in the Sultanate is manifesting itself in the contemporary era. The naval base at Duqm is officially termed a support facility and will include a drydock capable of receiving British Royal Navy submarines and new Queen Elizabeth class aircraft carriers, the largest in British history. In contrast to Juffair in Bahrain, where the ships will have to dock out of port as a result of the shallow waters surrounding Bahrain, Duqm will allow naval ships to dock inside the port.[73] This recommitment to Oman began during Theresa May's Conservative administration. In August 2017, Sir Michael Fallon, former UK Defence Secretary, signed a *Memorandum of Understanding and Services Agreement* with his Omani counterpart, Sayyid Badr, which ensured that expert private sector British engineering influence is present as the port expands and sent a message to Oman that Britain is committed to the future security of Oman. This also secured British expert power in the Sultanate. The importance of Duqm Port for Britain's Middle East defence policy was further demonstrated in 2018 when the joint *Saif Saarea* exercise was undertaken, and the UK Joint Logistics Support Base established with the aim of bringing together Britain's three armed forces under one command structure whilst operating in Oman. The base does form an important element of contemporary British policy, but foreign influence in Omani defence infrastructure is present, most notably by the Chinese Government.

> Clearly Duqm will be a strategic position for the armed forces (British and others). Although the port is Chinese built, along with the base in Bahrain, the port will form one important node in future British defence policy.[74]

British smart power in Oman is an integral part of the move to reassert British influence East of the Suez in the 21st century. As such, May's government committed

> over the next decade [to] spend £3 billion on defence in the Gulf region. That will very much help us build up our maritime land and air bases in Oman and give us a persistent and increasingly permanent naval defence there.[75]

This commitment has been retained by the government of Boris Johnson but could be impacted by spending cuts in the coming years resulting from the Covid-19 outbreak. Other than in Bahrain, Oman is a rare example in the world where Britain is expanding its defence commitments as opposed to drawing them down. The British military operated more bases in Oman than in any of the other Gulf states prior to 1971 and retained an overt military presence for longer in the country as a result of commitments during the Dhofar War. The recent pledge to Duqm is likely an attempt to protect and build upon the defence influence that Britain has in Oman: influence that did not weaken significantly as a result of withdrawal. Duqm Port is also a politically astute decision as Britain's largest overseas military base is termed as a joint UK–Omani facility; one of the main reasons for Harold Wilson choosing to withdraw from East of the Suez was because of the international criticism arising from Britain's sole operation of numerous defence bases in the Gulf. A crucial element of the post-withdrawal defence relationship is its cooperative nature, where Britain's increasingly permanent presence is secured by the acceptance of the Omani authorities of the development of Duqm Port. This cooperation is arguably based upon a British soft power legacy of attraction that has developed in Oman.

Sultan Qaboos spent most of his life training and ruling alongside Britons that he trusted, supported by the British Government, firstly via the Residency and then the government directly, and Qaboos remained committed to cooperating closely with Britain. He also witnessed British and Omani troops successfully defending Oman's interests together, and possibly felt a sense of gratitude to the British, resulting in the invitation to establish a permanent base at Duqm. To accept the stationing of British troops and ships in Oman, Qaboos and his advisors must have a respect and trust for British defence policy; this is a method through which British soft power is used to achieve foreign policy aims in the Gulf and soft power in action, both as a result of the historic role as defender of Oman and the contemporary cooperation. This gratitude to Britain may have been lost as Haitham took the throne, because he has not had the same threats to his rule as Qaboos, nor has the new Sultan had to make decisions regarding the permission to base British troops in Oman.

3.6.2 *A relationship built on its legacy*

Britain's military relations with Oman are undoubtedly one of the most historic and successful of any between Britain and an allied power, the foundations of which were established in 1820,[76] and the 'protection of UK interests and ability to tackle regional threats is impossible without the British Gulf position.'[77] This historic defence relationship would not have emerged if it were not for the Persian Gulf Residency and the methods through which historic British Governments secured their position in the region. In Oman's case, this is manifested as British long-term military support for the ruling Al Said dynasty, the recruitment of thousands of Omani nationals into the British-commanded Trucial Oman Scouts military force, the education of senior Omani military leaders in Britain and the loaning of British officers to lead and train the Omani military, using British-manufactured weapons and machinery to jointly overcome the uprising in the Dhofar region. More so than with any of the other Middle Eastern states, the security relationship between Britain and Oman has proved remarkably versatile, adapting from a position of hard Anglo-centricity power in which the British Government made the majority of defence decisions in the Sultanate as the sole supplier of weapons and manpower to the SOAF, to a more modern security relationship based on Omani attraction to British defence and foreign policies and shared values, with elements of Oman's ability to wield power over British policy makers.

British officers are now seconded to the Omani military at the request of Omani officials and these LSPs are largely now trainers rather than overt commanders. British defence manufacturers now have to compete to sell equipment to Oman with an increasing number of suppliers from numerous countries around the world, but there still appears to be an affinity by senior Omani royals to purchase from British companies, and there has been a recent transition from a one-sided military education relationship where Omanis were sent to British military academies for training to one where British officers are now gradually being accepted into Oman's own army officer training school and Omani troops are permitted to serve in the British armed forces on an equal footing with British and Commonwealth personnel. As the bilateral defence relationship has modernised and developed, it has emerged as one that is more equal, with both states continuing to train alongside each other through both large- and small-scale joint training exercises and Oman has been chosen as a host base for Britain's flagship aircraft carriers. Underpinning the whole defence relationship, however, is a strong commitment by both governments to the relationship, with many British politicians increasingly praising the development of relations, including this speech by Diana Johnson MP:

> I am particularly pleased to see British support for the development of the port in Oman, which will help Oman's economy and will provide a vital berthing point for our new Queen Elizabeth-class aircraft carriers. Intelligence sharing supports our fight against terrorism at home and abroad, and that co-operation is underpinned by strong governmental relationships.[78]

Britain's security influence in Oman has certainly diminished as a result of withdrawal, but the unique circumstances that bound the two states together at the point of withdrawal, and the strong economic position held by British companies and individuals in the Sultanate at that point, have enabled the relationship to modernise and develop into one more suited to the 20th and 21st centuries. Oman is the best example of a security location where Britain has successfully transitioned from an overt hard military power to a collaborative soft power, and the strong security relationship is the most prominent example of the British legacy in the Arabian Gulf.

In the UK's *Integrated Review of Security, Defence, Development and Foreign Policy*, published on 16 March 2021, the British naval base in Oman was identified as one of Britain's six 'strategic hubs' and the only one in the Middle East, committing the UK to invest in the base's facilities to 'give our forces reach, access, influence and insight.'[79] This arguably highlights a recognition within the government that the British presence in Oman is strong, secure, and a major factor in the projection of future British power in the Middle East. The review also shifted the focus of UK foreign and defence policy from one oriented towards soft power, as established by the Cameron and May administrations, back to a harder power focus where defence was put at the centre of the Global Britain agenda.

3.7 What impact will the succession from Qaboos to Haitham have on Britain's strategic influence in Oman?

The succession in Oman will undoubtedly have an impact on Britain's ability to exert influence over Omani decision-making, largely because of the loss of the direct legacy that was manifested through Qaboos. The military training that Qaboos undertook in Oman and his time serving in the British Army, using only British-manufactured arms, has not been replicated by Haitham, who, although a graduate of the University of Oxford, does not have the same direct military affiliation to Britain. In his first speech, Haitham vowed to follow the same foreign policy path set out by Qaboos, so if this does remain the case, the British Government will still be able to capitalise on channels through which influence can be utilised, but as the Deputy Prime Minister for International Cooperation Affairs, Asa'ad bin Tariq, is now the most senior official within the Government of Oman to train in a British military academy, it is likely that the British strategic capabilities will depend on his personal attraction to continue seconding cadets to Britain for training. As a result of the succession, it could be argued that any purely British hard power capabilities have been eroded in Oman. The relationship, whether the sales of arms and defence equipment, the secondment and training of LSPs, or joint training exercises between Britain and Oman will be dependent on the retention of a strong British soft power in the Sultanate. At the time of writing, there have been no significant developments in the bilateral strategic relationship since the succession took place, but the day after Haitham acceded to the throne, Boris Johnson and Prince Charles travelled to Oman to meet the new Sultan, accompanied by the Defence Secretary and the Chief of the Defence Staff. This was arguably an attempt by the British Government to ensure that the new Sultan was reminded of the commitment of Britain to Omani security and to secure the British position in the early years of Haitham's reign.

The gradual privatisation of strategic affairs will also contribute to the future strength of Britain's power to influence decisions in Oman. British officials have increasingly relied on the presence of British private sector companies operating in Oman since the dismantling of the Residency system. Large and influential UK-domiciled arms manufacturers such as BAE Systems, banks including HSBC, and energy organisations, such as Shell and BP, have increasingly taken over the responsibility to uphold the British presence in the country. Although many influential private companies such as these are no longer wholly British owned, they still retain major offices in the UK and enjoy significant government support for their activities. The commercialisation of influence lends itself to a soft nature of power, but joint training exercises are hard power. The future of the British influence in Oman is increasingly taking on smart power characteristics, which is the trajectory of power projection in the post-colonial international system. If Britain is able to adjust its power capabilities to suit Oman's evolving strategic needs, then the influence can be retained despite increased competition from other states and the loss of a sympathetic ruler.

The first demonstration of the British Government's continued commitment to Omani security (and the security of the wider Indian Ocean) since Haitham's accession was on 12 September 2020, when Defence Secretary Ben Wallace announced a £23.8 million investment in the UK logistics hub at Duqm Port and the subsequent tripling of the size of the base in preparation for the future deployment of British troops and aircraft carriers to Oman.[80] This investment, at a time of economic recession in Britain, was arguably an overt attempt to ensure that the new Sultan was reminded of Britain's continued commitment to Omani security.

3.8 Policy implications arising from Britain's strategic influence in Oman

The British strategic influence in Oman is arguably the strongest of any of the UK's other bilateral relationships in the world, more so than the Anglo-American relationship in many ways because of the specific power-centric nature of that with Oman. The British Government has ensured that policy remains attractive to Omani decision makers since withdrawal, and this is evident in the strength of bilateralism between the two states; however, the relationship has largely remained weighted towards Britain. Defence partnerships have proven an important method through which Britain can exert its influence in the Gulf, and the British Government has implemented policies that have remained appealing to Oman. As a result of the overt willingness that the British Government has demonstrated to Oman since 1975, most importantly manifested in the joint training exercises that have taken place since 1986, future policy has to continue to reflect this commitment. Future defence policy relating to Oman has to continue to demonstrate to Omani policymakers that Britain still wishes to train Oman and share military skills to assist with local strategic development.

The strategic aspect of the bilateral relationship with Oman cannot be understood in isolation. British policy since at least 2015 has taken a cross-governmental approach. All British activities in relation to Oman involve more than one governmental department. The three *Saif Saarea* military exercises involve both the MOD and FCDO, and related activities including the sale and financing of arms sales to the Omani military involve the DIT and private sector in Britain. Similarly, the preservation of the British economic presence in the banking and energy sectors requires collaboration between the FCO, DIT, and the private sector. As the British Government has identified cross-departmental cooperation as a key tenet of the 'Global Britain' agenda, Britain's influence in Oman should be considered as a successful example of this in action. The British strategic presence in Oman is multifaceted and evident in many areas of society, but it is more focussed and less diverse in Bahrain.

Notes

1 Risso, P., *Oman and Muscat: An Early Modern History*, (London, Croom Helm, 1986), p.220.
2 Letter from Colonel F.A. Wilson, Political Resident in the Persian Gulf, to the Secretary to the Government of India's Foreign Department (Bushire, 4 May 1895), p.6. in File 35/10 '*Attack on Muscat by Shaikh Salih, 1895*', British Library: India Office Records and Private Papers, IOR/R/15/1/391, in Qatar Digital Library <https://www.qdl.qa/archive/81055/vdc_100000000193.0x00016c> [accessed 4 December 2018].
3 Interview with a retired British Ambassador to Oman (*Retired Ambassador A*), (London, 18 October 2018).
4 See Onley, J., Britain and the Gulf Shaikhdoms, 1820–1971: The Politics of Protection, Center for International and Regional Studies – Occasional Papers 4. Georgetown University School of Foreign Service in Qatar, Doha (2009), p.6.
5 Defence Review report produced by Colonel R. Lea (Defence Attaché, Oman) for Duncan Slater (British Ambassador, Oman), 30 July 1984. FCO 8/5511 (1984), TNA.
6 '*Gulf security is our security*', *British PM tells GCC summit*, Arab News, <http://www.arabnews.com/node/1021016/middle-east> [accessed 12 December 2018].
7 HL Deb 9 March 2017 vol 779, *Armed Forces: East of Suez*.
8 *Security in the Gulf is vital to keeping Britain safe*, The Military Times, <https://www.themilitarytimes.co.uk/defence-security/security-in-the-gulf-is-vital-to-keeping-britain-safe/> [accessed 7 December 2018].
9 Ibid.
10 UK Ministry of Defence and Foreign & Commonwealth Office (2017), *UK's International Defence Engagement Strategy*, (London, Ministry of Defence UK), p.11.

11 Gardner, N., 'The Limits of the Sandhurst Connection: The Evolution of Oman's Foreign and Defense Policy, 1970–1977', *The Journal of the Middle East and Africa*, 6:1 (2015), pp.45–58.
12 Interview with a serving senior British diplomat (*Diplomat A*), (Muscat, 28 November 2018).
13 *UK's International Defence Engagement Strategy*, p.13.
14 HL Deb 21 January 2016 c WA4954.
15 HL Deb 21 January 2016 c WA4953, document: *Foreign nations trained at RMA Sandhurst*.
16 FOI2018/15984: Omani and Bahraini seconded officers at RAF College Cranwell and Britannia Royal Naval College, 14 January 2019.
17 Ibid.
18 It was only possible to collate data for the years 2012–2016 due to FOI release restrictions for some years.
19 FOI2017/08782: Number of foreign cadets represented at RMA Sandhurst, RNC Britannia and RAF Cranwell, 18 October 2017.
20 Interview (*Retired Ambassador A*).
21 Allen, C. and Rigsbee, W.L., *Oman under Qaboos: From Coup to Constitution, 1970–1996*, (London, Frank Cass Publishers, 2000), p.101.
22 FOI 0471-17 (FCO), 28 July 2017. Available at: <https://assets.publishing.service.gov.uk/government/uploads/system/uploads/attachment_data/file/638782/FOI_0471-17_response.pdf>.
23 FOI 2015-02237: PSNI Training Assistance to Other Countries for Last 5 Years (PSNI). Available at: <https://www.psni.police.uk/globalassets/advice--information/our-publications/disclosure-logs/2015/organisational-informationgovernance/psni_training_assistance_to_other_countries_for_last_5_years.pdf>.
24 FOI 0417-17.
25 'Conflict, Stability and Security Fund: Annual Report 2016/17 – A Cross-Government Approach to Tackling Insecurity and Instability', (London, HM Government, 2017), p.15.
26 Interview with a senior general in the Royal Oman Police (*ROP general*), (Muscat, 29 November 2018).
27 HC Deb 15 December 1986 vol 107 c371W.
28 Interview with a former British diplomat (*former Diplomat A*), (Oxford, 9 November 2018).
29 Nye Jr., J.S., 'Get Smart: Combining Hard and Soft Power', *Foreign Affairs*, 88:4 (2009), p.161.
30 HC Deb 30 January 1986 vol 90 c1117.
31 Lecture at the Anglo-Omani Society, '*Oman and Its Neighbours*' (London, 15 November 2018).
32 Interview with a serving senior British diplomat (*Diplomat B*), (Muscat, 24 November 2018).
33 Interview (*Diplomat A*).
34 See: https://www.wired.co.uk/article/middle-east-gchq-base-oman.
35 Cordesman, A.H., *Bahrain, Oman, Qatar, and the UAE: Challenges of Security*, (New York, Perseus, 1997), p.205.
36 Interview (*former Diplomat A*).
37 Interview with a retired Omani Brigadier General in the Sultan's Armed Forces (*Retired Brigadier General A*), (Muscat, 29 November 2018).
38 Interview with a retired Colonel in the Trucial Oman Scouts (*Retired TOS Colonel*), (Muscat, 27 November 2018).
39 Interview (*Retired Brigadier General A*).

40 HL Deb 11 December 2017 vol 787 c1426.
41 Nye Jr., J.S., 'Soft Power', *Foreign Policy*, 80 (1990), p.167.
42 Cypher (number: 140800Z) from Charles Treadwell (British Ambassador, Oman) to FCO and MOD UK, 14 October 1975. FCO 8/2479 (1975), TNA.
43 See reference to the agreement between Oman and the UK that supported this: Letter from Luce to Carrington entitled 'Oman: Defence 1980', 7 March 1981. FCO 8/3965 (1981), TNA.
44 This was the most senior rank that Omanis served at prior to the introduction of the Omanisation policy.
45 Annex to the Annual Report produced by the British Naval and Air Attachés in Muscat entitled 'Annual Report on Naval Matters – 1980', 3 March 1981. FCO 8/3965 (1981), TNA.
46 Annual Report produced by the British Defence Attaché, Muscat entitled 'Annual Report for 1980', 3 March 1981. FCO 8/3965 (1981), TNA.
47 Annex to Annual Defence Review produced by N.J.J. Cocks (Naval Attaché, Oman) for Colonel R. Lea (Defence Attaché, Oman), 30 July 1984. FCO 8/5511 (1984), TNA.
48 Annex to Annual Defence Review produced by N.J.J. Cocks.
49 Letter from Lindsay to DS11 entitled 'Visit by Secretary of State for Defence to Oman: Brief on LSP', 2 January 1981. FCO 8/3968 (1981), TNA.
50 Report by the Directors of Defence Policy entitled *British Military Assistance to Oman – 1976*. DEFE 24/2106 (1976), TNA.
51 Letter from Margaret Thatcher to HM Sultan Qaboos bin Said, 15 July 1982. FCO 8/4368 (1982), TNA.
52 Report by Gamp to Air Plans 2, 30 July 1981. FCO 8/3969 (1981), TNA.
53 Interview (*Retired TOS Colonel*).
54 Ibid.
55 '*Oman, UK review military ties; sign pact on loaning of forces*', Times of Oman. Available at: <https://timesofoman.com/article/132054> [accessed 10 December 2018].
56 Interview with a retired British Ambassador in Oman (*Retired Ambassador B*), (London, 15 November 2018).
57 '*BAE Systems invests in Omani youth development*', Times of Oman. Available at: <https://timesofoman.com/article/135325> [accessed 8 December 2018].
58 '*BAE signs funding deal for Chevening scholarships for Omanis*', Times of Oman, <https://timesofoman.com/article/136644> [accessed 8 December 2018].
59 Interview (*Retired Brigadier General A*).
60 See: https://www.globalsecurity.org/military/world/europe/eurofighter-sales.htm for Eurofighter Tycoon and F-16 prices and http://www.senat.fr/rap/a13-158-8/a13-158-814.html for Dassault Rafale costs.
61 See: <https://www.marketscreener.com/quote/stock/BAE-SYSTEMS-PLC-9583545/company> [accessed 1 March 2021].
62 Letter from Duncan Slater (British Ambassador, Oman) to S.L. Egerton (Arabian Department, FCO), 19 October 1983. FCO 8/5023 (1983), TNA.
63 Letter from Duncan Slater.
64 Telegram from Geoffrey Howe (Secretary of State for Foreign and Commonwealth Affairs) to FCO MED, 15 March 1984. FCO 8/5517 (1984), TNA.
65 Briefing and Personality Notes produced by Patrick Wright Esq. (RN Dales), FCO: *Briefing notes for PM Callaghan and Sultan Qaboos meeting on 14 July 1976*, 12 July 1976. DEFE 24/2106 (1976), TNA.
66 Minutes produced by A.G. Munro for MOD UK (Marketing): *Tri-Service Fixed Communications Project, Oman*, 5 October 1983. FCO 8/5022 (1983), TNA.

66 *Strategic power, defence, and security*

67 Telegram from Duncan Slater (British Ambassador, Oman) to FCO MED and MOD UK. FCO 8/5022 (1983), TNA.
68 Letter from K.P. Jeffs (Defence Sales) to UK Secretary of State for Defence: *Oman: Chieftain Tanks*, 13 October 1981. FCO 8/3972 (1981), TNA.
69 Ibid.
70 Letter from C.J. Treadwell (British Ambassador, Oman) entitled 'RAF Detachment Salalah' to I.T.M. Lucas (FCO MED), 14 October 1975. FCO 8/2479 (1975), TNA.
71 Interview (*Retired Ambassador B*).
72 Ibid.
73 Tossini, J.V., 'The UK in Oman – A new support facility for the British Armed Forces', UK Defence Journal. Available at: <https://ukdefencejournal.org.uk/the-uk-in-oman-a-new-support-facility-for-the-british-armed-forces/> [accessed 26 December 2018].
74 Interview (*Retired Ambassador A*).
75 HL Deb 9 March 2017 vol 779 c1472.
76 Some historians would refer to 1763 as the beginning of defence cooperation between the Omani Sultans and East India Company, as EIC ships used Muscat as a safe harbour and then coaling base from this point, but this research accepts that Britain's direct military intervention into Omani affairs only started in 1820.
77 Interview with a senior diplomat in the FCO's Arabian Directorate (*FCO Diplomat A*), (London, 12 October 2018).
78 HC Deb 4 May 2016 vol 609 cc92WH-93WH.
79 HM Government, *Global Britain in a Competitive Age: The Integrated Review of Security, Defence, Development and Foreign Policy*, (London, HMSO, 2021), p.73.
80 'Defence Secretary announces investment in strategic Omani port' [online]. London, Ministry of Defence, 2020, [viewed 16 September 2020]. Available at: https://www.gov.uk/government/news/defence-secretary-announces-investment-in-strategic-omani-port.

Bibliography

'*BAE signs funding deal for Chevening scholarships for Omanis*', Times of Oman, <https://timesofoman.com/article/136644> [accessed 8 December 2018].

'*BAE Systems invests in Omani youth development*', Times of Oman, <https://timesofoman.com/article/135325> [accessed 8 December 2018].

'Conflict, Stability and Security Fund: Annual Report 2016/17 – A Cross-Government approach to tackling insecurity and instability', (London, HM Government, 2017), p.15.

'Defence Secretary announces investment in strategic Omani port' [online]. London, Ministry of Defence, 2020, [viewed 16 September 2020]. Available at: <https://www.gov.uk/government/news/defence-secretary-announces-investment-in-strategic-omani-port>.

'*Gulf security is our security', British PM tells GCC summit*, Arab News. Available at: <http://www.arabnews.com/node/1021016/middle-east> [accessed 12 December 2018].

Allen, C. and Rigsbee, W.L., *Oman under Qaboos: From Coup to Constitution, 1970–1996*, (London, Frank Cass Publishers, 2000).

Annex to Annual Defence Review produced by N.J.J. Cocks.

Annex to Annual Defence Review produced by N.J.J. Cocks (Naval Attaché, Oman) for Colonel R. Lea (Defence Attaché, Oman), 30 July 1984. FCO 8/5511 (1984), TNA.

Annex to the Annual Report produced by the British Naval and Air Attachés in Muscat entitled 'Annual Report on Naval Matters – 1980', 3 March 1981. FCO 8/3965 (1981), TNA.

Annual Report produced by the British Defence Attaché, Muscat entitled 'Annual Report for 1980', 3 March 1981. FCO 8/3965 (1981), TNA.

Briefing and Personality Notes produced by Patrick Wright Esq. (RN Dales), FCO: Briefing notes for PM Callaghan and Sultan Qaboos meeting on 14 July 1976, 12 July 1976. DEFE 24/2106 (1976), TNA.

Cordesman, A.H., *Bahrain, Oman, Qatar, and the UAE: Challenges of Security*, (New York, Perseus, 1997).

Cypher (number: 140800Z) from Charles Treadwell (British Ambassador, Oman) to FCO and MOD UK, 14 October 1975. FCO 8/2479 (1975), TNA.

Defence Review report produced by Colonel R. Lea (Defence Attaché, Oman) for Duncan Slater (British Ambassador, Oman), 30 July 1984. FCO 8/5511 (1984), TNA.

FOI 0471-17 (FCO), 28 July 2017. Available at: <https://assets.publishing.service.gov.uk/government/uploads/system/uploads/attachment_data/file/638782/FOI_0471-17_response.pdf>.

FOI 2015-02237: PSNI Training Assistance to Other Countries for Last 5 Years (PSNI). Available at: <https://www.psni.police.uk/globalassets/advice--information/our-publications/disclosure-logs/2015/organisational-informationgovernance/psni_training_assistance_to_other_countries_for_last_5_years.pdf>.

FOI2017/08782: Number of foreign cadets represented at RMA Sandhurst, RNC Britannia and RAF Cranwell, 18 October 2017.

FOI2018/15984: Omani and Bahraini seconded officers at RAF College Cranwell and Britannia Royal Naval College, 14 January 2019.

Gardner, N., 'The Limits of the Sandhurst Connection: The Evolution of Oman's Foreign and Defense Policy, 1970–1977', *The Journal of the Middle East and Africa*, 6:1 (2015), pp.45–58.

HC Deb 15 December 1986 vol 107 c371W.

HC Deb 30 January 1986 vol 90 c1117.

HC Deb 4 May 2016 vol 609 cc92WH-93WH.

HL Deb 11 December 2017 vol 787 c1426.

HL Deb 21 January 2016 c WA4953, document: Foreign nations trained at RMA Sandhurst.

HL Deb 21 January 2016 c WA4954.

HL Deb 9 March 2017 vol 779 c1472.

HL Deb 9 March 2017 vol 779, Armed Forces: East of Suez.

HM Government, *Global Britain in a Competitive Age: The Integrated Review of Security, Defence, Development and Foreign Policy*, (London, HMSO, 2021).

Interview with a former British diplomat (former Diplomat A), (Oxford, 9 November 2018).

Interview with a retired British Ambassador to Oman (Retired Ambassador A), (London, 18 October 2018).

Interview with a retired British Ambassador in Oman (Retired Ambassador B), (London, 15 November 2018).

Interview with a retired British Ambassador in Oman (Retired Ambassador B), (London, 15 November 2018).

Interview with a retired Colonel in the Trucial Oman Scouts (Retired TOS Colonel), (Muscat, 27 November 2018).

Interview with a retired Omani Brigadier General in the Sultan's Armed Forces (Retired Brigadier General A), (Muscat, 29 November 2018).

Interview with a senior diplomat in the FCO's Arabian Directorate (FCO Diplomat A), (London, 12 October 2018).

Interview with a senior general in the Royal Oman Police (ROP general), (Muscat, 29 November 2018).

Interview with a serving senior British diplomat (Diplomat A), (Muscat, 28 November 2018).

Interview with a serving senior British diplomat (Diplomat A), (Muscat, 28 November 2018).

Interview with a serving senior British diplomat (Diplomat B), (Muscat, 24 November 2018).

Lecture at the Anglo-Omani Society, 'Oman and Its Neighbours'. (London, 15 November 2018).

Letter from C.J. Treadwell (British Ambassador, Oman) entitled 'RAF Detachment Salalah' to I.T.M. Lucas (FCO MED), 14 October 1975. FCO 8/2479 (1975), TNA.

Letter from Colonel F.A. Wilson, Political Resident in the Persian Gulf, to the Secretary to the Government of India's Foreign Department (Bushire, 4 May 1895), p.6. in File 35/10 *'Attack on Muscat by Shaikh Salih, 1895'*, British Library: India Office Records and Private Papers, IOR/R/15/1/391, in Qatar Digital Library <https://www.qdl.qa/archive/81055/vdc_100000000193.0x00016c> [accessed 4 December 2018].

Letter from Duncan Slater (British Ambassador, Oman) to S.L. Egerton (Arabian Department, FCO), 19 October 1983. FCO 8/5023 (1983), TNA.

Letter from K.P. Jeffs (Defence Sales) to UK Secretary of State for Defence: Oman: Chieftain Tanks, 13 October 1981. FCO 8/3972 (1981), TNA.

Letter from Lindsay to DS11 entitled 'Visit by Secretary of State for Defence to Oman: Brief on LSP', 2 January 1981. FCO 8/3968 (1981), TNA.

Letter from Luce to Carrington entitled 'Oman: Defence 1980', 7 March 1981. FCO 8/3965 (1981), TNA.

Letter from Margaret Thatcher to HM Sultan Qaboos bin Said, 15 July 1982. FCO 8/4368 (1982), TNA.

Minutes produced by A.G. Munro for MOD UK (Marketing): *Tri-Service Fixed Communications Project, Oman*, 5 October 1983. FCO 8/5022 (1983), TNA.

Nye Jr., J.S., 'Get Smart: Combining Hard and Soft Power', *Foreign Affairs*, 88:4 (2009), pp.160–163.

Nye Jr., J.S., 'Soft Power', *Foreign Policy*, 80 (1990), pp.153–171.

Oman, UK review military ties; sign pact on loaning of forces, Times of Oman, <https://timesofoman.com/article/132054> [accessed 10 December 2018].

Onley, J. (2009), Britain and the Gulf Shaikhdoms, 1820–1971: The Politics of Protection, Center for International and Regional Studies – Occasional Papers 4. Georgetown University School of Foreign Service in Qatar, Doha.

Report by Gamp to Air Plans 2, 30 July 1981. FCO 8/3969 (1981), TNA.

Report by the Directors of Defence Policy entitled British Military Assistance to Oman – 1976. DEFE 24/2106 (1976), TNA.

Risso, P., *Oman and Muscat: An Early Modern History*, (London, Croom Helm, 1986).

Security in the Gulf is vital to keeping Britain safe, The Military Times, <https://www.themilitarytimes.co.uk/defence-security/security-in-the-gulf-is-vital-to-keeping-britain-safe/> [accessed 7 December 2018].

Telegram from Duncan Slater (British Ambassador, Oman) to FCO MED and MOD UK. FCO 8/5022 (1983), TNA.

Telegram from Geoffrey Howe (Secretary of State for Foreign and Commonwealth Affairs) to FCO MED, 15 March 1984. FCO 8/5517 (1984), TNA.

Tossini, J.V., '*The UK in Oman – A new support facility for the British Armed Forces*', UK Defence Journal. Available at: <https://ukdefencejournal.org.uk/the-uk-in-oman-a-new-support-facility-for-the-british-armed-forces/> [accessed 26 December 2018].

UK Ministry of Defence and Foreign & Commonwealth Office (2017), *UK's International Defence Engagement Strategy*, (London, Ministry of Defence UK).

4 Britain's shifting strategic power in Bahrain since 1971

4.1 Introduction

The British strategic legacy in Bahrain is one of the longest lasting of all of the Gulf states, and although the bilateral security relationship has gone through several highs and lows throughout history, a legacy has endured. Historically, the British relationship with Bahrain was predicated on the East India Company's relations with the ruling Khalifa family, the gatekeepers to Bahrain's economy and power. Shaikh Salman bin Ahmad Al Khalifa offered his support to Britain's endeavours in the Gulf in return for occasional protection from the Bombay Marine in 1805, but it was ultimately refused by the Government of India. According to James Onley, between 1805 and 1861, the Political Resident for the Persian Gulf received at least 21 requests for protection by British gunboats from Bahrain,[1] a significant number from such a small and sparsely populated country at the time. It was not until 1816, when Political Resident William Bruce agreed that Britain would take a neutral position in the conflict between Bahrain and Oman, that Britain became indirectly involved in Gulf affairs. A marked shift in this security relationship occurred in February 1820, when the *General Maritime Treaty of 1820* was signed between Sir William Grant Keir and Bahrain's rulers, stipulating that the Residency would enforce an anti-piracy and anti-slavery agenda in the region, and all ships operating in the Gulf had to be registered with the Residency and fly red and white flags.[2] The Political Resident, based in the Persian port of Bushehr until 1946 and answerable to both the British and Indian governments, emerged as one of the most influential British figures in the Gulf and the determinant of the strength of the British–Bahraini security relationship. From 1946, the Residency was relocated to Manama, putting Bahrain at the centre of the British sphere of influence in the Middle East. From the early years of Britain's presence in Bahraini affairs, an element of coercive power was used to secure influence; British protection could be withdrawn if Bahrain did not accept the hegemony imposed by the Residency.

After 30 years of refusal, Britain extended full military protection to Bahrain in 1861 when Shaikh Muhammad bin Khalifa Al Khalifa started to shift his allegiance to Persia and the Ottoman Empire. When Shaikh

DOI: 10.4324/9781003302001-5

Muhammad signed the *Perpetual Truce of Peace and Friendship* with the British representatives, the foundations of the existing UK–Bahraini relationship were arguably laid, and Britain emerged as a hard power. The treaty, which effectively established Bahrain as an exclusive protectorate of the Residency, promised Bahrain British protection in return for the state rejecting relations with any country other than those within the British Empire.[3] At this point in the relationship, Britain's influence in Bahrain was underpinned by its unrivalled hard power in the region, with Bahrain's rulers requesting military protection concurrently from the Royal Navy and Bombay Marine in return for following exclusivity rules stipulated by British officials. Although this strong hard power ultimately benefited Bahrain, with Bahrain guaranteed protection from attacks and invasions, Britain and India also gained from this relationship.

Bahrain's influence over British policy decision-making was also evident. Although initially reluctant to guarantee the security of Bahrain, the island had a geostrategic importance for Britain, located at the centre of the region and opposite the key Persian ports of Bandar Abbas and Bushehr, the latter being the base of the Residency until it moved to Manama in 1946. Britain's influence in Bahrain after the relocation of the Residency to Manama should have been further secured; however, the growth of anti-imperialism sentiments across the Middle East and developments within British foreign and defence policy that took the focus away from the Gulf – Indian independence, the Malaya Emergency, and the Suez crisis – arguably impacted upon the authority of the British Government in Bahrain.

4.1.1 *A continued power legacy or loss of influence?*

As the decades have passed since 1971, Britain has retained a commitment to Bahraini security, albeit to varying extents during periods of Conservative and Labour governments. Rather than withdrawing from Bahraini security affairs in 1971, the relationship evolved and emerged as a contemporary avenue through which Britain could exert influence over domestic affairs. During the Residency era, all elements of Bahraini defence and security were exclusively within Britain's sphere of influence, grouped together under the auspices of a protectorate. Since withdrawal, with commitment on both sides to ensure that the relationship endured, the various individual security treaties, military developments, and defence sales agreements have emerged as an effective remedy to the rapid and somewhat destructive declaration of withdrawal in 1968, albeit leaving British influence significantly weaker than it was before 1971.

4.2 How have Britain's military and security education capabilities affected influence in Bahrain?

The strategic education relationship between Britain and Bahrain is multifaceted and the security dimension is undoubtedly one method through which Britain is able to retain some semblance of influence in the Kingdom, albeit much less than in Oman. In the immediate years following withdrawal,[4] despite Bahrain no longer being treaty-bound to restrict its relations to Britain alone, military officers and princes were still routinely sent to British academies for training. Similarly, throughout much of the 1970s and 1980s, the Bahraini police force was trained in-country by seconded British advisors. One of the most prominent examples of senior Britons being kept in position to train and lead security efforts in Bahrain was that of Colonel Ian Henderson, who was responsible for the Bahraini General Directorate for State Security Investigations between 1966 and 1998. Henderson was initially recruited by the Residency on the advice of the British Government, and the acceptance of the rulers in Bahrain to retain this most overt connection to the British legacy demonstrates the extent to which the Government in Bahrain still trusted and required Britain for domestic security. His continued role in Bahraini affairs was in direct contrast to the official stance taken by the British Government throughout much of the 1980s. In a 1987 discussion about a military partnership between British and Bahraini officials, the UK MoD made a clear rebuttal to requests from Bahrain, stating that 'the possibility of direct liaison would raise security problems, would not be something we would willingly initiate ourselves and would in any case be handled outside the committee framework.'[5] There was an obvious contradiction between what both governments officially said and what actions they took in relation to permitting Britons to work in security training and management jobs. The refusal to agree to these requests arguably diminished the expert power available to Britain, not providing advisors on request both diminished the perceived reliability of the British Government in Bahrain and limited the Bahraini attraction to what Britain could offer.

The British role as the preferred provider of security education was a crucial element in the wider balance of power between the two historic allies, and this influence which was held by the British Government was crucial for the preservation of British influence and a strong soft power asset. The privileged position that British military academies had over Bahraini affairs was, however, no longer guaranteed because of the increased influence of US academies and the tactics that they taught to cadets. In 1978, seven years after British troops officially withdrew from East of the Suez, Bahrain was still requesting training from British forces, specifically the SAS with their expertise in maintaining domestic stability in nearby Oman and Aden; 44 SAS troops were operational in 1958 and 1959 during the Jebel Akhdar War, a number of troops were active in the so-called 'Keeni-Meeni Operations' in Aden between 1963 and 1967, and the SAS played a crucial role in *Operation Storm* during the Dhofar Rebellion in Oman between 1970 and 1977. Although sending SAS trainers to Bahrain would have been a boost for Britain's influence in Bahrain in the short term, policymakers in Westminster and diplomats in Manama were divided over the benefits of allowing British troops to move back to the country after Wilson's commitment in 1968 that Britain's time in the Gulf had finally come to an end. A diplomatic telegram sent by Ivor Lucas, Head of the Middle East Department at the FCO in 1978, offered one point of view on the SAS training dilemma in Bahrain:

> Problem:
> 1 Should the SAS train the Bahrain special forces in anti-terrorist and anti-guerrilla activities at Bahraini expense?
>
> Argument:
> 2 Despite the ending of our special treaty and defence relationship with Bahrain and the other Gulf states in 1971, these countries wish to maintain their defence links with us and to develop their forces along British lines with British training. To provide such training is evidence of our continuing interest in the area at a time when the Arab Sheikhdoms of the Gulf feel exposed by events in Iran. Our readiness to help also brings longer-term political and commercial advantages.[6]

At this time, the SAS was at the forefront of Britain's projection of power capabilities in the Gulf and the primary military asset that the British Government had in the region; the SAS retained a presence in the Gulf throughout the withdrawal period, primarily because of its involvement in the Dhofar War in Oman. The SAS also remained the go-to agency for Britain's military training of local elite armies in the region for much of the 1970s. Frank Judd, Labour Minister of State at the FCO, justified the British Government's decision to permit military training in Bahrain in an answer to a written question in the HoC. Judd wrote:

> Britain no longer has a formal defence treaty with any country in the Arabian Peninsula. We do, however, have frequent discussions with many countries in the area, and pursue civil and military co-operation with them under arrangements agreed with the Governments concerned. At the time of the British military withdrawal from the Persian Gulf in 1971, treaties of friendship were signed with Bahrain, Qatar and the United Arab Emirates. These provide for consultation 'on matters of mutual concern in time of need.'[7]

4.2.1 The effects of political divisions in Britain

Despite the Labour administration's commitment to providing Bahrain with the requested training support after withdrawal, there was evidently a lack of urgency to send a training force, perhaps demonstrable of the divisions within the party over supporting the divisive Bahraini administration.

74 *Strategic power, defence, and security*

B.A. Major, a diplomat in the FCO's Middle East Department, wrote in a DipTel to Lawrence Walker that

> you will probably not be surprised to learn that the BDF is not alone among overseas defence forces in its wish to receive the benefit of the training of the SAS ... The Bahrainis would then have to wait in the queue of other customers.[8]

Although the fact that a number of different countries had requested military training in 1978 is evidence of the SAS being a strong soft power asset for the British Government, with hard power undertones, Bahrain was not given priority. The reluctance within Labour to upholding relations with Bahrain has continued, with the Blair administrations prioritising affairs with other Middle Eastern states over Bahrain, particularly Kuwait during the second Gulf War, and few developments of note emerged during the Brown government. Despite this reluctance to offer direct assistance to Bahrain during the 1970s, the rulers of Bahrain still persisted with their requests. The British Embassy in Bahrain reported various requests from the highest levels in the Government of Bahrain for training. In 1978, L.E. Walker sent a telegram to London stating:

> When I called the Chief of Staff yesterday he told me he would very much welcome our help in arranging for the commanding officers of the two BDF 'Special Forces' units to receive training with the SAS whom he regards, you will be pleased to hear, as the elite force anywhere in the world in its particular field of specialized activity.[9]

The recognition that Britain was losing its privileged position in Bahrain, the gradual decline in influence starting at the point of withdrawal, came when the Conservatives were elected to power. In 1980, during the first Thatcher administration, it became evident that the British Government was making a concerted effort to redevelop closer security relations with Bahrain. After two years of Bahrain's military officials openly requesting assistance from the SAS, but likely more requests at the minor level between junior ministers and army generals, the British Government signalled its commitment to Bahraini defence and Britain's place in the Kingdom's post-withdrawal defence infrastructure by agreeing to a six-week SAS training exercise in Bahrain. This was a recognition by the British Government of the expert power that arises from seconding troops to share tactics with their Bahraini counterparts. The SAS training would follow three stages:

OP Consolidate SAS training:
   The training comprised of three phases:
   a   Phase 1. Two weeks duration – including basic weapon training and selection of students.

b   Phase 2. Three weeks duration – including two separate concurrent sniper and assault group courses.
c   Phase 3. For weeks duration – consisting of specialised methods of entry, command group training, option training, including abseiling, familiarisation visits, and two exercises.[10]

Although Britain withdrew militarily from Bahrain in 1971, and much of the training that was previously exclusive to British military trainers was replaced largely by the United States, this small-scale SAS training exercise was the first step towards a gradual British reinvolvement in Bahraini defence affairs and a concerted effort to preserve the diminished influence that Britain had retained. The presence of the SAS training group in Bahrain was a significant victory for British influence in the Kingdom and the wider Gulf. Both British officials and Gulf rulers were worried that withdrawal would signal the final death knell to Britain's role as defender of the Gulf.

British hard power assets, such as physical armies and military hardware, would be more difficult to deploy to Bahrain after withdrawal than before because of the changing power dynamics in the Gulf since 1971. Direct military deployments also commonly led to warfare, which would not have been accepted in Britain or Bahrain as a result of Britain giving up this commitment in 1971. According to Colin Gray, 'soft power cannot sensibly be regarded as a substantial alternative to hard military power ... An important inherent weakness of soft power is that it utterly depends upon the uncoerced choices of foreigners.'[11] Thus, it could be assumed that the Thatcher administration, knowing that they no longer had permanent military assets in Bahrain at their disposal, utilised a small secondment of SAS trainers to ensure that Britain did not lose its trusted status as a military ally and expert advisor to Bahrain on military affairs. Britain's influence of power seemingly shifted from hard power prior to withdrawal, to purely soft power between 1971 and 1980, and then a hybrid combination of the two from 1980 onwards. The key question underpinning the British Government's decision-making process in relation to strategic relations with Bahrain has always been connected to how best to protect the British influence in the Middle East, and Conservative politicians have arguably taken a more interventionist stance than their Labour counterparts.

4.2.2 *British commitment and re-engagement in Bahrain*

In 1983, the deployment of an SAS training team was expanded further with a larger scale and more formal Royal Marines training programme. This formalisation seemingly ingrained British expert power influence into the bilateral relationship. As further evidence of a lasting soft power influence in Bahrain, the British Government was asked to provide a Royal Marines Training Team (RMTT) to train the Bahrain Defence Force, comprising volunteer troops. Although the RMTT was to be sent from Britain at the request of the Government of Bahrain, the British Government stipulated

76 *Strategic power, defence, and security*

that all members of the team would remain under contract from the UK MoD and thus answerable only to the British authorities. It was also made clear that members of the RMTT would under no circumstances take part in any warfare or hostile acts whilst serving in Bahrain. The historic role of British troops in Bahrain was one of defending the region in times of conflict, so the limitations placed on the RMTT in 1983 represented the marked shift that took place as a result of withdrawal a decade earlier. The Memorandum of Understanding signed between the British and Bahraini governments stated that:

> The United Kingdom Government will endeavour to make available volunteers of the regular Armed Forces of the United Kingdom to form a Royal Marines Training Team ... to assist in the training and development of the Bahrain Defence Force. ... They will act only in advisory and training capacities and will in no circumstances take part in hostilities or other operations of a warlike nature ... members of the RMTT will be responsible only to the Government of the United Kingdom.[12]

Britain's willingness to agree to this request was undoubtedly an attempt to reinvigorate and secure a contemporary influence in Bahrain, and to demonstrate to the rulers of the Kingdom that, although the majority of British troops had withdrawn from the Gulf, the region was still important to the British Government and allies in the region were still respected. This training was extended in 1984 to the Bahraini police force, when minor training activities were undertaken in Britain for a small number of Bahraini police officers with regional police forces, including West Yorkshire Metropolitan Police. The agreed plan was for three NCOs to spend one month in Wakefield and

> for the majority of the time the officers are attached to the force, they will be working with Operational Officers on road traffic patrols ... a period of attachment at the Accident Investigation Branch, Traffic Management Department and Force Control ... The officers will also attend specific law lectures at the Force Driving School.[13]

The non-military training programmes offered by the British Government form part of a wider technical assistance programme, established in 1973, and encompassing various types of education that ultimately contributed to Britain's strategic influence over Bahraini affairs.

> The major part of our technical assistance is concentrated in the education sector, where we support about 19 teachers of English and technical subjects ... British technical assistance experts also work in the civil aviation, health, natural resources and labour sectors. ... The

Bahrainis have particularly valued the long-standing assistance we have provided.[14]

The provision of technical training was used as a way to preserve what limited influence the British Government had been able to retain in the immediate years after withdrawal, but what was a sign of the increasing reluctance to keep paying the costs for this type of assistance in an independent state, British representatives recommended 'that we [the British Government] should seek to maintain our technical assistance programme in Bahrain but phase financial responsibility on Bahrain over 4 years.'[15] These recommendations by Britons who were aware of the situation in Bahrain were seemingly an attempt to secure the expert power influence that had developed since 1820.

As with many bilateral security activities with Bahrain, there has been vocal criticism about this cooperation from the opposition backbenches in Parliament. Some 28 years after 1983, and demonstrable of the continued British training activities in Bahrain, Labour MP Kevin Brennan asked the Minister for the Armed Forces, Nick Harvey whether British forces have played any role in training Bahraini troops involved in 'repression.' The Minister responded as such:

> We do not believe so, but we have trained staff over a period of years in those countries, and it is impossible to say with any certainty what they have subsequently gone on to do. When engaging in training programmes, we do our utmost to spread British principles and approaches to military activity, and have done so for many years, in the hope that that will rub off on the countries we are training.[16]

The response from Nick Harvey is symbolic of the soft power influence that various British governments have attempted to exert upon Bahrain over the decades since withdrawal. By working with the armed forces of Bahrain, training them in British techniques and military tactics and sharing best practices that British trainers have learned whilst serving in the British armed forces, it is believed that Bahraini decision makers will become attracted to British military principles and thus more likely to develop their armed forces on a British model. This is not a new tactic. British Agents and Residents utilised Britain's exclusivity agreements with Bahrain to train and command the Trucial Scouts in British tactics throughout the Residency era, thus instilling a British military ideology into the developing Bahraini Defence Force.

In 2017, Viscount Younger told the HoL

> we believe that we are thinking in 21st-century terms. Let me say a little more about the build-up of our presence in the Gulf. It is very important

78 *Strategic power, defence, and security*

to have a strong defence presence with the naval facility in Bahrain, HMS 'Jufair' ... We are also building more short-term training teams to build our partners' capacity.[17]

Short-term training teams that can be raised and disbanded at short notice and to react to changing governmental priorities could be interpreted as the 21st century equivalent of the presence of a permanent presence of British trainers in Bahrain, and a less divisive opportunity for the British Government to demonstrate its commitment to assisting Bahrain with its security development.

4.2.3 Education as an attempt to retain influence

A number of cadets are sent to British military academies from Bahrain each year, with a number of princes and senior government officials training at Sandhurst. Documents suggest that the number of Bahraini cadets at RMA Sandhurst has been consistently greater than those at both RAF Cranwell and Britannia Naval College, perhaps highlighting the larger size of the Royal Bahraini Army within the BDF over the navy and air force, but also the influence of the British Army in Bahrain to attract cadets to Britain's premier officer training academy. The number of officer cadets at Sandhurst has been small and relatively inconsistent, with Tables 4.1–4.3 demonstrating that some years had more cadets than others, with larger numbers as the 2010s progressed. British expert power, particularly in naval and aviation academies, is evidently weaker and has been superseded by American training power.

The number of Bahrainis seconded to train in British military academies has fallen drastically since withdrawal, but elite forces are still considered for training, albeit without the guarantee of a place. In April 2019, the first all-female police bodyguard unit in Bahrain was trained in Britain, believed to be the first all-female unit in the Gulf. The influence and mindset that trainers in these academies imparted upon these cadets was an important soft power capability, but there was also power play by Bahrain. When requesting training from the MoD, the Bahraini authorities argued that, as British military personnel based in Bahrain are targets for non-state actors in the Middle East, it is beneficial for Britain to agree to this training in the UK. This demonstrated an ability by Bahrain to exert soft power influence onto Britain. The police cadets would only spend a month in a British academy, but they would learn British tactics and re-establish Britain's role as an indirect protector of Bahraini assets, possibly including senior royals. The British training of Bahrain's police force is not widely publicised either in Britain or Bahrain, largely because of the opposition to cooperating with Bahrain within some section of British society and politics, but it is an important aspect of British soft power that should not be underestimated.

Table 4.1 Number of Bahrainis seconded to Sandhurst, 2005–06 to 2016–16

Number of Bahrainis seconded to Sandhurst for officer training[18]											
2005–06	2006–07	2007–08	2008–09	2009–10	2010–11	2011–12	2012–13	2013–14	2014–15	2015–16
5	2	3	4	5	4	4	10	4	11	14

Table 4.2 Number of Bahrainis seconded to Britannia Royal Naval College, 2005–06 to 2015–16

Number of Bahrainis seconded to Britannia Naval College for officer training[19]											
2005–06	2006–07	2007–08	2008–09	2009–10	2010–11	2011–12	2012–13	2013–14	2014–15	2015–16
≤5	≤5	≤5	≤5	≤5	≤5	≤5	≤5	≤5	≤5	≤5

Table 4.3 Number of Bahrainis seconded to RAF Cranwell, 2005–06 to 2015–16

Number of Bahrainis seconded to RAF Cranwell for officer training[20]											
2005–06	2006–07	2007–08	2008–09	2009–10	2010–11	2011–12	2012–13	2013–14	2014–15	2015–16
0	0	0	0	0	≤5	≤5	≤5	≤5	0	0

The British Government has funded several police training missions for Bahraini police officers to spend time with various British police forces to learn best practices that can be replicated in Bahrain. Following a similar theme to Oman, Bahrain's police force receives training funding from the British Government through the CSSF, which is money allocated to both development and conflict-affected states – Bahrain is neither of these. There are fluctuations in this security training, with cooperation reducing when there are large-scale protests in Bahrain. In 2017, Lord Ahmad of Wimbledon, a Minister at the FCO, responded to a written question confirming that CSSF spent £1.52 million on Bahrain and 'in 2016–17, the UK continued to work with the Government of Bahrain – including through the Conflict, Stability and Security Fund (CSSF) – to encourage progress on human rights in areas which included focusing on building effective and accountable institutions, strengthening the rule of law and justice reform;'[21] police training would be considered justice reform. Just like with Oman, Northern Ireland Cooperation Overseas (NI-CO), a publicly owned arm of the Northern Ireland Assembly, was paid by the CSSF to train Bahraini police officers. In 2016, Northern Ireland's Minister for the Economy, Simon Hamilton, told the assembly that 'since 2012, NI-CO has received funding of £1.457 million from the FCO for projects in Bahrain.'[22] This training by NI-CO for the Bahraini police was in the areas of community policing and command and control tactics, areas of policing where the PSNI has significant experience.

From 2013, several missions visited Bahrain to research where the country's police needed assistance, and in June 2014, the first delegation of Bahraini police officers visited Belfast on a 'study visit.' During the visit, the officers were taken to high-risk neighbourhoods in Belfast in armoured personnel carriers, trained in the chains of command used during times of trouble in Northern Ireland, crowd management and intelligence gathering in the lead up to protests. NI-CO has also organised several visits by Bahraini prison officers to HMP Maghaberry to train them in control-and-restraint techniques, fast incident management, the separation of high-risk inmates and the detection of drugs in inmate's cells, all areas that this prison regularly deals with.[23] Requesting assistance from an agency in the UK that is experienced in the skills that Bahrain wants to learn is an effective method of influence management by the FCO and evidence of retained British expert power over Bahraini domestic security decision-making. The strength of British soft power in Bahrain is dependent on the British Government complying with requests from the Government of Bahrain for development assistance; as Britain is no longer the only country offering expertise and training in policing tactics, it is important that Britain is able to remain a go-to ally when required. As Bahrain has requested assistance from NI-CO, via the FCO, it is a sign that British security influence is still present in Bahrain and expert power is still able to sway decision-making amongst Bahraini decision makers. Britain needs contracts with Bahrain to secure influence in the Gulf, so it could be argued that Bahraini soft power within the British Government resulted in the FCO spending money allocated to supporting other commitments on Bahrain through the CSSF; a commitment by the FCO to the bilateral relationship with Bahrain.

The concept of power in the strategic education realm is predicated on the establishment of groupthink within the senior ranks of the Government of Bahrain. Bahraini officials need to be sufficiently attracted to British tactics that they choose to invite British officers to establish the foundations of their own domestic education infrastructure.

4.3 To what extent does bilateral military cooperation between Britain and Bahrain contribute to the power discourse?

Military cooperation between Britain and Bahrain has undoubtedly survived withdrawal, as this bilateral cooperation was an element of the relationship that was prominent throughout the Residency era, but it has been significantly weakened. The cooperation has not necessarily taken the form of joint military exercises, as in Oman, but has emerged as a more passive advisory role. This is a position of influence that has actually changed little since the appointment of Charles Belgrave in 1926. Partially as a result of the legacy of Britain, but also because of the continued impact of British soft power in the Kingdom, British individuals have arguably emerged as the most important determinant of the strength of this military cooperation. This advisory role has shifted from a position where the Residency took for granted the right for British troops to collaborate with Bahrain, to one where the British Government had to rely on its soft power capabilities to attract offers of cooperation from the Government of Bahrain. To guarantee continued cooperation in the military sphere, whether on a large or small scale, the British military had to offer something that their Bahraini counterparts required, a form of reward power.

Numerous international organisations, including Transparency International, claim that the decisions regarding which states Bahrain cooperates with within the security sphere are made by a small number of government and military officials who are close to the King through the 14-member Supreme Defence Council, where meetings are held independent of parliament, and through which all defence procurement is decided in lieu of public tenders.[24] Therefore, as is the case with much of the bilateral relationship, the personal exposure of these Bahraini decision makers to British military procedures and hardware is the most important determinant of the strength of British influence in the Kingdom. This could explain why the British Government offers support to defence manufacturers to market their hardware extensively in Bahrain, and why Bahraini cadets have been routinely accepted into some training academies since the 1970s, albeit in smaller numbers than those from Oman, both of which will be discussed in more detail later.

Military partnerships – the term 'partnerships' being the key to understanding the post-withdrawal landscape in which cooperation takes place – are imperative for the preservation of Britain's authority in Bahraini security affairs. The bilateral partnership can be understood as between individuals or governments; individual relations forming a prominent element of British power projection capabilities in the post-withdrawal Gulf. In 1984, the Bahraini Chief of Staff asked the British Government for assistance with the development of defence plans for the future of Bahraini security, coming at a crucial time when Iran and Iraq were at war and Bahrain's rulers feared the increasing interventionism of the Islamic Republic. It is significant that Bahrain turned to Britain at a time of security threats, demonstrating that a mindset still existed amongst decision makers that they could turn to Britain for help at times of greatest need. A government document reported:

> During DMAO's visit to Bahrain in August 1984 he was asked in strict confidence by the Chief of Staff of the Bahrain Defence Force (BDF), Brigadier Shaikh Khalifa bin Ahmed bin Salman Al Khalifa, for assistance in the design of some permanent defence work that formed part of a new Bahraini defence plan. This request indicated considerable trust in the UK ... The Chief of Staff said he wanted advice from the British in three separate areas:
>
> a   Type design of a permanent protected fire position for batteries of 155mm US M198 Howitzers.
> b   Type designs for the components of a permanently fortified strong point to be occupied by a reinforced infantry platoon.
> c   Options for offshore obstacles to impede or canalise landing craft or hovercraft.[25]

Considering the understanding of soft power as the ability of a state to influence another state without force, requests from senior Bahraini officials directly to the British Government is potentially symbolic of a strong soft power presence in some areas of strategic relations. These requests also arguably constitute a sense of respect within the Government of Bahrain for British tactics and military experience, resulting in Bahraini decision makers wanting to instil British tactics into their own defence infrastructure. Requests such as this are antithetical to the idea that withdrawal has taken away any opportunities to exert influence over Bahraini domestic affairs.

4.3.1 How should Bahraini requests for British assistance be understood in terms of power?

In 1987, the Government of Bahrain asked the British Government to assist with intelligence gathering as part of a formal military partnership. The fact that Bahraini decision makers willingly requested British cooperation is evidence of tangible trust by Bahraini decision makers in British security expertise, with Bahrain attracted to the intelligence procedures used by the British Government and the desire to implement these tried-and-tested procedures into domestic intelligence processes. Although cooperating closely on intelligence matters would ensure that Britain retained an influential foothold in the realm of Bahraini security, the UK MoD was reluctant to agree to a position where individual Britons would be responsible for intelligence gathering in a country that was, at the time, so divisive within the international community; this is a common issue that often undermines efforts to foster closer relations between the two states. The attitude within the MoD towards intelligence cooperation with the Bahrainis, one of reluctance to become too engaged or involved in the intricacies of liaising with the General Directorate for State Security Investigations in the late 1980s, was a continuation of the attitude that had emerged at the point of withdrawal. Although there was continued security cooperation between Britain and Bahrain after 1971, there was no great push within the British Government to emerge as a major intelligence player in the state. Costs and political sensitivities likely played a part in British decision-making. A diplomatic telegram from the MoD in 1987 outlined the main reasons why the British intelligence community would not be willing to collaborate too closely with their Bahraini counterparts, the main reason being the risk that Britain would be drawn into dealing with the sectarian divisions if it reclaimed its historic position as the determinant of intelligence policy in Bahrain. The telegram stated:

> On the question of core membership, your proposal to include someone on the military assessments side presents some difficulty. We would not wish to be drawn into making formal detailed threat assessments for Bahrain.[26]

Intelligence cooperation and the attraction that Bahraini decision makers have for Britain's reputation as a strong intelligence gathering nation is only one element of the relationship, but security cooperation is more complex than just this one factor. Each of Britain's relations with the Gulf states is different, partly the result of differing historic relations, but also because of the development of each state since 1971 and their varying requirements for British expertise. The security relationship between Britain and Bahrain is most certainly unique and this is something that was acknowledged by Shaikh Mohammed, the Bahraini Foreign Minister in 1987. Shaikh Mohammed told British diplomats that he wanted a bilateral committee unlike any other that Britain had with other Gulf states. By doing this, the Foreign Minister was signalling his desire to work more closely with Britain than with other countries and to re-establish Bahrain as the first port of call for Britain's activities in the Gulf. In 1987, the US had firmly established itself as the hegemon in Bahrain as a result of its largest naval base in the Middle East being located in the former British base in Jufair, so it is significant that one of the most powerful government officials in the Kingdom approached Britain to advocate a security committee of this kind.

In 1987, Bahrain was increasingly being threatened by the relatively new revolutionary government in nearby Iran and US President Ronald Reagan had committed to the basing of STINGER air defence systems on American ships based at Jufair,[27] demonstrating their pledge to defend Bahrain from attacks. A DipTel sent on 22 September 1987 detailed the request that Shaikh Hamad made to David Miers, the Assistant Under-Secretary for Foreign and Commonwealth Affairs responsible for the Middle East at the time:

> Between Shaikh Hamad's meetings with the Prime Minister and myself, Miers talked to the Bahraini Foreign Minister. Shaikh Mohammed asked us to make proposals, implying that we must already have committees of this kind envisaged for other Gulf states. He was told that we did not. He made it clear that Bahrain did not want a political/economic/technical joint committee of the kind we had with Oman and the UAE.[28]

Prior to withdrawal, the British authorities took for granted the influence that they had over Bahraini policy making, but Harold Wilson's main aim for withdrawal was to take Britain out of the decision-making processes of the Gulf states, and thus also take the responsibility for regional issues away from Britain. Despite this, the Bahraini authorities evidently wanted to bring Britain back into their domestic processes, echoing the apprehension in 1968 to the initial declaration to withdraw and the attempts made by Emir Isa at that time to change Wilson's mind on withdrawal.

In 1987, Crown Prince Hamad told an official at the British Embassy in Manama that 'he had invited General Moore to act as his personal consultant, to advise him on all aspects of the BDF's planning and development.'[29] There was no intention at the point of withdrawal that Britons would continue to cooperate with Bahrain on an overt advisory level as this would represent a failure to end the British presence East of the Suez. Nonetheless, the most senior officials within the Government of Bahrain were evidently still attracted to the knowledge that British advisors could bring to Bahrain, securing the influence that many believed had been severely weakened by withdrawal. However, British advisors who wanted to retain their positions of influence in Bahrain were now reliant on the British Government's retention of close ties with Bahrain. Not only did this shift signify the loss of British power and direct influence in Bahrain, but it also suggests that Bahrain was now able to exert its own soft power influence on British authorities. To understand how Bahrain is able to utilise its own soft power influence in Britain, it is necessary to discuss one of Bahrain's key assets.

The geostrategic location of Bahrain, across from Iran and close to security hotspots in the Middle East, is attractive to British policymakers and therefore Bahrain holds significant leverage within the relationship. The bilateral relationship should not, however, be simplified. The close friendship between both royal families adds an extra dimension to the association between both states. Both states absolutely want the other to be safe and prosperous.

It seems that the British Government was not convinced about the Bahraini aims of the committee and was perhaps more evidence of a British reluctance to become more involved in domestic Bahraini security affairs. British officials were wary of why Bahrain wanted to establish a committee. The theme that emerged from reports and diplomatic minutes from the time was that Bahrain wanted a counterbalance against Iranian aggression, training, and support if Iran invaded, advice on the purchase of weapons and to diversify the defence community within Bahrain away from US advisors. Again, this demonstrates the willingness of Bahraini officials to deviate from their flourishing relationship with the US and an attraction that they had for continuing their close cooperation with Britain in the security sphere. FCO minutes defined the joint committee as:

> Bahraini [aims] for the Committee (Joint UK-Bahrain Defence Committee) are [ill] defined. They may want:
>
> a   More conspicuous military contract with the UK at the present juncture to deter Iran and to balance their current surfeit of US military VIPs;
> b   Shaikh Hamad wants advice on planning for emergencies (e.g. infiltration by Iranian guerrillas) and equipment purchase.[30]

A codified military contract with Bahrain, based on the framework set out by Shaikh Hamad and his cabinet, would have granted Britain a level of influence at the highest levels not seen since 1971. Yet again, the strength of Bahrain's attraction to British defence and security expertise came to the fore; British soft power evidently remained strong despite withdrawal less than two decades prior. Theorists of soft power define joint partnerships and committees as an effective way to secure influence in another state. Although the proposed defence committee would have been defined by its links to military hard power, the sharing of security advice and the deterrence that would arise from the signing of a defence agreement with Britain, which would be in force alongside an existing contract with the US, was very much soft power in nature. Professor Urs Matthias Zachmann told a HoL enquiry on British soft power that soft power can be used as a cover for hard power – a different take on the notion of smart power. Soft power can be viewed as a 'liberal compensation' by states for the 'lack in hard power to pursue its national interests abroad.' When relations between two states are under strain (because of domestic human rights issues in Bahrain and the resulting reluctance within British politics to cooperation with the Kingdom) 'soft power can at best soften an otherwise uncompromising antagonism and render attitudes more ambivalent.'[31]

As British hard power has been diminished in Bahrain by withdrawal, soft power has emerged as a way to secure influence in the state. Military cooperation and shared security initiatives that are voluntarily entered into by both parties is a way for Britain to collaborate with Bahrain on a military level without the stigma attached. In an increasingly interconnected world, states can no longer act alone to counter military threats, necessitating the expansion of defence ties between Britain and Bahrain. A strategic consultant at The Institute for Government, Jonathan McClory, told the HoL that the development of power *with* states is just as important as holding power *over* states when these states are developing their soft power capabilities.[32] British influence in Bahrain is ultimately dependent on relations between the two states, and rather than coercing Bahrain to agree to cooperate with British troops, these security partnerships need to be organically formed as a result of a willingness by both states to join forces for the common good.

4.3.2 The financial element of UK–Bahraini strategic cooperation

The financial element is also an important aspect of military cooperation between Britain and Bahrain that requires further assessment. The communication of power through financial commitments made to security cooperation contributes to the strengthening of influence, but restrictions on funding, either because of financial restraints as a result of budget cuts imposed by the British Government or the result of an unwillingness to allocate money to supporting collaboration with Bahrain for politically ideological reasons, can weaken this power. Britain has historically not had to commit money to military cooperation with Bahrain for the purpose of maintaining influence because the presence of the Residency essentially guaranteed this, but since withdrawal, other states that were previously barred from cooperating with Bahrain, the most obvious example being the US, have spent significantly more on the development of this influence than Britain. The US sent US$65 million of military aid to Bahrain under *Section 1206* of the National Defense Authorization Act of 2006 between 2006 and 2015, and a total of US$400 million since 1993.[33] This is perhaps evidence of complacency by the British Government in the way that it deals with the defence relationship with Bahrain, and is in direct contrast to dealings with Oman, where substantial funding is provided for the *Saif Saarea* training exercises and the credit guarantees to underpin the sale of arms to the Sultanate. The comparative scale of cooperation also limits how much support Britain can offer to Bahrain.

When an agreement had been signed in 1983 for Royal Marines to train their Bahraini counterparts, the Government of Bahrain had to commit a majority of the funding for this training cooperation. The fact that Bahraini policymakers requested a training mission to be sent from Britain highlights an attraction for the skills and experience that the Marines could impart upon the Bahraini special forces, but as is common in this relationship, there was an element of reluctance by the British Government to take on the full financial burden and the requirement of Bahrain to find money to support exercises such as this arguably weakens the British negotiating hand when other powers are offering something similar for less or no money. It could also be argued that Bahraini funding was a sign of the relationship shift as a result of withdrawal. Elite British troops were no longer used to secure the sphere of influence around the world, as was the case prior to 1971, but rather had become open to the international system and had to have a strategic benefit for Bahrain. The Memorandum of Understanding signed between the British and Bahraini governments for the Marines training mission stated that:

> The full cost of the RMTT will be shared between the Government of Bahrain and the Government of the United Kingdom according to the principle that the Government of Bahrain will pay in country costs and half of the out of country costs of the team; the Government of the United Kingdom the balance ...[34]

It is both understandable and evident that Bahrain has developed close strategic relationships with numerous countries other than Britain since the Kingdom was able to do so in 1971, and this diversification in Bahrain's network of allies has arguably resulted in a weakening of the ties that bound Britain and Bahrain together for over 150 years prior to withdrawal. The relationships that have emerged between Bahrain and other states around the world is a factor that undoubtedly has an impact on the strength of British influence and power in Bahrain, particularly in the areas of military and security relations. The most notable competition to British influence has emerged from the US and Saudi Arabia.

The permanent British naval base, HMS Jufair, was officially opened on 13 April 1935 as a result of lobbying by Belgrave to the ruler of Bahrain, Shaikh Hamad, and remained an important element of the British strategic relationship with Bahrain until 1971 when the base was handed over to the US Navy. The US leased space in the base from 1941 to enhance the strategic footprint of the US Middle East Force when they entered the Second World War. Although at this point, Britain's exclusive presence was under threat as a result of the Royal Navy's invitation to permit American incursions into what was considered Britain's sphere of influence, HMS Jufair was still under the control of the Royal Navy and all activities in the base were overseen by the Residency authorities. This historic cooperation between British and US navies in Bahrain, with the US Navy, the junior partner at the time as a result of Britain's control of access to the region, came to an end in 1971 and the US immediately claimed the position as the primary partner. A senior British diplomat responsible for the Gulf claimed

88 *Strategic power, defence, and security*

that 'Britain is able to lobby Bahrain in private on domestic human rights issues, but Saudi influence is greater on Bahraini foreign policy decisions than any other country.'[35]

Military cooperation between Bahrain and Saudi Arabia is a contemporary example of Bahrain's willingness to be pragmatic about its foreign policy, demonstrated by Bahrain's involvement in the Saudi-led intervention in the Yemeni civil war, sending 15 fighter jets to bomb Houthi bases[36] and soldiers since 2015, and the Saudi-led intervention in Bahrain to suppress an anti-government uprising in March 2011, when over 1,000 Saudi troops and 150 military vehicles (along with 500 Emirati policemen as part of the GCC-wide Peninsula Shield Force) were sent from Saudi Arabia across the King Fahd Causeway to Manama. This intervention was preceded by a similar action in 1994. Before 1971, British Residents and advisors to the Emir would have been called upon to quell any uprisings as they held the levers of power over the security forces, but after 1971, and the loss of direct British influence, the Bahraini authorities had to rely on assistance from neighbouring states that had a vested interest in the stability of the major financial base in the GCC and the preservation of the Sunni leadership in a state with a majority Shia community.

4.3.3 *Limitations of bilateral cooperation*

Although the security relations between the US and Bahrain are complex and worthy of further analysis in their own right, this is the factor that has the most impact on contemporary British power in the Gulf. There are no notable examples of large bilateral military engagements between Britain and Bahrain since withdrawal on the scale of the *Saif Saarea* exercises in Oman, and although the opening of HMS Juffair in April 2018 does suggest a re-engagement by Britain, the 'Mina Salman Support Facility' is not as large as the former British base that is now home to the US Naval Forces Central Command and United States Fifth Fleet, and the future of the base is dependent on continued acceptance of a British presence by Bahraini rulers. The small size of Bahrain compared to Oman, of course, also restricts where joint defence training can take place.

The military strategy of subsequent British Governments since 1971 has ultimately been focused on the protection of British interests abroad. Former Defence Secretary Liam Fox told the Royal United Services Institute in 2010 that 'the first duty of Government ... is to protect our way of life and provide security for our citizens.'[37] This strategy has extended to international cooperation, including joint military training exercises with the Gulf states. The frequency and strength of military exercises with Bahrain since withdrawal are significantly fewer than those with Oman, and this offers some sense of the opportunities open to the British military to cooperate. One of the limited joint exercises between British and Bahraini forces, although led by the US, is *Exercise Neon Falcon*, an annual trilateral naval exercise first held between June and December 1995, expanding to include a French naval contingent in 2000. The *Joint Force Quarterly* reported that

> Neon Falcon, which is [also] held in Bahrain, focuses on chemical, biological, and radiological defense for naval, naval air, and Special Operations Forces. British and French units as well as U.S. and Bahrain forces participated in Neon Falcon '00 which included a field training exercise to refine operational tactics, techniques, and procedures.[38]

The Defence Select Committee's thirteenth report stated that the Royal Navy's vessels that took part in the 2000 exercise included the aircraft carrier *HMS Illustrious*, nuclear submarine *HMS Triumph*, and the destroyer *HMS Gloucester*.[39] The fact that Britain now has to take part in joint exercises with other states is evidence of the loss of British hegemony and Bahrain's development of new relationships.

Prior to withdrawal, British military strategy in Bahrain took on largely hard power characteristics, with a strong arms and manpower presence in the state, but in the years immediately following withdrawal, this presence was diminished to a negligible level. From 1995, the gradual re-engagement in Bahraini military affairs resulted in the British Government having to utilise its smart power capabilities – working to attract Bahrain's authorities to requesting cooperation with the Royal Navy and respect for Britain's military hardware (soft power) – to exert some influence over the future direction of Bahraini military affairs. The nature of the development of Britain's strategic posture within the international system also affects Bahrain's cooperation with the British forces.

The Conservative–Liberal Democrat coalition government refocused military protection from one dictated solely by the central government to one that became adaptable to regional requirements, including in the Gulf. The 2010 *Strategic Defence and Security Review* announced that the British military would 'retain their geographical reach and their ability to operate across the spectrum from high-intensity intervention to enduring stabilisation activity.'[40] The smart power capabilities of the British military do contribute to the British presence in Bahrain by demonstrating commitment to Bahraini priorities and 'that ability to partner even in the most challenging circumstances is one of the UK's key attributes and sources of influence.'[41] The legacy has, however, been diminished and the historic privileged position in domestic affairs has been lost to the US.

As Britain has gradually lost strategic ground in the Gulf, cooperation with the Bahraini authorities on military matters has become more important for Britain's projection of power capabilities in the Middle East. Unlike the unrivalled historic influence that Britain enjoyed, where British politicians and civil servants were able to determine the strategic agenda in Bahrain, the contemporary influence in this area is predicated on requests from Bahrain – continued trust. Despite withdrawal from all military matters in Bahrain in 1971, it is evident that Britain has been able to retain a limited sentiment within the mindset of Bahraini decision makers, perhaps the result of various Residents' and Belgrave's instilment of British defence policy into Bahraini affairs for over 150 years and the foundations of the modern military structures in Bahrain emerging from the foundations left behind by the British. The most prominent symbol of the retention of this British influence was undoubtedly the request by the Government of Bahrain to the MoD to re-establish a permanent naval base at HMS Juffair in 2014, opening on 5 April 2018, and the emergence of a new cooperation between these two long-term allies. The permanent assignment of up to 500 British naval personnel in the base, and large aircraft carriers at anchor offshore, is a physical symbol of Britain's cooperative hybrid power in Bahrain. It was arguably soft power influence that led to the Bahraini authorities inviting Britain back into the military affairs of the Kingdom in 2014, with smaller scale advisory cooperation by seconded Britons laying the foundations for this re-engagement.

4.3.4 Bahrain's perception of risk and the resulting degree of cooperation with Britain

Bahrain's willingness to cooperate in the military sphere with Britain is, in part, dependent on the perception of risk within Bahrain and the assessment of future threats to Bahraini security. These calculations offer the British Government a channel through which influence can be further advanced. Martin Shaw described the field of modern warfare as threat reduction before it emerges by attacking potential risks to security where they originate.[42] The risk calculation offers an explanation of why British strategic decision makers have decided to re-pivot towards a cooperative stance with Bahrain, as most of the recent threats to British security have arisen within the Middle East; Bahrain is an ally in the fight against non-state actors including Al-Qaeda and Daesh. This dependence on Bahrain's will explains how the Kingdom has been able to develop its influence over British strategic policy, but not how it impacts British power. A consensus in international political theory is emerging, which argues that military cooperation cannot be considered alone when assessing power projection, because an increasingly interconnected world has reduced the pure power of warfare. Anne-Marie Slaughter's argument that the 'measure of power in interconnectedness' and war cannot be separated from economics, diplomacy, and society[43] offers the most coherent explanation of how risk and power plays out within the international system. It could be argued that British military cooperation with Bahrain is susceptible to fluctuations in the wider relationship, as is the power of Britain to influence domestic strategic policies in Bahrain.

In Bahrain, the entry of other states into what was formerly the British strategic sphere of influence until 1971 has inevitably had an impact on

Britain's influence in the Kingdom. As British manufacturers have closed, there have been fewer options from UK manufacturers for Bahraini decision makers to choose. Until 2003, the Bahraini police force used British Vauxhall and Rover vehicles, but the government has increasingly opted to purchase replacements from Japanese company Toyota, US company Chevrolet, and French company Renault as British companies have been purchased by foreign buyers.

Although Britain was invited to re-establish a permanent military base in Bahrain, this base and the military personnel stationed there are negligible in comparison with the US presence, with the US 5th fleet jointly headquartered at the Naval Support Activity Bahrain (NSA Bahrain) alongside the US Naval Forces Central Command. A possible explanation for the willingness of Bahraini authorities to allow such a large and overt US military presence in their country, aside from the fact that the US is the only major superpower in the world and a strong military power, is the hard power deterrent that this presence provides for Bahrain against aggression from regional states, particularly Iran. The US presence at HMS Jufair since 1971 is also deemed important by Bahrain's rulers as it guarantees regime survival for the Al Khalifa family. This role was held by Britain until withdrawal, so it is unsurprising that talks between Bahraini and US decision makers about the US takeover of HMS Jufair began shortly after Wilson declared his intention to withdraw British forces from Bahrain in 1968. It could be argued, therefore, that the US took the place that Britain had held for over a century, becoming the protector of Bahrain and thus also able to influence security decision-making in the state. This, combined with the relative absence of Britain from Bahraini affairs for more than four decades, has certainly damaged Britain's ability to influence policy making in Bahrain and weakened the cooperation between the two allies on security matters.

4.4 How have British arms sales contributed to the retention of British power in Bahrain?

Sales of defence equipment to Bahrain has arguably proven to be the most influential power asset for Britain since withdrawal, both on an economic and strategic level, and could offer a different explanation regarding how strategic cooperation is developing since withdrawal. Prior to withdrawal, Britain was the only supplier permitted to sell weapons and defence-related equipment to Bahrain as a result of the exclusivity agreements that were enacted as part of the protectorate agreement. After 1971, this exclusivity was lost and suppliers from countries that were previously off-limits to the Bahraini authorities – the US, France, Germany, and Italy – quickly began supplying the Bahraini military and police force with weapons and equipment. The entry of these powerful states undoubtedly weakened Britain's influence on Bahraini defence economics, and British diplomats and representatives of manufacturers have had to work hard to attract orders from Bahrain since that time. Defence and security sales to Bahrain are a key priority for the British Government, with significant emphasis put on attending defence shows and promoting British manufacturers in the country. Although Britain is still one of a handful of major defence suppliers to Bahrain, albeit no longer the only one, this contemporary demand and supply relationship has not always proceeded smoothly. In 1981, the Assistant Chief of Staff in Bahrain, Colonel Abdulla, told the new Second Secretary at the British Embassy in Manama, Simon Collis, of his frustration at the limitations to Britain's defence sales. Collis wrote in a letter to the FCO about his first meeting with the Colonel:

> When I saw Colonel Abdulla, the Assistant Chief of Staff, yesterday he saw fit to give me as a new arrival, the benefit of his views on UK/Bahrain relations in the defence field. On defence sales his attitude was one of, I think, genuine disappointment. Bahrain's first though was to turn to the UK, but there were two constraints:
>
> i   The BDF could not always select their own equipment;
> ii The UK would not always sell equipment to them.
>
> ... he then cited Blowpipe as an example of this last point.[44]

Britain was, in 1981, at least, still considered an important go-to country when Bahrain was looking to modernise its weapons, but internal divisions within the British parliament likely erected barriers. This is a theme that is proving the main determinant of the strength of the bilateral relationship; soft power influence can only be effective for Britain if limitations are not applied to the various elements of the relationship. Critics of the theory of soft power argue that it is difficult to differentiate between soft and hard power in international relations, and whilst this may be true when considering the sales of arms, which are hard power assets, without a soft power presence in Bahrain, policymakers would be unlikely to opt to purchase from British suppliers. There is an undeniable correlation between soft power economics and the supply of arms from Britain to Bahrain. These orders could be tied to referent power. British technology and the reliance that Britain has demonstrated to Bahraini security contributes to the future development of the relationship. Throughout the 1980s, there was evidently still interest in British equipment at the highest levels of the Bahraini Government, despite the frustrations, as Crown Prince Hamad told A.S. Kemp in 1983:

> Our main defence interest in Bahrain is in the area of defence sales. The Bahrainis are showing serious interest in a range of UK equipment, including Hawk aircraft and Valiant tanks.[45]

In the 1980s, Bahrain still considered Britain the most important supplier of military aircraft during times of modernisation. Indeed, the British Government conceded that defence sales were the overriding priority for diplomats. This shift away from viewing Bahrain as a key geostrategic asset before 1971, where the protection and defence of Bahrain and use of the island as a deterrent from attacks on other Gulf states was as much a priority as weapons sales, to a situation where defence sales were considered the only British interest in Bahrain is an important indicator of how Britain viewed itself in the Gulf and how the pillars that underpinned Britain's influence in Bahrain developed after withdrawal. Prior to withdrawal, Bahrain was the location of one of Britain's largest naval bases anywhere in the world, HMS Jufair, and Britain was largely the only defence supplier to the country – the result of both the exclusivity agreements that ingrained Britain's supremacy in Bahrain and the presence of senior British officials in Manama, promoting British weapons to decision makers.

It could be argued that focusing mainly on one element, weapons sales, simplified the relationship and gave British officials based in Bahrain a specific focus, was more cost-effective for the British Government, and could be considered a more tangible measurement when assessing the strength of Britain's contemporary relationship with Bahrain. Referent power also became more important as technology and weapons became the main method to attract Bahraini cooperation. This focus on defence economics has continued within the British Government since the early 1980s, with the *2015 Strategic Defence and Security Review* highlighting defence prosperity as the third major objective for national security. Integrating prosperity into defence policy aimed to ensure that all defence policies benefited the national income of the UK and contributed to the national budget. The argument made by the government was that strong defence exports would result in a more productive and sustainable defence economy in Britain, and thus a greater British influence around the world. The review stated that the government will:

> Establish a team in UKTI dedicated to supporting the negotiation and delivery of government-to-government deals by departments. These deals offer customers simplicity, reliability, access to our skills and advice, and a wider relationship with the UK. They are increasingly in demand from our partners. ... Make support for exports a core task for the MOD, with responsibility for managing all strategic defence export campaigns, overseen by the Defence Secretary and a new senior official post. This will create additional capacity to support these campaigns, including the training of international customers. We will adopt a more flexible approach to charging potential customers when supporting export campaigns where this is in our national interest.[46]

94 *Strategic power, defence, and security*

4.4.1 *An emerging British dependence on arms sales to Bahrain?*

It has become evident that the British Government is focused on re-establishing British defence manufacturers as the preferred supplier to international security forces. Britain lost significant influence in Bahrain when US suppliers moved into their former economic sphere of influence. In 2018 alone, a major deal for rocket launchers worth US$300 million was approved by the US Senate.[47] British manufacturers have to commit significant sums of money to marketing their equipment to the Bahrainis, suggesting that in the area of defence sales, Britain is no longer as influential as it was before 1971. Defence economics currently underpins this important relationship, but it seems that these sales are more important to the British than the Bahrainis. The importance of Bahrain to British prosperity provides the Kingdom with significant influence over Britain, as a dependence has developed within the relationship. This dependence, and the resulting economic effects within the British economy, has established a reverse power dynamic; the Government of Bahrain now holds significant leverage over British policymaking.

The Government of Bahrain needs to guarantee its own security by purchasing weapons from trusted suppliers, and British manufacturers are undoubtedly aware of the influence that this bestows upon them. There has to be an element of smart power involved in the marketing of arms to Bahrain – attracting orders by selling reliable products that are cost-effective and supported by the British Government (soft power) and being able to supply weapons and equipment at times of greatest need in Bahrain and being able to sell required parts, missiles, and technology upgrades throughout the life of the arms (hard power).

Between 2008 and 2017, British defence manufacturers exported a total of £88.9 million worth of arms and related equipment to the Bahraini armed forces.[48] The value of approved export licences fluctuated depending on the political situation in Bahrain throughout the period. In 2010, when the Conservative–Liberal Democrat government was elected in the UK, the number of approved export licences to Bahrain increased by 179 on the amount approved during the 2008–09 Labour government. This was a significant increase to such a divisive state. The number of licences dropped to the lowest level in 2011, corresponding with the Bahraini anti-governmental uprisings, but then increased again and remained relatively stable until 2017, when Theresa May's government attempted to further reinvigorate

Table 4.4 Number of approved arms export licences from the UK to Bahrain

Number of approved arms export licences for Bahrain from the UK Government[49]										
2008	2009	2010	2011	2012	2013	2014	2015	2016	2017	2018
52	72	251	73	213	135	115	92	138	373	238

its relations with Bahrain, at which point export licences increased to their highest level in a decade. Table 4.4 demonstrates this trend.

Nick Ritchie discussed the implications of political shifts within the UK on international security priorities. He wrote that

> under New Labour (the Blair and Brown period between 1997 and 2010) the concept of national security moved beyond traditional ideas focused on the threat, use and control of military force and territorial protection to encompass a range of threats and risks, including pandemic disease, natural disasters, global poverty, climate change, transnational crime and failing states. ... Under Blair, Labour translated international interdependence and the rise of truly global security challenges into a globalized national security role for the UK.[50]

This internationalisation of British security priorities has continued to influence British foreign policy since, and this can be found in the marketing of arms and the number of export licences approved to sell British arms across the Gulf and, by extension, the enhancement of British power in the region.

If the economic aspect of soft power is predicated on the value and quantity of arms sales between states, the Conservatives have attempted to improve Britain's influence in Bahrain by using arms sales to recommit to a state that had been neglected throughout the previous decade. British suppliers have had to compete against competitors from other countries since 1971, and because Bahrain has now diversified its supply chain, it has gained leverage and influence over British policy making. Nye suggested that 'arms recipients have sought to diversify their purchases in order to gain leverage over the major or sole supplier.' Although more companies are able to supply arms to Bahrain, 'when arms are supplied from outside, the supplier often has leverage through technical assistance, spare parts, and replacements.'[51] Decision makers within both the British Government and private companies are likely aware of the increased influence that they would gain as more arms are sold to Bahrain at times when the government there is looking to modernise and expand its armaments.

Although the UK is no longer the largest arms supplier to Bahrain, the soft power influence that has developed in the Kingdom over 150 years cannot be matched by any other ally. However, this has not hindered the expansion of arms sales to Bahrain from other states that were historically barred from trading with the state and the gradual reduction in the British influence, suggesting that a 'legacy' is not a guaranteed channel of influence.

4.4.2 Convergence between defence economics and strategic priorities

British defence sales is arguably the point of convergence between British strategic and economic priorities in Bahrain, and seemingly the most

96 *Strategic power, defence, and security*

important legacy for Britain. Although this influence has diminished as a result of the intervention of other states into the Bahraini defence procurement process, the presence of British manufacturers in the state has remained stable despite withdrawal. Military expenditure on weapons and vehicles in Bahrain is significant. According to data released by SIPRI, defence spending in Bahrain in the 2017–18 year was US$1.4 billion[52] with total GDP in the same year totalling around US$71 billion. Although this is only a small fraction as a percentage of GDP, the market is important for British companies in an increasingly competitive region. Government spending on defence in states that do not build their own weapons and equipment is dependent on two factors, a risk analysis of potential threats, in the case of Bahrain, this would-be Iran and domestic opposition to the ruling regime, and the deterrence capabilities that importing arms would have. It is these considerations that both the DIT DSO and British defence manufacturers capitalise on when marketing their equipment to the Bahraini authorities.

Between the years 2007–08 and 2018–19, there have been no UKEF agreements for defence-related equipment exports from British manufacturers to Bahrain, but in the same period, a buyer credit was awarded by the British Government in 2016–17 worth £1,709,583,352 for BAE Systems to export Typhoon and Hawk Aircraft to Oman,[53] and in 2018–19, three buyer credits and export insurance policies were awarded for defence exports to Qatar – £736,844,923 for BAE Systems and MBDA UK to export Typhoon aircraft, weapons systems, and Hawk aircraft, £2,256,326,224 for BAE to export Typhoon and Hawk aircraft, and £559,838,820 to export weapons systems for Typhoon aircraft.[54] The lack of arms export financing offered to Bahrain was arguably either a symptom of the lack of a desire by the Government of Bahrain to purchase from Britain, in which case, the historic influence as a reliable arms supplier had diminished, or the result of an unwillingness by British officials to commit to selling weapons to the Kingdom, thus highlighting the effect that domestic political opposition has on trade policy. There have also been budget cuts across governments in Bahrain since the start of the 21st century, so competition to supply Bahrain has intensified. Whilst the UK was not financing large arms deals with Bahrain, major competitors including France and the US were.

In 2015, the French *Ministère de la Défense* reported that 27 arms export licences were approved worth €27,924,577 in 2009, 26 in 2010 worth €18,280,596, 9 in 2011 worth €17,338,096, 17 in 2012 worth €5,147,900, and 18 in 2013 worth €4,602,116.[55] Although arms sales could be defined as a form of hard power, offering financial inducements to gain orders is a soft power method of international relations that the British Government can utilise to enhance its influence in other states, but this has not been used effectively in relation to Bahrain. If decision makers in Britain are not utilising their ability to offer export guarantees to market large-scale arms contracts to Bahrain, then it is inevitable that the government there will turn to other countries offering financing, and as a result, it could be argued that Britain's reputation as a trusted supplier to the Kingdom has been declining since 1971. Domestic opposition within the UK to arming a divisive Bahraini administration is also a contributor to the reduction in influence.

On 20 June 2019, a Court of Appeal judgement mandated that the British Government stop the granting of future export agreements for any equipment that could be used in the Yemen War, including all weapons sold to Bahrain.[56] Until the war in Yemen ends, defence economics is unlikely to be a contributing factor to the development of British influence in Bahrain regardless of the strength of British soft power. This also limits the impact of British referent power in Bahrain, as the main type of British power is dependent on the availability of technology (including arms) to attract Bahraini interest.

4.5 How do British public relations companies employed by Bahrain's Government affect Britain's power in the Kingdom?

The Bahraini economy became the first in the Gulf to privatise its strategic advisory affairs. The British–Bahraini relationship has modernised since withdrawal, shifting from one based on government-to-government expertise sharing to one based on private–public partnerships. The preservation of influence in Bahrain is no longer solely in the hands of British government officials, and instead has been transferred to private consultancy companies who are directly contracted by the Government of Bahrain to advise on specific topics. Statistics indicate that since 2011, the Government of Bahrain has hired at least ten British private PR companies to advise on several areas of development.[57] A number of these large London-based companies work with governments around the world. The likes of Bell Pottinger, M&C Saatchi and G3 have been awarded substantial advisory contracts worth a total of US$30,537,048.[58] The PR firms have been hired to assist the Government of Bahrain to both develop domestic policies and to manage the Kingdom's image on the international stage. From the perspective of the British Government, the involvement of London-based PR companies in Bahrain can only be seen as a positive. Bahrain's active involvement with British PR companies arguably replicates the advisory role that British officials held in the country during the Residency era.

Historically, British Agents, Residents, and advisors assisted Bahrain with developing its domestic economic and strategic affairs, but after 1971, this position of direct governmental influence on Bahraini affairs reduced. The PR companies that have been hired by the Government of Bahrain could be described as an unofficial arm of the British Government, as they have replaced the economic advisory position that British policy officials held. Large British PR companies have close links to the British Government as many consultants are MPs and Lords. This is an indirect avenue for British officials to push for changes in the Kingdom that ultimately benefits Britain.

98 *Strategic power, defence, and security*

The presence of a relatively significant number of private PR companies since 2011 is evidence of Britain's strong soft power capabilities in the state, something that has seemingly survived withdrawal and the intervention of other countries into Bahraini domestic affairs.

As a key aspect of the theory of soft power is the ability to retain a presence through an individuals' attraction to the skills and expertise of an organisation during times of need, it could be argued that the strong and consistent presence of British PR companies since 1971 is evidence of influential British power in Bahrain. These collaborations could be categorised as covert rather than overt, as these PR firms are not publicly accountable, nor is their presence evident within Bahraini society or openly acknowledged by officials. This is in direct contrast to the historic position where British advisors to the Royal Court and the Residency openly held power over domestic decision-making. PR firms hired by the Government of Bahrain are a crucial element of British expert power in Bahrain affairs and an indirect avenue for the British Government to exert influence.

4.5.1 The financial aspect of advising

The cooperation between the Government of Bahrain and private British PR companies correlates with the direct financial assistance provided by the British Government to Bahrain. There are no limitations on how Bahraini ministers can spend the funding received from Britain. Bahrain receives an undisclosed amount of funding under the auspices of the *Magna Carta Fund* – the FCO's funding programme that aims to promote the implementation of policies that bring target countries in line with international standards in the areas of freedom of religion or belief, prevention of torture, prevention of the death penalty, freedom of the media, international justice, responsible business practices, and online freedoms[59] – through which Bahrain is considered 1 of 30 human rights priority countries. An FCO report produced on the fund stated that:

> the UK will continue to work with the Government of Bahrain to support the Bahraini-led reform agenda. We welcome the Government of Bahrain's commitment to continue, into 2017 and beyond, with implementing its own series of socio-economic reform programmes which are designed to improve opportunities for all Bahrainis and which include developing new ways that all citizens can hold government institutions to account.[60]

Much of the funding allocated to Bahrain is spent on PR and consulting fees, a significant amount of which goes to British agencies. Although not officially disclosed, these British PR companies are arguably prioritised to work with the Government of Bahrain to achieve the fund's stated aims.

British consultants working with senior Bahraini officials are a mainstay of the modern bilateral relationship.

The rapid shift from Britain's advisory hegemony to a situation where local rulers willingly opted to contract British agencies, despite competition from other countries, is an important indicator of the continued ability of Britain to influence Bahraini affairs. There are, however, a number of American PR companies that are quickly emerging as preferred bidders for many strategic projects in Bahrain, with the largest and most prominent being McKinsey & Company. They have an office in Manama and advise the Government of Bahrain on economic and strategic topics relevant to Bahraini development. The significant presence of American companies in Bahrain suggests that the British influence has not remained hegemonic, but the fact that there is a British footprint in Bahraini public relations at all contradicts the claim that withdrawal has ended Britain's responsibilities in the Kingdom – the responsibilities have just shifted from the British public sector to private companies. These private companies are able to adapt their capabilities to suit Bahraini priorities more efficiently than governments, ensuring that Britain remains relevant in Bahrain and attractive to local decision makers in the future – soft power.

4.6 Shifting power balances and the future of UK–Bahraini strategic affairs

When Harold Wilson declared in 1968 that all British assets would be withdrawn from Bahrain, he was referring to the closure of British military bases and the termination of the Bahraini reliance on Britain for protection. It is questionable whether or not his ambitions to withdraw from East of the Suez by 1971 has been a success, as British arms manufacturers have never wholly stopped supplying Bahrain's military and domestic security forces with weapons, nor were British security advisors prevented from being directly employed by the Government of Bahrain after 16 December 1971. The strategic relationship between Britain and Bahrain has shifted from one where British Residents and advisors enjoyed almost unrivalled influence over defence and security policymaking to a situation where Britain has to rely on the continued willingness of the rulers of Bahrain to cooperate on issues of defence. This is a shift from British hard power to soft power, and a recognition that the Government of Bahrain now holds just as much power as Britain within the contemporary relationship. The re-opening of a permanent naval base at Juffair could be interpreted as a reaffirmation of Britain's new role in the Gulf, as a strong military power that is committed to assisting the regional states with their protection, but without the treaty foundations that existed between 1820 and 1971.

The precarious nature of the British presence in Bahrain, having to rely on strong government-to-government relations and the desire of the local rulers to foster this continued presence, has required an adaptation in British

100 *Strategic power, defence, and security*

Gulf policy and a willingness to meet Bahrain's strategic priorities as they emerge. The notion of security in the contemporary era has become a soft power political issue that is increasingly impacted by the interests of states involved, the threats facing the states, and the values of decision makers involved in the security process.[61] This is a marked change in the way that Britain has interacted with Bahrain since 1971, as the overriding priority for the British Government was the security of British interests in the region, not the values of Bahraini rulers.

Despite withdrawal, Britain has remained committed to Bahraini security, with more emphasis on individuals and the private sector since withdrawal. This demonstrable commitment is a contributing factor to Britain's attractiveness in Bahrain. A senior British diplomat remarked that

> there remains an affinity to close cooperation with the UK because of the demonstrable British understanding of the region. The UK has been tied to the security of the Gulf for over two centuries, and the current Gulf position shows commitment to Bahrain's security.[62]

This smart power, a combination of working to attract cooperation from Bahrain and the physical deployment of military assets in the Gulf, is an important element in Britain's contemporary Gulf policy.

4.6.1 The internationalisation of Britain's security presence in Bahrain

The presence of the *United Kingdom Maritime Component Command* in Bahrain and the opening of the UK Naval Support Facility on 5 April 2018 is about more than just securing the influence of Britain in the Kingdom, the combined presence is an important element of Britain's defence capabilities and a 'strong shadow presence around the Gulf; not an evident imperial-style footprint, but a smart presence with facilities, defence agreements, rotation of training, transit and jumping-off points for forces that aim to be more adaptable and agile'[63] than the previous British base at HMS Jufair between 1935 and 1971.

The British military presence in Bahrain is also more dependent on international events than it has ever been before. Since President Donald Trump withdrew the US from the *Joint Comprehensive Plan of Action* (also known as the Iran Nuclear Deal) on 8 May 2018 – the deal between Iran and the US, UK, France, Germany, China, and Russia that was intended to limit Iran's enrichment of weapons grade nuclear material – Iran has become increasingly aggressive towards British trade shipping passing through the Gulf. As the waters of the Gulf remain one of the most important passageways for British oil trade, with an average of three large ships passing through the Strait of Hormuz every day and annual trade worth US$554 billion,[64] the naval base in Bahrain has taken on increased importance. Britain's naval presence in the Gulf is part of the Combined Maritime Forces' CTF 152 operations, a grouping of ships from the Gulf states, US, Britain, Australia, and Italy. Although Britain can no longer independently protect trade through the region, as it did until the Second World War, the British contingent in the CMF could be described as a re-engagement by the Royal Navy in Gulf affairs and an increasing British re-influence in the Gulf. Bahrain has become reliant on British protection and agreed to pay the running costs of HMS Juffair as a result. Britain is the only European state with a significant permanent naval presence in Bahrain, and according to Leo Docherty, an MP on the Defence Select Committee,

> we must remember that some 20% of the world's oil flows through the strait of Hormuz. That is astonishing. The area of operations of the Combined Maritime Forces is at the epicentre of global trade, and we have a disproportionately positive impact on that.[65]

Politicians in Britain are aware of the importance of the presence in Bahrain for the projection of British power and an opportunity to deal with security issues in the Middle East before they affect domestic affairs in the UK.

On 8 July 2019, the British Government announced that it was raising the threat level for British-flagged ships passing through the Gulf to 'critical,' resulting in immediate extra insurance criteria and costs being applied to all trade ships in the region flying the red ensign. This was followed on 10 July by the attempt by three high-speed Iranian Revolutionary Guard boats to interfere with the passage of the BP oil tanker, the *British Heritage*, as it passed through the Strait of Hormuz. One of the Royal Navy's frigates stationed at HMS Juffair between 2019 and 2022, *HMS Montrose*, was engaged to protect the tanker. The British Government announced that a second Type 45 destroyer ship, *HMS Duncan*, would be deployed to the Gulf and stationed at HMS Juffair on 12 July 2019 and on 16 July announced that the Frigate *HMS Kent* would be deployed to Bahrain from mid-September of the same year. 'Besides HMS Montrose, a type 23 frigate, the Royal Navy has four minesweepers and the Royal Fleet Auxiliary Ship Cardigan Bay in the region.'[66] Although this deployment is likely a reactionary tactic to deter future Iranian aggression against British commercial shipping passing through the Strait of Hormuz, the importance of Britain's new permanent naval base in Bahrain for Britain's projection of power and deterrence in the region is once again coming to the fore.

The role that Royal Navy ships played in the defence of the Gulf between 1820 and 1971, shadowing trade ships and ensuring their safe passage through the pirate-filled waters of the Gulf is seemingly being replicated by the contemporary British naval contingent stationed there today. The British naval presence in Bahrain is significantly weaker and less influential today than it was before 1971, and the strength of the deterrence that it is able to exert is now reliant on a combination of a willingness by the

102 *Strategic power, defence, and security*

Bahraini authorities to host HMS Juffair, the US and other allied countries to contribute to the CMF CTF 152, and the support of the Gulf states on the Arabian side of the region.

4.6.2 A contemporary relationship and a power shift

To uphold its presence in the Gulf, the Royal Navy is reliant on Bahraini payments for the upkeep of HMS Juffair. This British reliance on Bahrain is resulting in Bahrain holding some soft power within the sphere of British policymaking. The economic influence that Bahraini authorities hold over Britain by paying for a naval base that is increasing in importance for Britain's defence capabilities in the Gulf is a marked shift in the relationship since 1971. Whereas Bahrain was solely reliant on the Residency and Royal Navy for protection and the longevity of the ruling regime until 1971, granting Britain unrivalled influence in Bahrain, the post-withdrawal situation has resulted in Britain being reliant on Bahraini goodwill and situational threats to Bahraini security from rival states and regional non-state actors necessitating a British military presence in the Kingdom. The presence of a British naval taskforce in Bahrain is both important for Britain's projection of power in the region, particularly at a time when western states are having to choose to support or reject sanctions against Iran, and the defence of Bahraini interests in the region. It could be argued, therefore, that Bahrain supports the British naval presence in HMS Juffair to protect its own interests, but prioritises its relations with the contemporary regional hegemon, the US.

The model of the new British naval base in Bahrain, which was gifted to the Royal Navy by King Hamad in 2016 to commemorate the 200th anniversary of the bilateral relationship, has been lauded as the future model on which all of Britain's international military bases should be based. Leo Docherty told the HoC that the base

> is not just about the Royal Navy, because the capacity for the Army to stay as a company group at the UK naval facility in Juffair presents tremendous training and partnership opportunities with the Bahraini army, which would be to its benefit and to ours. That spirit of enduring partnership is the driver behind all this.[67]

The future of Britain's power projection in the Gulf, manifested through the new base, is contingent on joint working efforts between the Royal Navy and Army. The Minister for the Armed Forces in 2018, Mark Lancaster, told the house that

> the UK NSF is a joint asset and operates under Permanent Joint Headquarters command within the Operation Kipion joint operational area. The facility's primary function is to provide appropriate

levels of real-life support to personnel deployed to Bahrain, whether permanently shore-based, on contingent operations, on a deployed maritime unit or on short-term theatre visits.[68]

The base might be considered a bastion of power projection by the British Government, but it is shared with 33 coalition states through the auspices of the Combined Maritime Forces, led by the US Fifth Fleet. To utilise this presence to bolster Britain's influence in Bahraini security affairs, the Royal Navy has to ensure that it remains relevant to the evolving priorities in the waters of the Gulf. The permanent basing of the UK's Mine Countermeasure Force, comprising 'four mine countermeasure vessels supported by a Royal Fleet Auxiliary ship ... is very much considered the jewel in the crown of the force by the Americans.'[69]

As the US has expanded its influence in Bahraini defence affairs since 1971, they have emerged as the principal defender of Bahrain, replacing Britain as the hegemon, and as a result, the British Government has to utilise its main assets to attract favour with both the Bahraini authorities and the American military commanders based in the Kingdom.

4.6.3 A model for future international cooperation

The British naval presence in Bahrain is the meeting point between economic and strategic responsibilities in the Gulf, a priority that has changed little since 1820. The influence that the Royal Navy exerts upon the Gulf from its base in Bahrain is limited, but this overt military influence is an attempt to demonstrate a commitment to both Gulf states and hostile actors that the British Government is willing to work with allies in the region to protect commerce. The presence of military assets in the region could also be described as hybrid power. After withdrawal, Britain withdrew most of its physical naval assets – warships and personnel – from Bahrain when the base was handed over to the Americans. It is only in recent years, since the re-opening of HMS Juffair, that the British Government has committed to a physical re-engagement in the waters of the Gulf by stationing a number of the most advanced and powerful ships in the Royal Navy in Bahrain.

Nye differentiated between the two types of power, hard and soft, by the extent to which physical force is involved in the development of influence in the affairs of other states. Based on this understanding of power, the contemporary influence of Britain in Bahrain, from a strategic perspective, is being actively achieved by a growing naval presence. The re-deployment of physical military assets to Bahrain – hard power – undoubtedly results in a soft power benefit for British influence in the region. The Government of Bahrain can see the commitment that the British Government is putting into defending Bahraini economic interests and those of the other Arab Gulf states. Although there have been significant changes in Britain's capabilities in the Gulf since 1971, the recent re-pivot by Britain back to Bahrain could only be possible because of the historic footprint left behind by the Royal Navy and the proven impact that they had on the defence and development of the Gulf as one of the world's most important trade routes. The power that Britain can utilise in Bahrain is largely referent in nature, with the British Government becoming dependent on technology produced by arms manufacturers to continue to attract Bahrain to cooperate with Britain. Expert power also plays a role, particularly in relation to the commissioning of advising from British PR companies.

Notes

1 Onley, J., *Britain and the Gulf Shaikhdoms, 1820–1971: The Politics of Protection*, (Doha, Center for International and Regional Studies, 2009), p.5.
2 Commis, D., *The Gulf States: A Modern History*, (London, I.B.Tauris & Co Ltd, 2012), p.78.
3 Khuri, F.I., *Tribe and State in Bahrain: The Transformation of Social and Political Authority in an Arab State*, (Chicago, IL, Chicago University Press, 1981), p.32.
4 Withdrawal from Bahrain took place in 1971, when the Residency was abolished, unlike in Oman where the strategic withdrawal was delayed until 1975 as a result of the British involvement in the Dhofar conflict.
5 Diplomatic Telegram from MoD (UK) to Mr Kelly, 21 October 1987. FCO 8/6530, TNA.
6 Diplomatic Telegram from I.T.M. Lucas (Middle East Department, FCO) to Mr Weir, 13 December 1978. FCO 8/3116 (1978), TNA.
7 HC Deb 25 July 1978 vol 954WA.
8 Diplomatic Telegram from B.A. Major (Middle East Department, FCO) to L.E. Walker, 5 September 1978. FCO 8/3116 (1978), TNA.
9 Diplomatic Telegram from L.E. Walker to B.A. Major, 31 August 1978. FCO 8/3116 (1978), TNA.
10 Final Report – OP Consolidate by HQ D SAS and SAS Group, 21 January 1980. FCO 8/3500 (1980), TNA.
11 Gray, C.S., *Hard Power and Soft Power: The Utility of Military Force as an Instrument of Policy in the 21st Century*, (Carlisle, PA, Strategic Studies Institute, 2011), p.viii.
12 Memorandum of Understanding between the Government of the United Kingdom of Great Britain and Northern Ireland and the Government of the State of Bahrain concerning the provision of a Royal Marines Training Team to assist in the training and development of the Bahrain Defence Force. FCO 8/4970 (1983), TNA.
13 Letter from C. Lund, Chief Superintendent of the West Yorkshire Metropolitan Police to M. Blomfield at the Home Office, 31 May 1984. FCO 8/5451 (1984), TNA, p.1.
14 Report by the Ministry of Overseas Development – Bahrain Technical Assistance, 3 September 1975. OD 34/405, TNA.
15 Diplomatic Telegram from Wright to Rednall. OD 34/404, TNA.
16 HC Deb 10 October 2011 vol 533 c 11.
17 HL Deb 9 March 2017 vol 779 c 1471.
18 HL Deb 21 January 2016 vol 4953WA (Document: HL4953 – Foreign Nations trained at RMA Sandhurst).
19 FOI2018/15984.

20 Ibid.
21 HL Deb 26 September 2017 WA1626.
22 Northern Ireland Assembly, 5 December 2016, AQW 5387/16-21.
23 See: National Preventative Mechanism, *Report on an unannounced inspection of Maghaberry Prison (11–22 May 2015)*, (London, Her Majesty's Inspectorate of Prisons, 2015).
24 See: 'Bahrain - Government Defence Anti-Corruption Index 2015', (2016), sec. Political 16. Available at: <http://government.defenceindex.org/generate-report.php?country_id=6257> [accessed 25 November 2019].
25 Report by MoD (UK): Bahrain Special Project. FCO 8/5447 (1984), TNA.
26 Diplomatic Telegram from MoD (UK) to Mr Kelly, 21 October 1987. FCO 8/6530 (1987), TNA.
27 *Public Papers of the Presidents of the United States* – Ronald Reagan: July 4 to December 31 1987, (Washington, DC, Federal Register Division, National Archives and Records Service, General Services Administration, 1987), p.1418.
28 Diplomatic Telegram – No. 122 from Howe (FCO, London) to British Embassy, Bahrain, 22 September 1987. FCO 8/6530 (1987), TNA.
29 Diplomatic Telegram No. 193 from British Embassy Bahrain to FCO, 22 September 1987. FCO 8/6530 (1987), TNA.
30 Minutes: Bahraini proposal for a bilateral military committee, 13 October 1987. FCO 8/6530 (1987), TNA.
31 Parliament. House of Lords: The Select Committee on Soft Power and the UK's Influence, *Persuasion and Power in the Modern World*, (HL 2013–14), (London, The Stationery Office, 2014), pp.52–53.
32 Ibid.
33 Katzman, K., *CRS Report: Bahrain: Unrest, Security, and U.S. Policy*, (Washington, DC, Congressional Research Service, 2019), p.19.
34 Memorandum of Understanding, FCO 8/4970 (1983), TNA.
35 Interview with a senior diplomat in the FCO's Arabian Directorate (FCO Diplomat A), (London, 12 October 2018).
36 'UAE, Kuwait, Bahrain, Qatar, Jordan deploy warplanes against Houthis', *Al Arabiya News*, Dubai, 26 March 2015. Available at: <http://english.alarabiya.net/en/News/middle-east/2015/03/26/Saudi-Arabia-30-UAE-fighter-jets-deployed-for-Yemen-campaign-.html#> [accessed 28 May 2019].
37 Liam Fox, 'Strategic Defence and Security Review', speech delivered at the Royal United Services Institute, (London, 14 June 2010).
38 Institute for National Strategic Studies, *Joint Force Quarterly*, (Washington, DC, National Defense University, 2000), p.45.
39 *Defence – Thirteenth Report*, Evidence (Memorandum submitted by the Ministry of Defence – 20 March 2000), p.24.
40 Ministry of Defence, *Securing Britain in an Age of Uncertainty: The Strategic Defence and Security Review*, (London, HMSO, 2010), p.17.
41 Ibid., p.16.
42 Shaw, M, *The New Western Way of War*, (Cambridge, Polity, 2005), pp.94–95.
43 Slaughter, A-M., 'America's Edge: Power in the Networked Century', *Foreign Policy*, 88:1 (2009), p.94.
44 Letter from S.P. Collis to J.H. Turner (Middle East Department, FCO), 11 May 1981. FCO 8/3902 (1981), TNA.
45 Minute: Letter from Crown Prince Hamad of Bahrain by A.S. Kemp to MoD (UK) and FCO MED, 25 April 1983. FCO 8/5028 (1983), TNA.
46 HM Government, *National Security Strategy and Strategic Defence and Security Review 2015: A Secure and Prosperous United Kingdom*, (London, HM Government, 2015), pp.77–78.

47 See: Gould, J., 'US Senate rejects effort to stop Bahrain arms sale', *Defense News*, November 2018. Available at: <https://www.defensenews.com/congress/2018/11/15/us-senate-rejects-effort-to-stop-bahrain-arms-sale> [accessed 21 May 2019].
48 Campaign Against the Arms Trade, 'UK export licences applied for military goods to Bahrain'. Available at: <https://www.caat.org.uk/resources/export-licences/licence-list?status=approved&destinationSearch=all&region=Bahrain> [accessed 28 November 2019].
49 Ibid.
50 Ritchie, N., 'Rethinking Security: A Critical Analysis of the Strategic Defence and Security Review', *International Affairs*, 87:2 (2011), p.357.
51 Nye, Jr., J.S., 'Soft Power', *Foreign Policy*, 80 (1990), p.163.
52 Stockholm International Peace Research Institute, *Trends in World Military Expenditure, 2018*, (Stockholm, SIPRI, 2019), p.8.
53 UK Export Finance, *Annual Report and Accounts, 2016–17*, (London, Export Credits Guarantee Department, 2017), p.213.
54 UK Export Finance, *Annual Report and Accounts, 2018–19*, (London, Export Credits Guarantee Department, 2019), p.167.
55 Ministère de la Défense, *2015 France and Arms Trade Control*, (Paris, Délégation à l'information et à la communication de la défense, 2015), p.24.
56 See: *Campaign Against Arms Trade vs The Secretary of State for International Trade*, [2019] EWCA Civ 1020, (London).
57 For a full list of PR companies hired by the Government of Bahrain, see Bahrain Watch's database. Available at: <https://bahrainwatch.org/pr/> [accessed 13 May 2019].
58 Ibid.
59 See: Foreign & Commonwealth Office, *Magna Carta Fund for Human Rights and Democracy: Rules Based International System Fund – Call for Bids and Summary of Thematic Areas of Interest*. Available at: <https://assets.publishing.service.gov.uk/government/uploads/system/uploads/attachment_data/file/707887/CALL_FOR_BIDS_AND_SUMMARY_OF_THEMATIC_AREAS_OF_INTEREST_updated_pdf.pdf>.
60 Foreign & Commonwealth Office, *Human Rights & Democracy: The 2016 Foreign & Commonwealth Office Report*, (London, HMSO, 2017), p.33.
61 See: Smith, S., 'The contested concept of security', in K. Booth, *Critical Security Studies and World Politics*, (Boulder, CO, Lynne Rienner Publishers, 2005), pp.27–62.
62 Interview with a senior diplomat in the FCOs Arabian Directorate (*FCO Diplomat A*), (London, 12 October 2018).
63 Stansfield, G. and Kelly, S., Briefing Paper: *A Return to East of Suez? UK Military Deployment to the Gulf*, (London, Royal United Services Institute, 2013), p.1.
64 See: Osler, D., *Hormuz blockade would mean $554bn hit to seaborne trade*, Lloyd's List Maritime Intelligence. Available at: <https://lloydslist.maritimeintelligence.informa.com/LL1127721/Hormuz-blockade-would-mean-$554bn-hit-to-seaborne-trade> [accessed 12 July 2019].
65 HC Deb 20 November 2018 vol 649 c264WH.
66 Oliphant, R. and Ensor, J., *Britain' recommends heightened security' for ships in Straits of Hormuz after Iran tries to block oil tanker*, The Telegraph. Available at: <https://www.telegraph.co.uk/news/2019/07/11/royal-navy-fends-iranian-seizure-british-oil-tanker-persian> [accessed 16 July 2019].
67 HC Deb 20 November 2018 vol 649 c 265WH.
68 HC Deb 20 November 2018 vol 649 c 266WH.
69 Ibid.

Bibliography

'Bahrain - Government Defence Anti-Corruption Index 2015', (2016), sec. Political 16, <http://government.defenceindex.org/generate-report.php?country_id=6257> [accessed 25 November 2019].

'UAE, Kuwait, Bahrain, Qatar, Jordan deploy warplanes against Houthis', *Al Arabiya News*, Dubai, 26 March 2015. Available at: <http://english.alarabiya.net/en/News/middle-east/2015/03/26/Saudi-Arabia-30-UAE-fighter-jets-deployed-for-Yemen-campaign-.html#> [accessed 28 May 2019].

Campaign Against Arms Trade vs The Secretary of State for International Trade, [2019] EWCA Civ 1020, (London).

Campaign Against the Arms Trade, 'UK export licences applied for military goods to Bahrain' Available at: <https://www.caat.org.uk/resources/export-licences/licence-list?status=approved&destinationSearch=all&region=Bahrain> [accessed 28 November 2019].

Commis, D., *The Gulf States: A Modern History*, (London, I.B.Tauris & Co Ltd, 2012).

Defence – Thirteenth Report, Evidence (Memorandum submitted by the Ministry of Defence – 20 March 2000).

Diplomatic Telegram – No. 122 from Howe (FCO, London) to British Embassy, Bahrain, 22 September 1987. FCO 8/6530 (1987), TNA.

Diplomatic Telegram from B.A. Major (Middle East Department, FCO) to L.E. Walker, 5 September 1978. FCO 8/3116 (1978), TNA.

Diplomatic Telegram from I.T.M. Lucas (Middle East Department, FCO) to Mr Weir, 13 December 1978. FCO 8/3116 (1978), TNA.

Diplomatic Telegram from L.E. Walker to B.A. Major, 31 August 1978. FCO 8/3116 (1978), TNA.

Diplomatic Telegram from MoD (UK) to Mr Kelly, 21 October 1987. FCO 8/6530, TNA.

Diplomatic Telegram from MoD (UK) to Mr Kelly, 21 October 1987. FCO 8/6530 (1987), TNA.

Diplomatic Telegram from Wright to Rednall. OD 34/404, TNA.

Diplomatic Telegram No. 193 from British Embassy Bahrain to FCO, 22 September 1987. FCO 8/6530 (1987), TNA.

Final Report – OP Consolidate by HQ D SAS and SAS Group, 21 January 1980. FCO 8/3500 (1980), TNA.

FOI 2018/15984: Omani and Bahraini seconded officers at RAF College Cranwell and Britannia Royal Naval College, 14 January 2019.

Foreign & Commonwealth Office, Human Rights & Democracy: The 2016 Foreign & Commonwealth Office Report, (London, HMSO, 2017).

Foreign & Commonwealth Office, Magna Carta Fund for Human Rights and Democracy: Rules based international system fund – Call for bids and summary of thematic areas of interest. Available at: <https://assets.publishing.service.gov.uk/government/uploads/system/uploads/attachment_data/file/707887/CALL_FOR_BIDS_AND_SUMMARY_OF_THEMATIC_AREAS_OF_INTEREST_updated_pdf.pdf>.

Gould, J., 'US Senate rejects effort to stop Bahrain arms sale', *Defense News*, November 2018. Available at: <https://www.defensenews.com/congress/2018/11/15/us-senate-rejects-effort-to-stop-bahrain-arms-sale> [accessed 21 May 2019].

Gray, C.S., *Hard Power and Soft Power: The Utility of Military Force as an Instrument of Policy in the 21st Century*, (Carlisle, PA, Strategic Studies Institute, 2011).
HC Deb 10 October 2011 vol 533 c 11.
HC Deb 20 November 2018 vol 649 c 265WH.
HC Deb 20 November 2018 vol 649 c264WH.
HC Deb 25 July 1978 vol 954WA.
HL Deb 21 January 2016 vol 4953WA (Document: HL4953 – Foreign Nations trained at RMA Sandhurst).
HL Deb 26 September 2017 WA1626.
HL Deb 9 March 2017 vol 779 c 1471.
HM Government, *National Security Strategy and Strategic Defence and Security Review 2015: A Secure and Prosperous United Kingdom*, (London, HM Government, 2015).
Interview with a senior diplomat in the FCO's Arabian Directorate (FCO Diplomat A), (London, 12 October 2018).
Katzman, K., *CRS Report: Bahrain: Unrest, Security, and U.S. Policy*, (Washington, DC, Congressional Research Service, 2019).
Khuri, F.I., *Tribe and State in Bahrain: The Transformation of Social and Political Authority in an Arab State*, (Chicago, IL, Chicago University Press, 1981).
Letter from C. Lund, Chief Superintendent of the West Yorkshire Metropolitan Police to M. Blomfield at the Home Office, 31 May 1984. FCO 8/5451 (1984), TNA.
Letter from S.P. Collis to J.H. Turner (Middle East Department, FCO), 11 May 1981. FCO 8/3902 (1981), TNA.
Liam Fox, 'Strategic Defence and Security Review', speech delivered at the Royal United Services Institute, (London, 14 June 2010).
Memorandum of Understanding between the Government of the United Kingdom of Great Britain and Northern Ireland and the Government of the State of Bahrain concerning the provision of a Royal Marines Training Team to assist in the training and development of the Bahrain Defence Force. FCO 8/4970 (1983), TNA.
Ministère de la Défense, 2015 France and Arms Trade Control, (Paris, Délégation à l'information et à la communication de la défense, 2015).
Ministry of Defence, *Securing Britain in an Age of Uncertainty: The Strategic Defence and Security Review*, (London, HMSO, 2010).
Minute: Letter from Crown Prince Hamad of Bahrain by A.S. Kemp to MoD (UK) and FCO MED, 25 April 1983. FCO 8/5028 (1983), TNA.
Minutes: Bahraini proposal for a bilateral military committee, 13 October 1987. FCO 8/6530 (1987), TNA.
National Preventative Mechanism, *Report on an Unannounced Inspection of Maghaberry Prison (11–22 May 2015)*, (London, Her Majesty's Inspectorate of Prisons, 2015).
Northern Ireland Assembly, 5 December 2016, AQW 5387/16–21.
Nye Jr., J.S., 'Soft Power', *Foreign Policy*, 80 (1990), pp.153–171.
Oliphant, R. and Ensor, J., *Britain 'recommends heightened security' for ships in Straits of Hormuz after Iran tries to block oil tanker*, The Telegraph. Available at: <https://www.telegraph.co.uk/news/2019/07/11/royal-navy-fends-iranian-seizure-british-oil-tanker-persian> [accessed 16 July 2019].
Onley, J., *Britain and the Gulf Shaikhdoms, 1820–1971: The Politics of Protection*, (Doha, Center for International and Regional Studies, 2009).

Osler, D., 'Hormuz blockade would mean $554bn hit to seaborne trade', Lloyd's List Maritime Intelligence. Available at: <https://lloydslist.maritimeintelligence.informa.com/LL1127721/Hormuz-blockade-would-mean-$554bn-hit-to-seaborne-trade> [accessed 12 July 2019].

Parliament. House of Lords: The Select Committee on Soft Power and the UK's Influence, *Persuasion and Power in the Modern World*, (HL 2013–14), (London, The Stationery Office, 2014).

Public Papers of the Presidents of the United States – Ronald Reagan: July 4 to December 31 1987, (Washington, DC, Federal Register Division, National Archives and Records Service, General Services Administration, 1987).

Report by MoD (UK): Bahrain Special Project. FCO 8/5447 (1984), TNA.

Report by the Ministry of Overseas Development – Bahrain Technical Assistance, 3 September 1975. OD 34/405, TNA.

Ritchie, N., 'Rethinking Security: A Critical Analysis of the Strategic Defence and Security Review', *International Affairs*, 87:2 (2011), pp.355–376.

Select Committee on Soft Power and the UK's Influence, *Persuasion and Power in the Modern World*, 2014, Q368.

Shaw, M., *The New Western Way of War*, (Cambridge, Polity, 2005).

Slaughter, A-M., 'America's Edge: Power in the Networked Century', *Foreign Policy*, 88:1 (2009), pp.94–113.

Smith, S., 'The contested concept of security', in K. Booth (ed.), *Critical Security Studies and World Politics*, (Boulder, CO, Lynne Rienner Publishers, 2005), pp.27–62.

Stansfield, G. and Kelly, S., *Briefing Paper: A Return to East of Suez? UK Military Deployment to the Gulf*, (London, Royal United Services Institute, 2013).

Stockholm International Peace Research Institute, *Trends in World Military Expenditure, 2018*, (Stockholm, SIPRI, 2019).

UK Export Finance, Annual Report and Accounts, 2016–17, (London, Export Credits Guarantee Department, 2017).

UK Export Finance, Annual Report and Accounts, 2018–19, (London, Export Credits Guarantee Department, 2019).

Part II
Trade and the power of money

5 Omani prosperity and the British power dimension

5.1 Introduction

Britain and Oman have enjoyed economic relations since as early as 1646, with the protection and advancement of trade to British India being the main catalyst for the East India Company sending an envoy by the name of Philip Wylde to negotiate treaties with the country. The agreement between Wylde and Nasir bin Murshid, Imam of Oman, was undoubtedly the most important historic economic treaty signed between the two maritime powers.

Numerous treaties have been signed between the governments of Britain and ruling Omani Sultans since 1646, with the first to focus specifically on economic matters dating back to 1839. This first formal commercial treaty was made between the EIC and Said bin Sultan Al Said and it formalised the strong commercial ties that had developed between the two major maritime powers in the Indian Ocean. By this time, Britain had secured her position of power throughout the Indian subcontinent and developed the powerful Bombay Marine naval force (later renamed the Bombay Marine Corps, the Indian Navy, and the Bombay and Bengal Marine, amongst others). This treaty limited the tax and duties that Oman could levy on British imports into the Sultanate,[1] so although a relatively minor issue, it could be argued that it was from this point that the commercial balance of power began to shift in Britain's favour. A commercial treaty signed in 1891 between Sultan Faisal bin Turki and Political Resident Sir Edward Ross superseded this earlier agreement.[2] Similar subsequent treaties were signed on 5 February 1939[3] and 20 December 1951,[4] both of which reaffirmed a bilateral commitment to freedom of commerce and navigation between the two signatory states and 'most favoured-nation' status for commercial matters, providing various privileges and concessions in trade talks to both states. Although these treaties are no longer in force, the bilateral exclusivity in commerce having been terminated at the point of withdrawal, the legacy that was left behind by these influential intergovernmental agreements in the form of British enterprises that developed in Oman and a sentiment that still exists in the mindsets of Omani policymakers to favour Britain over other states is still

114 *Trade and the power of money*

undoubtedly a key contributor to the strong trading relationship. Although it is not possible to definitively argue that these commercial treaties are the main reason behind the development of the strong contemporary presence in Oman, it is plausible that the trust that developed between the two states and the foothold that individual Britons have been able to establish in Oman over the centuries does still play a significant role in the development of British power in Oman.

5.1.1 Economic diversification in Oman and the British connection

As the Omani economy embarked upon its diversification away from the British hegemony that had dominated the Sultanate for over a century, the soft power influence of other states quickly became apparent. Soft power strength is dependent on its covert nature, largely hidden from public view and criticism, but it is the result of a willingness by local rulers to replicate policies that are present in allied states. The pegging of the Omani riyal to the US dollar in 1986 at a rate of $1:0.3845 riyals and the resulting requirement to follow monetary policy of the US Federal Reserve is an example of non-British soft power having a major impact on the Omani economy.[5] The currency of a country is one of the most important assets through which external powers can influence domestic policy, both directly and indirectly. The pegging of the riyal to the US dollar suggests that the US holds significant influence over Omani monetary affairs, an important diversion by Qaboos away from the historic British influence that Britain had over the Omani domestic economy. This shift also contradicts the theory that Britain has been able to retain its influence in Oman because of the unchallenged hold that it has on domestic economics. The willingness of Qaboos to tie his currency to that of a state that has never played a significant role in the development of Oman arguably suggests that pragmatism is increasingly factoring into Omani decision-making rather than nostalgia and the continued presence of Britons in key positions within society.

The contemporary influence of Britain on Oman's economic affairs is significantly influenced by the sentiment within the British Government for the strengthening of Britain's influence in the Sultanate and agendas affecting the policy priorities of the FCDO, MoD, and DIT. Prosperity is a key tenet of Britain's foreign policy motives and has been since at least the start of Cameron's Conservative administration in 2010, but it could also date back to the start of Thatcher's first government in 1979 when emphasis was put on international trade and the development of the British domestic defence industry. In July 2018, the UK MoD released a report on the contribution of defence trade to British prosperity, entitled *Growing the Contribution of Defence to UK Prosperity*. The report concluded that

> the UK defence industrial sector is one of the world's strongest, with an annual turnover of £22 billion and supports 260,000 jobs, many of

which are highly skilled and well paid. The UK is also one of the world's leading, responsible exporters of defence capability, securing export orders worth £5.9 billion in 2016.[6]

Although a minor trade partner in terms of overall import–export statistics, Oman is one of the most important destinations for British defence exports, thus contributing to the strong defence industry in all regions of Britain. According to official statistics released by the DIT, in 2017, the UK was the world's third-largest defence exporter, accounting for a 12% market share, ahead of France, Germany, and Italy, which are the main competitors to Britain's defence influence in Oman.[7] The trading relationship and its impact on Britain's influence in Oman will be analysed in greater depth later in this chapter.

The economic priorities of Oman are also integral to which states the Sultan's government chooses to cooperate with and the extent to which they permit foreign powers to intervene in the economic affairs of Oman. Domestic rentierism and reliance on the energy sector for public finances has dictated many of the policies of Qaboos' government since his accession to power in 1970. According to the 2019 *Global Index of Economic Openness*, produced by the British think tank the Legatum Institute, resource rents contributed 27% of Oman's GDP in 2016.[8] This dependence on resource extraction and exports, as will be assessed later in this chapter, is a key reason for Britain's continued interest in the Omani economy and prosperity, particularly as British energy companies Shell and BP have historically held, and continue to hold, significant direct influence over Omani prosperity. The Legatum report also concluded that Oman ranks 53rd for its economic openness, just above the middle of the list.[9] Although the report does not focus specifically on the intricacies of Oman's economy, the ranking does possibly suggest that one reason for Britain's influence on the Omani economy is because of the lack of openness to greater external investment and a government that prefers to deal with countries that it is familiar with, which could be referred to as *Relational Power*. Qaboos' government undoubtedly felt comfortable dealing with Britain, and Haitham appears to be following a similar path.

This chapter will begin by assessing the bilateral defence trade between Britain and Oman and the influence of export financing for arms exports to Oman, including the power that arises from the economic commitment that Britain displays towards assisting Oman with its military modernisation; this is the main link between British soft and hard power in Oman and economic and strategic influence. The development of the contemporary British soft power influence on the Omani oil and gas industry will follow, including analysis of how the two major British energy companies contribute to British influence in the Sultanate. Economic diversification in Oman and the influence of other countries on this important process will highlight how much influence Britain has lost to states that have followed a similar diversification path and thus have developed soft power attraction amongst Omani decision makers, followed by an assessment of the future of UK–Omani economic relations and the importance of joint economic programmes and the pre-withdrawal legacy to the soft power that Britain enjoys.

5.2 Arms for influence. What impact does export financing have on British power in Oman?

The strength of the contemporary economic relationship between Britain and Oman is undoubtedly heavily dependent on military cooperation, and the value of arms sales from British manufacturers to the SOAF forms a major element of this. Oman has been one of the major purchasers of British-manufactured defence equipment since at least the 1960s, before which the British Government was jointly responsible for defending Oman alongside the Residency's own Trucial Oman Scouts, based in the former Trucial States. Defence trade with Oman since Sultan Qaboos' accession to the throne, but more so after the Dhofar War in 1975 when the majority of British troops withdrew from the Gulf, is the bellwether of the strength of the relationship – the more significant the defence sales from Britain to Oman, the stronger the economic relationship. The Defence & Security Organisation, a sub-section of the DIT,[10] is the body responsible for assisting and promoting British defence trade, and the Gulf is a major focus for the organisation according to annual departmental reports. However, with a workforce of approximately 500 and only two regional directorates that group diverse parts of the world into two categories – RD Americas, Pacific and East Asia and RD Africa, Europe, Middle East, Central and South Asia – the Gulf is seemingly not recognised as a particularly important export destination by the British Government who provides funding for DSO's activities. The extent to which British policy makers recognise the influence that comes from defence sales has fluctuated since the 1970s depending on the party in power in the UK, like many aspects of the wider relationship. Former Welsh Labour MP Ann Clwyd, a noted opponent of arms sales to the Gulf states, highlighted the incompatibility of 'promoting human rights and promoting arms exports ... a difficulty not with export controls, but with the mindset that prioritises export promotion. ... licences to Foreign and Commonwealth-designated countries of concern were valued at almost £12 billion.'[11] There is a notable difference in the sentiment towards arms exports amongst Conservative MPs, with Bob Seely arguing that 'denying sales ... may not achieve a great deal because [they] will simply buy the bombs from elsewhere.'[12] When considered in the wider power discourse, arms sales is on the hard power level of the scale, but the attraction that Oman has for British weapons correlates more with soft power, largely tied to referent power, as British arms technology is a major magnet for Oman's continued attraction to cooperation with Britain. The use of monetary inducements by the British Government could be considered one of the main soft power tools available to British manufacturers, but its effectiveness is dependent both on the support provided by the government and the desire of the Government of Oman for British arms.

5.2.1 The British commitment to arming Oman

In the years following withdrawal, the strength of Britain's influence as the largest defence supplier to Oman remained relatively consistent. In the late 1980s, Oman was the first country to commit to purchasing eight Tornado aircraft from BAE, 'the first export contract obtained for the aircraft [was] said to be worth over £250m'[13] although 'the order faced difficulties from the start and financial limitations forced the [Omani] government to cancel it in 1990 and substitute Hawk aircraft at a cost of £150 million,'[14] another British aircraft. There are numerous contributing factors to Oman's decision-making processes, many of which can be directly attributed to the legacy position that Britain developed in the Sultanate prior to Qaboos' accession to the throne, the most important of which are Qaboos' trust for Britain's expertise in the area of defence manufacturing, the commercial relationships that exist between British and Omani partners, and the financial support that underpins these sales.

One factor that contributes to the soft power strength of a country is the ease of doing business. As Oman's defence spending has been largely dependent on income from oil exports since Qaboos became Sultan, the Sultanate has not always been able to pay or barter with Britain for the weapons that it requires. Neighbouring Saudi Arabia uses its significant oil supplies to barter for weapons, including the controversial *Al-Yamamah Agreement* between BAE Systems and Saudi Arabia, which involved BP and Shell, whereby BAE supplied Tornado and other aircraft to the Saudi military in return for the delivery of around 600,000 barrels of oil to Britain per day in lieu of a monetary payment.[15] Oman does not have the ability to barter with its oil supplies because it does not produce the quantities that neighbouring states do, but also because of the increasing domestic need for oil, so the British Government offers buyer credit to Oman to facilitate defence trade via the Export Credits Guarantee Department (ECGD). 'The primary objective of ECGD is to assist exporters, project sponsors, banks, and buyers so that they can compete effectively in overseas markets where private sector assistance may be unavailable.'[16] Projects of low value (under £5 million) can be loaned directly to the Government of Oman by the British Government, but for deals worth over £5 million, the British Government underwrites loans from British banks, with the condition that there is a 20% involvement of the UK supply chain.[17] The commitment and risks that the British Government is willing to take if economic conditions in Oman result in a default on export loans are undoubtedly a sign to the Omani leadership that Britain, and British banks, trust Oman and respect the historic trading relationship so much that they put significant sums of money at risk.

The latest statistics[18] collated by the DIT show that the total value of British exports to Oman and Omani exports to the UK was £3.1 billion in the year 2017–18, £2.8 billion of which were UK exports to Oman, representing a 92.2% increase from the previous year. Both completed aircraft and aircraft parts accounted for 64.5% of exports to Oman.[19] Although official statistics do not breakdown the exports into sectoral categories, it is highly likely that major BAE Systems' defence contracts comprise a significant proportion of this large increase in British exports to Oman. Although Oman is only Britain's '50th largest trade partner, accounting for just 0.2% of the total UK trade balance,'[20] the historic legacy of close economic cooperation is an influential determining factor that affects the bilateral relationship and results in unique conditions attached to export deals with Oman.

According to the *UK Export Finance accounts 2016–17*, a buyer credit worth up to £1,709,583,352 was agreed so that BAE Systems could supply Oman with Typhoon and Hawk aircraft[21] until the end of 2018. The largest British credit agreement in the scheme's history is with Oman. UKEF has agreed credit with many countries since its establishment in 1919, but few agreements have dedicated such a substantial amount to one British company for the sole purpose of arms sales. This credit is arguably an overt attempt by the British Government to retain its strong position as the largest defence supplier to SOAF as a result of the increased competition since Qaboos' accession, but more so as Oman has increased its military spending on an almost annual basis. The argument could also be made that the financial commitment made by the British Government and the message that this sends to Oman's rulers, that Britain trusts Oman to pay back the loan within an agreed time period, is a major reason for the Sultanate still choosing to purchase military aircraft from Britain, not because of a nostalgia for the British presence in Oman or a sense that Qaboos owed Britain for the support provided during the Dhofar War. However, this major arms deal is demonstrable of a strong lasting British defence legacy in Oman because when the Government of Oman was searching for a squadron of new aircraft in the 2000s:

> it would have been cheaper, easier and a more integrated decision for SOAF to buy F16 jets from the US to join their other two F16 squadrons. Calls were made from the highest levels of the UK Government to the most senior figures in Oman asking SOAF to buy Typhoons from BAE so that factories could stay open across Britain. Oman then chose to buy Typhoons instead of F16s.[22]

This is a striking example of how the bilateral relationship has changed. It is now no longer wholly down to Britain to support Oman; Britain now relies on Oman to help in times of economic need. British soft power in Oman is the likely determining factor that led to this significant Typhoon order, but Oman is now able to exert soft power on Britain, a trait that the Sultanate did not have prior to the modernisations led by Qaboos. To persuade the British Government, through UKEF, to provide Oman with one of the world's largest credit loans needed to further modernise SOAF, Qaboos enticed Britain with the Typhoon order from BAE that created jobs in Britain. The contemporary shift in the balance of power away from Britain to Oman is an indicator of the extent to which Britain has lost its hegemonic influence in Oman as a defence supplier. However, the Typhoon deal was more expensive than the comparative F16 deal with the US-based General Dynamics, it meant that the RAFO was less coherent as there are now two F16 squadrons and one Typhoon squadron, and the Typhoon deal required a separate group of engineers trained to maintain Typhoons alongside those working on F16s. The only logical explanation for Qaboos choosing to purchase the Typhoon aircraft from BAE was because he really did want to help Britain, arguably the closest ally of Oman, just as Britain had helped Oman during the Dhofar War and as a symbol from Oman that they also value their close bond with Britain. There was no financial benefit for Oman's choice of the Typhoons, nor was the choice strategically coherent, so the decision could be understood as a power legacy. Nye specified that one key characteristic of effective soft power is the ability to get another state to do what you want by offering financial inducements;[23] this is essentially what UKEF does in Oman.

By offering to underwrite significant loans for Omani defence and infrastructure projects, it could be suggested that the British Government is inducing Oman to buy from British companies, thus achieving a priority for Britain through the creation of domestic jobs and the preservation of Britain's influence at the edge of the Gulf. According to a British trade representative based in Oman, 'UKEF is one of the best tools that the UK Government has. The ECGD is very commercially minded as the majority of employees are from banking and the private sector. UKEF gives the UK the edge on deals in Oman over competitors.'[24]

5.2.2 British export financing and the resulting influence

Export financing, an official contractual method of financial inducement, is the main type of support for arms sales offered by the British Government, but a more covert and non-monetary method is used that is not widely offered to other states. To retain Britain's defence export advantage in Oman, the British Government has occasionally resorted to offering the SOAF payments-in-kind, sending surplus defence equipment no longer in use by the British armed forces to Oman, likely in the hope that this will be interpreted by Omani decision makers as a commitment to Omani security and resulting in future defence deals. On 16th May 2018, Under-Secretary of State for Defence Guto Bebb told the HoC about a grant-in-kind that would be made to the RAO, comprising surplus assemblies and line replaceable units for the repair and maintenance of Challenger 2 tanks. The provision of this equipment is a direct response to a request made by the Royal Army of Oman to the UK defence attaché in Oman and is in support of National Security Council objectives. ... The total cost of the proposed UK package is £0.997 million.[25]

Prior to withdrawal, it was not uncommon for the British Government to donate military equipment to the TOS in support of their defence of the Gulf, but since Qaboos' accession, Oman has been a key buyer of British defence equipment and, as a result, there has been little incentive to send equipment to the Sultanate for free. The request from RAO directly to the Defence Attaché at the British Embassy in Muscat suggests that there is a strong defence relationship between the two states, but Britain's agreement to send £997,000 worth of Challenger 2 tank equipment at no cost is arguably the result of increasing competition and encroachment by rival suppliers into a country that many policymakers in Westminster still see as an element of Britain's sphere of influence.

The DSO is influential in its own right in Oman, with a section of the British Embassy's DIT office working solely on the defence trade and marketing British-manufactured weapons and military equipment to the Sultan's security forces; however, the DSO cannot operate in a vacuum, and it undoubtedly gains a lot of traction within Oman from the defence relations between the British and Omani militaries and the shared history and joint training campaigns that have taken place since 1986. The economic aspect of Britain's defence relations with Oman is inextricably linked to the strategic relationship between the two states. By using British weapons in operational training exercises, particularly in the *Saif Saarea* exercises, decision makers in the Omani security services are able to see this equipment in action and thus are more likely to opt to purchase from British manufacturers than from other countries where they have not seen the equipment in use. Between 2008 and 2017, the Middle East accounted for an average 57% share of UK defence exports[26] and although the official statistics do not explicitly divide these exports between countries in the region, Oman has been the second-largest buyer of British weapons and equipment for over a decade, the largest being Saudi Arabia, which received 36% of arms exports in the same period.[27] According to DSO data, between 1997 and 2017 'vehicles and other transportation [aircraft, ships and armoured vehicles] accounted for 70% of all arms exports'[28] to Oman from the UK. The DSO has been important in ensuring that British defence equipment remains at the forefront of the minds of decision makers across the Gulf. The arms industry is an asset that the British Government has available to bolster its influence in Oman, but the legacy that British companies hold as the main historic supplier undoubtedly plays a part. Since other foreign suppliers started to enter the Omani arms market after 1971, the British Government, in partnership with private sector suppliers located across the UK, have had to put more effort into marketing weapons and technology to Omani Government officials to mitigate the increasing competition.

5.2.3 *The power dimension to export finance*

The value that Britain places on its international trading relationships is demonstrated by the amount of money committed to the department responsible for fostering trading relationships around the world. According to Graham Stuart, Parliamentary Under-Secretary of State at the DIT in the May administration, 'at 1 April 2018, the Department for International Trade had a total workforce of 155 in the Defence and Security Organisation. Its current net budget for 2018–19 is £9.9m.'[29] The DIT has a miniscule annual budget in comparison with all but one other government departments, with total funding for the 2018–19 year of £360.6 million[30] This demonstrates that the DSO is only a tiny factor in the DIT's efforts to market British defence equipment abroad, and as the British Embassy in Muscat, where the DIT is based in the country, is just 1 of the 133 missions around the world, the impact that the DSO really can have in Oman is debatable. Thus, if the large defence trade surplus from Britain to Oman cannot be solely attributed to the work of DIT and DSO, there has to be an underlying reason for Britain's relative success in continuing to sell defence equipment to the Sultanate, and this is likely the presence of strong soft power influence, particularly referent in nature. In evidence submitted to the House of Lords' *Soft Power and the UK's Influence Committee*, Dr Christina Rowley argued that:

> Understandably, the UK does not want to project an image of itself as a colonial power, but nor should it want to deny that aspect of its history, and how its present place in the world is fundamentally built upon that colonial past. 'Owning up to' and owning those aspects of the UK's past and present that it is less proud of, as well as publicising the good – deploying honesty, modesty (perhaps even a touch of humility now and then), in its dealings with others, are likely to attract friends and establish enduring relationships with others in the world. ... States, groups and individuals are most secure when others too feel secure.[31]

It could be suggested, therefore, that the way the British Government interacts with the Government of Oman, not denying its historic colonial-style relationship with successive Sultans and dealing with Qaboos and the current government in an honest manner, contributes to the strong position that Britain enjoys as a major arms contributor to Oman. Although this legacy is an important contributor to British soft power influence in Oman and the strong presence of British arms in the Sultanate could be described as a hardening of soft power. This pivot back towards a position of hard power, albeit as a result of soft power attraction to British arms, stands in contrast to the commonly held belief amongst IR theorists that international politics is becoming increasingly soft power oriented. Investing in the development of Duqm Port, the largest naval base built in Oman since the 1960s, is another way that export financing is contributing to Britain's presence in the southern Gulf and the waters of the Indian Ocean. The support facility, a naval base that is open to the UK's largest ships and aircraft carriers, is jointly operated by the British company Babcock International and Oman Drydock Company, termed the *Joint Logistics Support Base*. When the joint investment worth US$110 million was announced, Labour MP, Diana Johnson, told the HoC that she was 'particularly pleased to see British support for the development of the port in Oman, which will help Oman's economy and will provide a vital berthing point for our new Queen Elizabeth-class aircraft carriers.'[32] This is an important element of Britain's defence dimension in Oman and the wider Gulf and a method of how soft power can be used to bolster Britain's hard power influence in the region. Where Duqm differs from the historic position that Britain held in Oman is the number of international navies that are permitted to use the base and the Chinese investment worth US$10.7 billion,[33] dwarfing the British FDI into Oman and taking Britain's place as the largest investor in the defence infrastructure if Oman Wanfang does ultimately invest the total amount committed.

5.3 What impact does the legacy of British exclusivity have on Oman's oil and gas sector?

The strategic location of Oman, at the entrance to the Gulf, has undoubtedly been a significant pull factor for British defence investments into the Sultanate since the mid-1800s, but the energy sector emerged as a critical industry in 1967, at a time when the British Government and individuals enjoyed indirect and direct power over the development of the oil industry. The petrochemical industry is the most important sector in Oman, sustaining tens of thousands of jobs in the country and the income from oil exports is the largest contributor to the national GDP. Figures suggest that at the point of Qaboos' accession to the throne in 1970, approximately 90% of Oman's government revenue was derived from oil exports by Petroleum Development Oman (PDO), the largest oil company and the main leaseholder of petroleum exploration sites in the country. At the time, PDO was 85% owned by Royal Dutch Shell, a dual listed company, registered in the Netherlands and the UK but with much of its operations in Oman overseen by British expatriates, with the remaining 10% owned by Compagnie Française des Petroles and 5% by Partex.[34] The commanding shareholding by Shell in PDO undoubtedly ensured that a British presence was secure within Oman, a country that had been effectively governed by a team of British advisors for over a century, and was a useful hard power asset for both the British Government and British private sector in the closing years of Sultan Sa'id's rule and during the transition period until Qaboos consolidated his domestic power.

It would not be amiss to suggest that commercial priorities for Shell took priority over political – there was likely no patriotic plan to try to keep Britain's foothold in the Omani oil sector to ensure that Britain could influence Omani governmental spending, but the British Government was not naïve to the fact. Even today, British diplomats are well aware that

> oil is still an important component of the prosperity agenda of both the UK and the Gulf states. It is important that Britain secures oil interests in the region because the energy sector is interlinked with broader prosperity and UK national security; if the oil industry is weak in the region, British interests could be at risk.[35]

The oil industry and the wider impact that fluctuating revenues has on the economy of Oman, and by extension the British economy, has arguably been one of the major issues concerning Britain's relations with the Sultanate since the turn of the 1970s. The foundations of Britain's influence over Oman's energy sector, however, can be traced back to the early 1930s, when oil companies began to take an interest in the potential for drilling in the region. Rupert Hay mentioned that the Political Residents were the main point of contact for interested oil explorers, and he 'has to closely watch all negotiations for new agreements or the amendment of existing agreements and ensure that nothing is decided which will seriously affect the position or the rulers of the British government.'[36] This relational power has continued regardless of the dismantling of the Residency system.

All oil exploration treaties signed with the local rulers were also, simultaneously, signed with the British Government through the Residency, and thus the British Government had a vested interest in the developments of Oman's oil industry. This secured the British influence over the oil industry at its foundation, ensuring that the sector developed in a way that was most acceptable to Britain.

5.3.1 The start of Omani nationalisation

The historic unrivalled influence that Britain enjoyed proved to be insecure and was not wholly retained after withdrawal. Perhaps evidence of the independence of the new Sultan from British oversight, or at least in preparation for the eventual withdrawal of the bulk of British expatriates after the cessation of fighting in Dhofar, the new Sultan took it upon himself to purchase a significant stake in PDO to be controlled by his new government. The 25% of PDO that Qaboos purchased on behalf of the Omani state on 1 January 1974 was purchased from Shell at market value at the time, and although this decreased Shell's control of PDO, it demonstrated that the new Sultan understood the importance of Shell to Oman; he willingly paid the true value for the shares, and Shell was delighted that the Sultan was willing to spend, unlike his father.[37]

In the same year, Qaboos purchased another 35% of PDO, again at the market value at the time, making the state the largest shareholder in Oman's main oil exploration and production company, shifting the balance away from the private sector to the public, from majority British control to Omani.

As a result of the partial nationalisation of PDO, Shell retained a 34% stake, Compagnie Française des Petroles had 4% and Partex was left with 2%, an ownership structure that has remained unchanged since 1974. As a large but now secondary shareholder in PDO, Shell, and therefore also the British Government, who was historically able to exert indirect influence over Omani oil affairs, have undoubtedly lost the ability to directly influence the decision-making of Oman where oil is concerned. Historically, British-registered oil companies had a combined majority stake in PDO throughout its history – firstly when PDO was a subsidiary of Iraq Petroleum Company, *Petroleum Development (Oman and Dhofar) Ltd*, in which Royal Dutch Shell and the Anglo-Persian Company (later renamed BP) held a 23.75% share each,[38] and then in June 1967, a month before oil was first exported from Oman, when Shell owned 85% of PDO. This is not to suggest that Shell has ever been directly answerable to the British Government as it has always been a private company and not solely registered in Britain, but a key tenet of British diplomacy is the utilisation of the private sector to achieve governmental aims abroad. When PDO became largely Omani state-owned, an important route for British intervention in Oman was seriously diminished.

Hydrocarbon contributions to Oman's GDP in the first half of 2018 stood at 37%, a 5.1% decrease from the same period in 2017,[39] but approximately 30% of which was attributable to PDO output. Therefore, in 2018, PDO contributed 30% of the national GDP of Oman, a large proportion for a single company. The *Ninth Five-Year Development Plan (2016–2020)*, written in 2015, states that 'oil revenues continue to constitute about (80%) of total revenues of the State General Budget, and proceeds from oil exports formed about (70%) of commodity export returns.'[40] This plan for economic diversification also states that 'non-oil activities are still dependent to a large extent on oil and gas production.'[41] Oman is still heavily reliant on the oil sector for public spending and investment. Table 5.1 demonstrates how Oman's oil production has increased significantly since the first exports in 1967, but also the proportionate decrease in the difference between the number of barrels of oil produced and those exported.

This trend highlights an increasing domestic demand for oil within Oman. This arguably suggests that the domestic reliance on PDO production is increasing, as the sectors that Oman is relying on for economic diversification – 'in Oman the growth strategy [is] centred on developing

Table 5.1 Oil production and exports data between 1967 and 2017

Oil production in Oman (1967–2017)[42]

Year	Annual oil production (millions of barrels)	Oil exports (millions of barrels)
1967	23	22
1968	88	88
1969	120	120
1970	121	121
1971	107	106
1972	103	103
1973	107	107
1974	106	106
1975	125	125
1976	134	134
1977	124	122
1978	115	115
1979	108	108
1980	104	102
1981	120	120
1982	123	119
1983	142	129
1984	152	135
1985	182	165
1986	204	187
1987	213	197
1988	227	212
1989	234	215
1990	250	229
1991	259	235
1992	270	253
1993	285	267
1994	296	271
1995	311	285
1996	323	296
2000	350	327
2005	283	262
2006	269	233
2007	259	222
2008	277	217
2009	297	244
2010	316	272
2011	323	269
2012	336	280
2013	344	304
2014	344	292
2015	358	308
2016	368	322
2017	354	294

its natural gas resources and tourism has just begun to bear fruit[43] – are dependent on oil to function and expand. As PDO remains the mainstay of the domestic economy, despite attempts to diversify, the British economic footprint in Oman also retains its significance. Shell's partial ownership of PDO is a hard power asset, through which senior British executives are able to exert their influence upon their majority Omani workforce, but the fact that Shell, a non-Omani company, has been able to retain a large shareholding in PDO that has remained unchanged for four decades is a sign that the Government of Oman values the expertise and oversight that one of the world's major energy companies brings to PDO. There is no evidence to indicate that Qaboos has permitted Shell to retain an influential place in Oman just because it is a British company with British expats in senior positions, rather this is because of the necessary expertise that Shell is able to share with PDO employees who are regularly seconded to work at Shell. There is undoubtedly an element of respect within the senior ranks of the Sultan's government for the important role that Shell and the British Government held when developing the domestic oil industry, and this respect for the British legacy and trust in Shell's reputation is a key tenet of the continued British soft power in Oman.

5.3.2 *The British role in Oman's energy market development*

The oil industry is more than just the main contributor to the GDP of Oman, PDO has played a significant role in the development of the careers and mindsets of the Sultanate's senior officials and ministers since it was established. Although Shell is a shareholder in PDO, and for half of the 20th century, Shell's representation in Oman was via PDO, there is a Shell office in Muscat's extensive PDO compound, responsible for coordinating Shell's PDO operations and the commercial Shell Oman Marketing Company SAOG (which is 49% owned by Shell) and Oman LNG LLC (30% owned by Shell). So, although Shell is no longer the majority shareholder in PDO, nor in Oman LNG, Oman's gas company, the footprint of Shell is still considerable enough to argue that there remains significant British influence in Oman's natural resource sector. The presence of a large British company at the centre of Oman's most important industry could be considered soft power in nature. Shell's executives share their skills with their Omani counterparts and invest in PDO's developments, but the longevity of Shell's shareholding is dependent on the Sultan's government continuing to respect these skills.

Oil remains the most important contributor to national GDP, but gas is emerging as a diversifier within the sector. A signal of the gradual shift away from the oil industry in Oman, and a major focus of the diversification agenda, is the development of the natural gas industry in Khazzan. Oman Oil Company Exploration & Production (OOCEP), in partnership with the British company BP, started the first phase of the development in September

2017, under budget and ahead of schedule. The Khazzan-Makarem gas field is expected to supply approximately 40% of Oman's domestic energy by 2030, with 'gas-in-place reported to be in the region of 2.8 trillion cubic metres' and at an initial upfront cost of $24 billion.[44] The first Khazzan project was jointly operated by the state-owned OOCEP, who owned 40% of the operations, and BP with 60%. Although the Omani state ensured that it retained a significant minority shareholding in Khazzan, it is important to acknowledge the majority share that BP owned, a private company registered in London and with influential support within British governments of various parties. This is the industry that is set to emerge as the key diversifier of the Omani economy.

The Khazzan gas project has seemingly followed the same path as that of PDO. The Government of Oman has permitted a private foreign company; in this case, a British company in the form of BP just like Shell in the oil industry in 1968, to retain a majority ownership of the developing industry until it becomes profitable. This symbol on the Omani side that the country is open to private companies was arguably an attempt by Qaboos to replicate a successful process of economic development that he witnessed in the oil industry at the point of his accession to the throne, with a British-registered company given the opportunity to expand its portfolio in Oman, make a profit from its Omani investments, and make autonomous decisions regarding which companies to use for the supply and maintenance of equipment. Although the majority ownership by BP in the Khazzan gas project undoubtedly gives Britain a significant amount of influence in the industry as it develops, the British influence has been weakened as a result of Oman's sale of a 10% share in the project in late 2018 to Petronas, the Malaysian state-owned energy company. 'For OOCEP, the deal "could be worth in excess of $1.3 billion," an important consideration as spending on Khazzan's second phase, Ghazeer, ramps up.'[45] As a result of the entry of Petronas, a rival company to BP operating under the rules of the Malaysian state, Britain's influence has been diminished similarly to when Qaboos part-nationalised PDO in 1974. Nye defined soft power as the attraction for what another state or company can offer in times of need, and Petronas has developed its own gas industry in a similar economic landscape as in Oman. BP does not share this necessary expertise and thus cannot offer the Government of Oman the specific economic expertise required at this time.

5.3.3 Competition to Britain's influence in Oman's energy markets

The engineering, procurement, and construction management for the first phase of Khazzan was undertaken by the American multinational Jacobs Engineering Group Inc., not a British company, which differs to when oil was first exploited in Oman during the final years of the Residency era, when all work was undertaken by British companies. During the Residency era, Oman had no option but to allow British companies to develop its oil industry. Since withdrawal, evidence demonstrates that Oman is more willing to diversify its economic relations with companies from other countries. Nevertheless, much like Shell with PDO, by cooperating with OOCEP, BP gains on two fronts. Firstly, the oil and gas supermajor gains influence in Oman and takes away a possible extra revenue source from Shell and other rivals, but they also have the opportunity to impart their own expertise upon OOCEP as the domestic gas industry is developing in the Sultanate.

The presence of BP in Oman's largest gas field is positive for British prosperity and important for the preservation of Britain's influence in an industry that will come to grow in importance for Oman's economic development. There was no guarantee that BP would have won the tender to work with OOCEP as the bidding process for the contract was open, as was the engineering and construction bid, with five companies shortlisted – American companies Bechtel, Jacobs Engineering and KBR, Australian company Worley Parsons, and former British company Amec Foster Wheeler. As Oman has become more interconnected within the global economy since 1971, it is inevitable that the Omani economy, in particular the developing natural resources sector that is crucial to the domestic economy, is also increasingly opening to companies from a number of different countries. This increased competition has, undoubtedly, had a negative effect on Britain's influence in Oman and the ability of the British Government to indirectly utilise the position of Shell and BP in the Sultanate to expand its soft power in Oman. Competition ultimately means that the British voice is no longer the only one within the Omani decision-making process and the power to influence can no longer be taken for granted.

British links with Oman's oil and gas industries and the influence that these companies have in the country should not be considered as solely one sided. Although the likes of Shell and BP need the contracts in Oman to exploit oil and gas resources to increase their profits, and the indirect influence that the British Government gains from this is invaluable. Oman also exerts power over Britain in its choice of companies working in the country. It is undeniable that senior officials in Oman know the extent to which British energy companies rely on their operations in Oman as other contracts around the world expire or face financial difficulties, and this grants Omani ministers significant power to dictate the shareholding and time frame of contracts, and the allocation of exploration licences to each company. The Government of Oman is arguably more pragmatic in the way that it conducts economic affairs now than before 1971, partly out of necessity as domestic reliance on income generated from the energy sector has continued to increase, but also because they can use oil and gas contracts to achieve international priorities and foster closer relations with states that were previously barred from cooperating with Oman by the Residency.

5.4 How has the Omani diversification agenda affected Britain's economic influence?

Although Oman still enjoys close economic relations with Britain, the accession of the new Sultan in 1970 and British political withdrawal from the Sultanate in 1971 has undoubtedly resulted in a gradual decline in the overt economic influence that Britain once enjoyed in the state. Opinions relating to the extent to which this influence has declined differ greatly across Omani society, making it difficult to get a true indication of the contemporary British economic footprint in Oman. The diversification agenda in Oman has been gradually picking up pace since around the turn of the century, but the oil sector still remains the most important contributor to Omani national income. A former British diplomat in the Gulf, now an advisor on regional economic affairs, warned that

> the failure of Gulf economies to adapt quickly to a post-oil era would result in their economies becoming less viable, it would affect jobs and continue to mean that there is a lack of jobs for restless young populations, and would lead to instability for the next generation of leaders.[46]

If Oman is unable to diversify its economy, British influence in the wider Gulf will arguably be damaged because Oman is a crucial economic gateway to the region for both the British Government and British companies. It is likely that Britain's diplomats and representatives in Oman are aware of this and relay their worries back to London. The recognition of this potential to lose ground in Oman is perhaps a major reason for both the hard and soft power efforts by the British Government when collaborating with the Sultan's government. The British Government has demonstrated its ability to find a balance between these two types of power, between a physical presence in the form of economic investments and assistance with the development of infrastructure that is integral to domestic economic diversification, and a more covert pressure imparted by British companies and the financial support provided by export finance to persuade the Government of Oman to diversify in sectors supported by British money.

5.4.1 Britain's necessary shift from hard to soft power

The shift from hard power to soft power is evident in many areas of the bilateral relationship, but the Sultan's willingness to now accept major economic assistance from a state other than Britain is testament to how much influence Britain has lost in Oman either as a result of, or despite the official withdrawal in 1971. Diversification is a delicate subject in the politics of the Gulf states, and this is no different in Oman, where the energy sector is the

130 *Trade and the power of money*

most significant contributor to the finances of the Sultanate and the largest provider of high-paid private sector jobs. As has previously been discussed, Shell has been the dominant private company within the Omani oil industry since before withdrawal and the company continues to invest in the sector, but financial support is being provided to BP to expand the gas industry and provide a new avenue for Oman to generate income.

Commodity dependence is an issue across much of the Middle East, and although Sultan Qaboos and his ministers have acknowledged this and asked other states for assistance, the shift from oil dependence to a diversified economy is not a journey that the British Government has expertise in. In a research paper produced by *The Oxford Institute for Energy Studies*, Adeel Malik argued that economies in the Middle East which have so far failed to diversify on a major scale

> suffering from the burdens of both history and oil. Whatever weak constituency of private production was inherited by these countries was further weakened after the discovery of oil. Even where rulers were more dependent on merchants prior to the discovery of oil … oil tied down the merchant class in state contracts and other forms of patronage.[47]

Malik also suggested that the private sector in the Gulf countries is still 'structurally dependent on the state.'[48] This is, indeed, the case in Oman. Despite attempts to diversify, the economy of Oman is still dependent on its energy sector. The British Government cannot assist with diversification because it has no relevant experience in the area. This is an important issue that potentially limits the influence that the British Government and British companies are able to exert upon the Omani diversification agenda. According to Ernest Wilson, smart power, which has defined Britain's dealings with Oman since the early 1980s, 'increasingly rests on a nation's capacity to create and manipulate knowledge and information.'[49] This is where Britain's reputation as a trusted consultative partner to Oman is limited, as the specific knowledge and expertise that the Government of Oman needs – how to shift the domestic economy away from a reliance on oil – is not a topic that British advisors are intricately familiar with.

5.4.2 Malaysian involvement in Omani diversification

The 9th Omani Five-Year Development Plan, implemented between 2016 and 2020, was largely focused on the restructuring of the domestic economy so that it is more suited to a future after oil. Under the banner of TANFEEDH (*Implementation*), the diversification model that has been chosen by the Sultan's ministers is modelled on a system that was formerly implemented successfully in Malaysia, a state that was reliant on its oil industry for national finances, and the choice to implement this specific model has necessitated the secondment of Malaysian officials who are knowledgeable about the process. The TANFEEDH process intends to develop a partnership between the public and private sector in Oman, with public enterprises and government departments supporting private sector expansion and investments, in the expectation that higher paid jobs will be created in the non-commodities industries, and the reduction of the burden on the state that will result from this. This diversification programme aims to increase the competitivity and viability of the logistics, tourism, and manufacturing industries, and to change the fundamentals of labour and finance in Oman. These are areas that the British Government is not as familiar with as many states that have now established relations with the Sultan's government. The implementation of TANFEEDH further demonstrated Qaboos' willingness to be pragmatic when developing his economy, rejecting traditional allies in favour of states that have demonstrable experience in areas that he required.

Through the auspices of the *Implementation Support and Follow-Up Unit*,[50] the Government of Oman identifies target economic areas and implements policies and programmes, with assistance from Malaysian advisers, and ensures that they are successfully implemented. TANFEEDH identified a number of target sectors to assist with diversification: manufacturing (petrochemicals, metals, non-metals, food production, and innovation); tourism (privatisation of nature and heritage sites, nature and adventure activities, culture and heritage, events, conferences and exhibitions, leisure, recreation and accommodation, marketing and promotions, and the tourism labour market); logistics (land transport, air transport, sea transport, and trade facilitation); job market and employment (unlocking demand, strengthening supply, coordination of supply, and demand); and business environment and finance.[51]

Whilst there may be opportunities for British private sector involvement in some of the areas identified for development and diversification, the Omani economy is now open to companies from around the world. It should not be concluded that the British presence has been wholly diminished as a result of the entry of other countries, the influence has just become less obvious and less direct than it was before withdrawal. The government appointed the multinational consultancy company KPMG to oversee the implementation of the TANFEEDH programmes. Although the company is now registered in Switzerland and has its head office in the Netherlands, the London office is heavily involved in working with the Gulf governments, and many of the senior analysts and consultants are British. It is not possible to assess the exact compilation of Britons working on KPMG's Oman operations, but there is certainly a British footprint critiquing the Sultanate's economic diversification.

5.4.3 Sectoral diversification and the British footprint

In its attempt to diversify away from oil, the Government in Muscat has identified the mining industry as one of five elements in its future-proofing agenda. There are large reserves of copper, chromite, zinc, and iron across Oman. Although Oman Mining Company LLC (OMCO), the state-owned mining company, was the first to exploit the country's resources in 1979, and it has been registered at the London Metal Exchange since its establishment, there has been a constant British influence over the development of the sector. Since the approval of a decree to permit full foreign ownership of companies in priority industries in March 2019 – including mining – British companies have emerged as frequent bidders for mining permissions. British company Savannah Resources was granted the first two licences to a foreign firm since the passing of the new law, with permission to open a copper mine for 1.7 million tonnes of 2.2% graded copper and a mine for 500,000 tonnes at a 4.5% grade across a 1,004 sq. km area within the Semail Ophiolite belt near Sohar.[52] The granting of the first foreign licence under the new regulations to a British company by Oman's Public Authority for Mining is demonstrable of an attraction by Omani decision makers to the proven expertise of British companies in this industry and the regulations within the UK that underpins this. It could be argued that Savannah is now reliant on a continued acceptance by the government in Oman in order to permit their presence in one of the most important diversifying industries, but Oman has also become reliant on a British company once again to successfully implement its economic diversification process.

Despite the reduced influence of Britain in Omani economic diversification efforts, it should not be deduced that Britain has no economic presence in Oman at all. In fact, there is a strong presence in the defence and non-oil commodities industries, particularly in the form of construction machinery, food products, and civil aircraft. There is also a strong British insurance and services presence in Oman. Competition from other European and Asian states is a barrier to the establishment of a larger British presence in sectors, such as education, banking, and non-military machinery sales.[53] The DIT is trying to establish Britain as an all-round economic power in Oman, but it is no longer possible for British companies to attempt to compete with India or China on construction projects because these countries can produce greater quantities of materials at lower costs and they have a much larger low-skilled workforce at their disposal. The DIT tries to sell British goods on their quality rather than price,[54] but Oman's attempt to rapidly diversify its economy away from a reliance on oil revenues has inevitably resulted in a weakening of British influence outside of two key sectors – defence and energy.

5.5 The future development of economic bilateralism and the role of FDI

Since Britain's withdrawal, Sultans Qaboos and Haitham have opened Oman up to investment from countries around the world, but there does seem to be a concerted effort by both Britain and Oman to build upon the economic legacy that has defined the bilateral relationship for over two centuries. There are several dimensions to this relationship, ranging from official cross-governmental programmes to the personal level between individual Omani and British business representatives. There are also several commercial and non-commercial friendship groups that promote UK–Omani relations in an attempt to establish greater personal and economic connections between stakeholders.

5.5.1 The multi-faceted nature of bilateral business representation

The business relationship between Oman and Britain is multi-faceted – there is a monarch-to-monarch relationship, government-to-government relationship, business to government relationship, and various business-to-business relationships. There is a common theme that links various British business groups in Oman together – the patronage of the ruling Sultan and his desire to strengthen the bilateral relationship manifested by his personal funding and founding of these groups. It is not uncommon for there to be numerous groups responsible for representing businesses of different countries operating in Oman,[55] and the sheer existence of groups representing non-British companies demonstrates the extent to which the former hegemonic economic influence of Britain in Oman has diminished since 1971. However, economics is an important soft power tool, as the preservation of a British economic presence ensures that Oman remains an important market for British companies.

The interconnectivity between the most prominent British business representative groups in Oman, namely the *Omani British Friendship Association*, the *Oman British Business* Council, the *British Ambassador's Advisory Group*, and the *British Business Forum* and their close ties to the ruling families in both Britain and Oman seemingly ensures that all aspects of UK–Omani business are represented and that there is a continuity in the economic links between Britain and Oman. The economic relationship is also maintained via a number of cultural and friendship groups with a less commercial focus, particularly the *British Council Alumni Association* in Oman and the *Anglo-Omani Society* in London, both of which have high-profile patrons and influential members in both governments and large businesses in Britain and Oman. These pro-British groups ensure that the British presence remains in the minds of decision makers within Oman, and the argument could also be made that the reverse is also the case within the British mindset for Oman. An element of soft power influence is attraction to what the partners have to offer and a desire to foster closer relations. These business groups try to ensure that British companies are given priority when Omani businesses are looking for partners on mutually beneficial projects. This represents a shift from the historic hegemonic position of British companies in Oman who were guaranteed first refusal on projects to a situation where British organisations have to compete in open competition.

134 *Trade and the power of money*

Although it is not uncommon for there to be groups representing British interests abroad, Oman is a rare example where Sultan Qaboos himself called for the establishment of a bilateral group to develop commercial relations between British companies in Oman and Omani companies in Britain. In 1991, the Omani British Friendship Association (OBFA), a business group that involves large companies in both states, was established to promote bilateral investments between the two countries. According to one of the senior representatives at OBFA, the group is a roundtable to promote investments from British companies into Oman and from Omani businesses into Britain. There are a number of conferences and receptions held throughout the year, each with a business theme, with the aim of bringing businesses from both sides of the relationship together to discuss investment opportunities and any issues on either side that could hinder the relationship.[56] The association includes the likes of HSBC, Shell, and a number of Omanis who have close commercial and personal ties to Britain. Although the ways in which the association is organised differ in both countries, taking a more formal appearance in Oman and less so in Britain, the bilateral group has seemingly benefited Britain more than Oman thus far. A number of large-scale Omani property investments in London have emerged from OBFA, including luxury hotel developments. British investments into Oman are still on a smaller scale.[57] Business groups such as OBFA are an important method through which the bilateral economic relationship between Britain and Oman is retained and strengthened, and the resulting Omani investments into the UK is possibly evidence that there is still a strong attraction within the Omani business community towards Britain.

Friendship groups are soft power tools through which Britain is able to retain an economic presence in Oman, and arguably a replacement for the historic presence of significant communities of British expatriates in the Sultanate who were responsible for promoting and ensuring that only British companies and individuals were awarded contracts to undertake projects in Oman, including drilling for oil, establishing a national currency for Oman, and building infrastructure.

5.5.2 The British Business Forum

The *British Business Forum* (BBF) is not unique to Oman as there are also three variations in neighbouring Saudi Arabia, two in the UAE, and one each in Kuwait and Qatar, but the BBF in Oman is part of a wider attempt by the British Government, via the embassy in Muscat, to build upon the commercial relations that have dominated the bilateral relationship for over two centuries and an element of the wider business representation framework that is in place to preserve UK–Omani economic relations. The BBF in Oman in its current format was established by Malcolm Ives, the trade representative at the British Embassy in the 1990s, building upon an existing British Gentleman's Club that acted as a forum for CEOs and directors of major British companies in Oman (including the British Bank of the Middle East – now part of HSBC, British Airways and British Aerospace – now BAE Systems) to meet and discuss business in Oman. These companies are no longer wholly British-owned, but do retain important ties to the British Government and are considered British flag-bearing corporations. The BBF, with British members either working in Oman or for British companies in the country, meets regularly and assists with the promotion of Oman as a place for British companies to invest during trade visits to the Sultanate. Although the BBF is now independently organised and financed, it is an obvious example of an organisation set up by an arm of the British Government in Oman – the trade department – to ensure that British commercial interests were represented. In the contemporary Gulf, non-governmental bodies such as this are an important method through which British individuals promote themselves and ensure that they remain relevant in an ever-changing region. The soft power impact of organisations such as BBF should also not be discounted, as by meeting to promote best practice in Oman, they are helping to indirectly attract Omani attention to British business.

5.5.3 *Representation of British interests in Oman*

Strategic communications consultancy, Portland, and the USC Center on Public Diplomacy measure the soft power strength of a country using an index called 'The Soft Power 30,' with one factor measuring the number of business and cultural missions abroad. In Oman, there is no shortage of organisations of this nature representing British interests, a contributing factor to Britain being chosen as the most influential soft power nation in 2015 and 2018, and second place in 2016, 2017, and 2019.[58] The future of Britain's economic influence in Oman will depend on both the future development of intergovernmental relations between Britain and Oman and the effort that British Government agencies put into marketing British goods and expertise in the Sultanate to ensure that Britain remains at the forefront of the minds of decision makers in Oman. Promotions in Oman by the British trade department are indicators of the importance that the British Government is putting on trade with Oman and the strength of British soft power in the country. These trade promotions are multidimensional, ranging from small-scale advertisements in Omani media to trade visits by British regional chambers of commerce, cooperation between British companies operating in Oman and the BBF, and more formal cooperation between British and Omani companies through the OBFA's Business Council. Each organisation organises regular events in both Oman and Britain to bring together decision makers responsible for investments in either country. These trade promotions are closely associated with ministerial visits by British trade ministers, with these high-profile visits symbolising the importance that the British Government puts on trading with certain states. Dr Liam Fox,

136 *Trade and the power of money*

Secretary of State for International Trade during the first May government, visited Oman between 20 and 22 November 2016 to meet Omani ministers, to sign the joint venture agreement between Babcock and the Oman Drydock Company to provide engineering and maintenance services to the Duqm naval dockyard, and to talk to Omani media about Britain's commitment to Oman and to emphasise how Britain is the largest foreign direct investor in Oman. Dr Fox also visited Oman between 9 and 10 April 2017 to meet the oil and gas minister to promote British involvement in the Duqm oil refinery. This ensured that the British presence remained at the forefront of Omani decision makers.

Prior to the formation of DIT, trade visits were undertaken by ministers responsible for the FCO and Business departments, under various guises. Over recent years, Oman has attracted many official ministerial visits from Britain, including by former Labour Minister of State at the FCO, Bill Rammell, between 19 and 22 October 2009 for bilateral meetings with Omani Government officials, Conservative Foreign Secretary Boris Johnson who visited in December 2017 and January 2018 and by Minister at the FCO responsible for the Middle East, Alistair Burt, in October 2018, alongside many non-ministerial visits by MPs on the Oman All-Party Parliamentary Group and various parliamentary select committees in the HoC and HoL over the years since 1971. Again, this ensured that the Sultan's cabinet remained aware of the assistance that Britain could offer.

5.5.4 The impact of British FDI into Oman on the power dynamics

These trade connections are an important way for Britain to ensure that its footprint remains constant in Oman and to further develop Britain's influence on the Omani economy. As British officials effectively controlled the Omani economy until 1971, there was arguably no requirement for Britain to market its goods and services in Oman, as exclusivity agreements meant that this British sphere of economic influence was not threatened by rival powers. After 1971, the British Government had no choice but to begin soliciting the Government of Oman and Omani private companies to ensure that domestic companies retained their privileged position in Omani economics. As the largest foreign direct investor in Oman, Britain has successfully remained one of Oman's closest economic partners – according to statistics recently released by the Omani National Centre for Statistics and Information (NCSI), the UK has remained the largest foreign direct investor in Oman since 1971, contributing more than double that of the second highest FDI contributor (United Arab Emirates). Since 2012, the value of British FDI into Oman in comparison with other countries is indicative of the responsibility that British officials believe they have for the state and the commitment to securing the resulting influence (see Table 5.2).

There are likely several reasons for Britain's retention of its position as the largest FDI investor into Oman, but soft power undoubtedly plays a role.

Table 5.2 The value of foreign direct investments into Oman, 2012–16

FDI into Oman (million Omani rials)[59]

Country	2012	2013	2014	2015	2016
United Kingdom	2,659.0	3,073.9	3,599.3	2,571.4	3,505.5
United Arab Emirates	1,023.6	1,156.8	831.7	846.0	1,020.0
Kuwait	223.5	243.7	341.3	387.6	407.5
Qatar	208.7	221.1	265.0	365.6	389.5
Bahrain	228.7	246.4	246.4	312.1	339.5
Switzerland	408.4	187.6	158.3	287.6	281.1
India	243.6	264.4	291.3	281.3	266.7
The Netherlands	122.7	141.3	203.0	253.8	253.6
USA	233.2	230.1	253.4	255.4	244.8
Other	1,044.4	1,160.9	1,349.0	1,328.6	1,388.5
Total	6,395.8	6,926.2	7,556.7	6,889.4	8,096.7

'Direct investments by British companies into Oman demonstrates a willingness to assist with domestic priorities but also to retaining the close economic ties between the two countries.'[60] If decision makers in Oman can see that Britain is committed to funding priority initiatives in their state, they are more likely to feel attracted to British companies and a sense that they owe British investors privileged access to projects within Oman. FDI has arguably emerged as a 21st century soft power replacement of the historic hard power gunboat diplomacy that dictated British relations with Oman. Relations between the two states are now dependent on the trading of goods and services rather than the military strength of Britain in the region. In 2018, Oman was ranked the fifth fastest-growing market for UK exports, with growth between 2010 and 2018 of 161.2% (with increases in exports of defence and construction machinery and services accounting for much of this increase), and although British exports to Oman in 2018 were only worth £1.6 billion of total £345.1 billion non-EU exports,[61] the growth of over 161% within eight years is a significant increase that could be explained in several ways.

The value of British exports to Oman started from a comparatively low base when compared with other states (for example, in 2018, the US imported £118.2 billion from the UK, Germany imported £55.4 billion, the Netherlands imported £44 billion[62]) and when assessing the importance of Oman to Britain from a purely trade perspective, statistics reveal that Oman is a minor export market. Britain also does not feature in the list of Oman's main export markets, with China accounting for 39% of all Omani exports at a value of $12.1 billion, India for 9.2% worth $2.9 billion, and the UAE for 7.2% valued at $2.3 billion. In fact, the British market accounted for only 0.41% of Omani exports at a value of $127 million in 2017.[63] When these statistics are analysed in detail, however, Oman is an important export market

138 *Trade and the power of money*

for British companies because of the nature of the products produced in Britain and the imports required in Oman. The main imports into Oman fall into the categories of machinery and transport equipment and manufactured goods, products that British manufacturers such as BAE Systems focus their export efforts on. The nature of Oman's imports from Britain perhaps explains why the British trade surplus with Oman was £3 billion in 2018, up £1.8 billion since 2016.[64] There is evidence of an increased demand for specialist oil and gas equipment, military and commercial aircraft and parts, and services to the energy and banking sectors – all areas that Britain has proven itself to be strong in.

Trade is an important asset that both the British Government and British companies are able to effectively utilise to strengthen Britain's influence in Oman and exert influence upon the Government of Oman to advance British values and best practices in the Gulf. There is an emerging theory that claims that the strength of a state's soft power in another state determines the amount of trade between the two countries. Research by Andrew Rose at the *National Bureau of Economic Research* in Massachusetts on the correlation between trade and soft power concluded that

> countries which are seen to be exerting a more positive influence in the world tend to sell more exports to their admirers, holding a host of other phenomena constant through the workhorse gravity model of trade. This result is economically and statistically powerful, and reasonably (though not completely) robust to a wide variety of potential econometric challenges.[65]

5.5.5 *FDI as one element of the wider bilateral relationship*

It is also important to understand that trade cannot be considered a solitary factor when assessing the strength of British investment influence in Oman. Robert and Shannon Blanton argued that there is a relationship between FDI and human rights projection within the global economy. 'Respect for human rights also creates an environment conducive to the development of human capital, with such countries generally more open, accountable and economically efficient.'[66] Similarly, Charles Oman concluded that governments that are more successful at attracting FDI follow the norms of good governance, including developing credible sound public finances.

> Investors often choose sites where the host government's strategy to attract investors is part of a broader process of mobilisation around a project of social and political reform in which the government redefines its role, turning away from rigid structures and exclusive relationships with vested interest groups in favour of greater transparency, democracy and market competition.[67]

A major criticism of FDI into the Gulf is that it is too oil-centric in nature and neglects human rights within the receiving country. This argument is difficult to support in the way that Blanton and Blanton claim, who suggested that 'economic growth may lead to instability by increasing the number of dissatisfied people prone to rebel, which would likely increase human rights abuse.'[68] Historic British investments into Oman to assist with the building of roads to the interior, construction of hospitals, schools, and airports arguably stand as a testament to the British support for economic growth, and although rebels within the Dhofar Province did rise up against the central government in the 1950s, it is widely accepted that this was because of a lack of investment into the province.

The large annual sums of FDI provided by Britain to Oman to assist with the Sultan's economic development projects could be considered hard power in character, but it is dependent on soft power attraction to be effective. Oman is also able to use its position as a trusted investment destination to attract increasingly larger FDI sums. 'When a multinational firm (MNC) establishes a subsidiary and opens a plant in a foreign country, the whole capital stock is at risk from violations of property rights and contracts.'[69] Oman's British-oriented contract laws, implemented during the Residency era, are attractive to decision makers within the British Government and private enterprise. Non-military export credits are important for securing British contracts to support Omani infrastructure projects, contributing to the large amounts of FDI sent to Oman and the influence of British companies there. Although the success of Oman's diversification policies is predicated on a gradual shift away from oil, one of the largest non-military export credit guarantees awarded by the British Government is a US$157 million contract to the Oman Oil Refineries and Petroleum Company SAOC to finance the purchase of goods and services from UK-based suppliers for the construction of a new petrochemicals plant in support of the Liwa Plastics Industries Complex. The project includes three developments: an extraction plant for natural gas at Fahud, a natural gas pipeline from Fahud to Sohar, and a petrochemical plant at Sohar port.[70] Officials within the British Government's ECGD understand the continued importance of the energy sector to Omani prosperity and have faith that the money will be repaid on time.

5.5.6 *External factors affecting Britain's economic influence*

The strength of the British trading relationship with Oman is now affected by a multitude of external factors that were not present before 1971, when Britain was still the unrivalled economic and strategic hegemon in the Gulf, many of which cannot be controlled by political policies implemented by the British Government or by sheer goodwill. The most prominent threat to British trade with the Sultanate that has seemingly emerged since the turn of the century is the encroachment of other states into what was considered the British sphere of influence for over 150 years. China has become the major export partner for Omani companies, followed by India and South Korea. Oman has evidently shifted its trade focus towards the emerging East and away from the established states in the West.

In a 2010 report produced by the Middle East Association, Foreign Office Minister and former confidante of Sultan Qaboos, Sir Alan Duncan, noted that 'the UK is losing market share, both to established competition and to emerging markets such as India, China and Korea. While British companies continue to win significant levels of new business, we could and should be doing more.'[71] Although this speech was made in 2010, the situation has not changed. The level of influence that British companies enjoy in Oman as a result of their trading relations with Oman, and the historic reliance that Oman had on British suppliers, has been reduced significantly and continues to decline as other states sign free trade agreements (FTAs) with the GCC and foster closer relations with Omani corporations. The role that Oman plays in regional affairs, mediating between Iran and Qatar and the GCC, and between Israel and other Middle Eastern states, should not be overlooked as a factor affecting the economic influence with Britain. The rift between Iran and the West would usually be considered a strategic issue – an attempt by western states to prevent Iranian production of nuclear weapons, resulting in serious economic sanctions being applied to Iran by the United Nations between December 2006, with the passing of Resolution 1737, until 16 January 2016. The influence that Oman holds in relation to Iran has been acknowledged by numerous politicians in Parliament for over a decade. Similarly, it has been acknowledged that Oman directly benefits from the internal GCC dispute with Qatar, with Baroness Goldie telling colleagues in a HoL debate that 'it is the case that air and sea routes for people and goods in and out of Qatar have been rerouted through Oman.'[72]

As one of the most influential economic actors in Oman, particularly in relation to the energy sector, the benefits for British influence in the wider Gulf as a result of Oman's strategic relations with Iran and Qatar are important. As key shipping routes are redirecting to Oman, and Oman is taking some of the business focus away from other states in the region, the British companies working in relevant industries in Oman are benefiting. Similarly, as the British Government tries to retain close ties to the Omani authorities, the accepted understanding of soft power claims that Britain would be able to exert influence over Oman's economic developments with Iran and Qatar.

5.5.7 *Domestic factors affecting Britain's economic influence*

Domestic economic policies implemented by Sultan Qaboos have also gradually reduced Britain's influence in the state, largely because the Sultan wanted to give the Omani people more influence over their own destiny; this has manifested as the 'Omanisation' programme that has been gradually implemented in the Sultanate since 1988. A significant element in the nine five-year plans that have been implemented since 1976, just five years after British withdrawal and the announcement of Sultan Qaboos' first national budget, is an attempt by the Government of Oman to ensure that Omani nationals are given priority in an increasing list of reserved jobs. The implementation of a stand-alone budget, as opposed to the state budget being inextricably linked to the Sultan's finances, as was the case with all Sultans before Qaboos, was a significant shift in domestic economic policy, and the process of Omanisation continued this marked transformation of Oman into the modern state of the late 20th century. Although the five-year plans were intended to modernise the Omani economy by attracting investments, foreign investment, stabilising and growing government finances, decreasing expenditure, and boosting defence and security, the restrictions placed on expatriate workers in restricted professions and the limiting of visas to foreign nationals looking to work in Oman undoubtedly resulted in a loss of Britain's ability to indirectly influence domestic Omani policy.

The loss of British jobs in Oman at the point of withdrawal, largely as the result of British political decision-making, has resulted in the loss of an avenue through which the British Government and British companies were able to exert their influence on Oman. Although there are still a small number of British consultants and technical experts working with the Omani Government in an advisory capacity, few of these are permanent positions and Omanisation policies prevent Britons from taking up positions restricted solely to Omani nationals. Omanisation, and the restrictions placed upon expatriate workers, including Britons, has certainly resulted in a loss of British power in Oman. Based on the definitions of power set out by Nye, physical assets (such as people) based in a country would be regarded as hard assets, and the influence that these workers can exert upon domestic Omani affairs would be regarded as indirect soft power. Thus, prior to withdrawal, British workers and advisors in Oman could be described as hybrid assets of power for the British Government, but after withdrawal and the gradual shift in the Omani economy towards employing Omani nationals rather than British expatriates, this hybrid power was diminished.

5.6 The power of British money in Oman

Anchoring this study on the concept of soft power, whereby it is assumed that the British economic legacy in Oman is built upon the gradual shift towards a less interventionist and more covert relationship, enables a critical analysis of the financial aspect of one of Britain's most important bilateral relationships. The theory of power is generally considered to be constructivist in nature, whereby the British position in Oman is historically constructed rather than a natural occurrence. Britain's economic legacy in Oman is one of, if not the most prominent relationship with any of the Gulf states. This important economic legacy is undoubtedly a remnant of the unrivalled direct influence that Britain had in Oman since the mid-18th century, utilising ports in Muscat as a coaling base for trade ships passing through the Gulf to India and the British colonies in Asia. Since that time, Viceroys and Governors in the Raj, Residents in the Persian Gulf, and British politicians have courted the many rulers of Muscat and Oman to ensure that Oman remained firmly within the British sphere of influence.

The consolidation of British power in the Sultanate from 1822, when the Residency was firmly established as the paramount decision-maker in the region, and more so after the First World War when Bertram Thomas was recruited by the Government of Oman as a local advisor, resulted in a British monopoly on all aspects of Omani economic affairs. This monopoly was beneficial for the preservation of British power in Oman but came at a financial cost as Omani Sultans proved reluctant to modernise the country using their own money, resulting in Britain having to contribute large sums at times. However, as the only economic power in Oman until withdrawal, British companies were firmly ingrained into the Omani economy by 1971, ensuring that a British presence, with the influence that this granted, remained in the Sultanate as Sultan Qaboos modernised and developed his country. This strong British presence in Oman post-withdrawal has arguably remained a mainstay of the bilateral relationship and a key indicator of the strength of Britain's influence on Oman in the future.

When considering the convergence between soft and hard power, manifested in the arms sales that British companies do with Oman, this constructivist approach could be considered more smart power than just hard or soft. The sale of arms to Oman and the British contribution to the development of the Omani military is hard power in nature as it involves direct military assistance and the sales of weapons to support the regime in power in Oman. However, Oman is now able to diversify who supplies the SOAF and Britain no longer enjoys the unrivalled hegemony that it once did. Qaboos' choice to sign significant arms deals with British manufacturers was not the result of low pricing or force, rather an attraction amongst decision makers for the quality and provenance of the weapons purchased from the likes of BAE. This continuation of British manufacturers supplying critical arms to Oman suggests that Britain is still an influential player in domestic economic affairs, and because of the nature of defence sales, the strategic element of the bilateral relationship also comes to the fore. It could be argued that the joint training exercises and legacy of the British assistance during the Dhofar War also contributes to sentiment amongst Omani decision makers that purchasing arms from British companies is the most suitable option.

As was the case with every aspect of the bilateral relationship between Britain and Oman, the economic influence that Britain holds in the Sultanate has undergone a significant shift since withdrawal. An area of influence that Britain has been able to retain, despite withdrawal, is inward investments into Oman. British companies have remained the largest foreign direct investors into Oman despite Britain directing efforts to only a small number of economic sectors since 1971, and the increased involvement of countries that were previously barred from cooperating with the Sultanate. FDI from Britain into Oman has remained relatively stable since at least the 1990s, at more than double the amount invested by the UAE, the second-largest investor, and since 2012, British FDI comprised between 37% and 47% of all FDI into the country. Investments are considered a strong indicator of power and influence by Nye, so although Britain is no longer the direct determinant of economic activity in Oman, these major investments ensure that Britain is still able to exert indirect influence over the economy. Rather than British individuals and companies deciding what sectors will be developed in Oman, British companies need to invest in projects that have already been decided and approved by the Government of Oman. Since the beginning of the 2010s, the strong British economic presence in Oman, and the trusted status of British companies in the country, has resulted in Britain emerging as a crucial partner for the development of a more sustainable Omani energy sector.

The succession of power in Oman, from Qaboos to Haitham on 11 January 2020, had the potential to further weaken the British influence, but the visit by PM Boris Johnson, the Secretary of State for Defence, Ben Wallace, Chief of the Defence Staff and Prince Charles the following day – the first non-Arab visitors to the new Sultan – sent a strong signal that the British Government was still committed to Oman. Haitham was head of the *Vision 2040* programme for the future economic diversification of Oman. He was also responsible for energy and tourism developments, through which he would have had significant exposure to Shell and BP, working with influential British energy companies on the diversification agenda. On an economic level, the new Sultan does not share the same mindset as Qaboos did, largely because he acceded to power after Oman had already developed international economic partnerships and the Sultanate no longer has a coterie of influential British expatriates in senior advisory positions. As Oman is increasingly courted by emerging Asian powers such as China and India, the lack of direct historic ties between the new Sultan and Britain to the same extent as with Qaboos is likely to test the strength of Britain's power to influence domestic Omani affairs.

5.6.1 *Implications of the continued British economic influence in Oman*

Britain's direct economic influence is stronger in Oman than in any other Middle Eastern state. This study has found that the economy of Oman is less complex than most others in the region, with fewer sectors, and thus British companies that are present in Oman have become established in position over decades. The continued foothold by British companies

144 *Trade and the power of money*

in Oman's predominant energy and banking sectors, and the unlimited export credit guarantees offered to British companies selling goods and services to Oman, implies that British power has remained consistent within the economy of the Sultanate. A recognition of this power presence, and the influence that accompanies it, is an important element of the British projection of economic power and a crucial asset for the British Government when trying to expand its trade and financial leverage after leaving the EU. The policy implications of this influence in Oman are significant, as the British Government has to implement policies that retain this economic influence in Oman, support existing companies operating in the Sultanate so that they do not lose their privileged status or the expert power that Britain gains from their position within Omani society, and ensure that the new Sultan remains as attracted to British commercial relations as his predecessor.

One important method for securing this economic influence takes a more cultural form. Indeed, non-defence education, including British Council English language schools and teacher secondments to Omani schools, British contributions to Oman's cultural sector, including cooperation between the English and Omani Football Associations, and British musicians being invited to perform at the Royal Opera House Muscat are all parts of the composite power relationship. The British economic presence in Oman is significantly more overt than in Bahrain, and the British economic commitment to Omani prosperity is also greater.

Notes

1 See: Aitchison, C.U., *A Collection of Treaties, Engagements and Sanads Relating to India and Neighbouring Countries (5th ed.)*, (Calcutta, Government of India Central Publication Branch, 1933), Vol. 11.
2 See: *British and Foreign State Papers, 1890–1891*, (London, HMSO, 1897), vol. 83, p.11.
3 See: United Kingdom Treaty Series, No. 29 (1939), Cmd.6037.
4 See: 'Muscat No.1 (1952), Cmd.8462.
5 Jeffreys, A. (ed.), *The Report: Oman 2014*, (Dubai, Oxford Business Group, 2014), p.33.
6 Ministry of Defence, Growing the Contribution of Defence to UK Prosperity: A Report for the Secretary of State for Defence, (Ministry of Defence, Government Communication Service, 2018), p.17.
7 See: DIT DSO, *Defence exports (based on orders/contracts signed): Estimated UK and competitor percentage market shares (2008 to 2017)*. Available at: <https://www.gov.uk/government/uploads/system/uploads/attachment_data/file/729935/Chart01.csv/preview> [accessed 17 March 2019].
8 Legatum Institute, *Global Index of Economic Openness 2019*, (London, Legatum Institute, 2019), p.72.
9 Ibid., p.62.
10 Formerly known as UK Trade & Investment.
11 HC Deb 17 September 2015 vol 599 cc389-390WH.
12 HC Deb 23 May 2019 vol 660 c854.

13 Smith, R. and Fontanel, J., 'Weapons Procurement: Domestic Production Versus Imports', in I. Bellany and T. Huxley (eds.), *Conventional Weapons and Western Defence*, (London, Frank Cass & Co. Ltd, 1987), p.83.
14 Allen Jr., C.H. and Rigsbee II, W.L., *Oman Under Qaboos: From Coup to Constitution, 1970–1996*, (London, Frank Cass Publishers, 2000), p.78.
15 See: Mason, R., *Foreign Policy in Iran and Saudi Arabia: Economics and Diplomacy in the Middle East*, (London, I.B.Tauris & Co Ltd, 2015), esp. pp.71–74.
16 Baker, J.C., *Financing International Trade*, (Westport, CT, Praeger Publishers, 2003), p.141.
17 Interview with a senior representative of the UK Department for International Trade (*Trade Representative A*), (Muscat, 11 March 2019).
18 At the time of writing, the most recent UK trading accounts available are those from the year 2017–18 due to the delays in the government publicly releasing official statistics.
19 DIT Analysis – Statistics Brief: 'Trade and Investment between the United Kingdom and Oman (data reported by the UK)', (London, Department for International Trade, 2018).
20 Ibid.
21 UK Export Finance, Export Credits Guarantee Department (UK Export Finance): Annual Report and Accounts 2016–17, (London, HMSO, 2017), p.213.
22 Interview, Trade Representative A.
23 Nye, J., *Bound to Lead: The Changing Nature of American Power*, (London, Basic Books, 1990).
24 Interview, Trade Representative A.
25 HC Deb 16 May 2018 vol 641 c WS687.
26 See: DIT DSO, *DIT DSO UK export statistics for 2017: tables*. Available at: <https://assets.publishing.service.gov.uk/government/uploads/system/uploads/attachment_data/file/732588/Tables_-_DSO_Statistics_2017_-_V2.xlsx>.
27 Dempsey, N., *UK Defence Industry Exports*, House of Commons Library Briefing Paper: 8310, 18 May 2018, p.10.
28 Ibid., p.9.
29 HC Deb 19 December 2018 c 202327W.
30 HC Deb 19 September 2018 c 173554WA.
31 Select Committee on Soft Power and the UK's Influence, *Persuasion and Power in the Modern World*, 11 March 2014, HL 2013–14, Ev 252. Oral and Written Evidence – Volume 2, p.805.
32 HC Deb 4 May 2016 vol 609 c 93WH.
33 Jabarkhyl, N. (2017), 'Oman counts on Chinese billions to build desert boomtown', *Reuters*, 5 September. Available at: <https://www.reuters.com/article/us-oman-china-investment/oman-counts-on-chinese-billions-to-build-desert-boomtown-idUSKCN1BG1WJ> [accessed 7 January 2020].
34 Interview with a senior executive at Royal Dutch Shell, Oman (*Shell Executive*), (Muscat, 25 November 2018).
35 Interview with a senior Gulf-focused diplomat at the UK FCO, (London, 10 September 2018).
36 Hay, W.R., *The Persian Gulf States*, (Washington, DC, Middle East Institute, 1959), pp.66–67.
37 Interview, Shell Executive.
38 The other shareholders being French company Compagnie Française des Petroles (23.75%), American company the Near East Development Company (23.75%), and Partex (5%).
39 See: *Oman's General Budget for 2019*, Times of Oman. Available at: <https://timesofoman.com/article/674400/Oman/Omans-General-Budget-for-2019> [accessed 7 March 2019].

40 A BRIEF of The Ninth Five-Year Development Plan (2016–2020): A Plan Building on Achievements and Laying Foundations for the Future, (Muscat, Government of the Sultanate of Oman Supreme Council for Planning, 2016), p.21.
41 Ibid., p.34.
42 Fasano, U. and Iqbal, Z., *GCC Countries: From Oil Dependence to Diversification*, (Washington, DC, International Monetary Fund, 2003), p.7.
43 Gavin, J., (2012), 'Price could be right as BP targets Oman tight gas deal', *Interfax: Natural Gas*, Moscow, 13 September. Available at: <http://interfaxenergy.com/gasdaily/article/12095/price-could-be-right-as-bp-targets-oman-tight-gas-deal> [accessed 18 March 2019].
44 'Petronas buys stake in Khazzan field in Oman', *Oil & Gas Journal*, 22 October 2018. Available at: <https://www.ogj.com/articles/2018/10/petronas-buys-stake-in-khazzan-field-in-oman.html> [accessed 18 March 2019].
45 Interview with a former British diplomat, now an advisor on Gulf economics (*Gulf economics advisor A*), (London, 24 September 2018).
46 Malik, A., 'The Politics of Diversification in the Middle East', *Forum: A Quarterly Journal for Debating Energy Issues and Policies*, 118 (June 2019), pp.18–21.
47 Ibid.
48 Wilson III, E.J., 'Hard Power, Soft Power, Smart Power', *The Annals of the American Academy of Political and Social Science*, 616 (2008), p.112.
49 The unit was established by Royal Decree No. 50/2016 on 17 October 2016.
50 See: Implementation Support and Follow-Up Unit, *2017 Annual Report*, (Muscat, Implementation Support and Follow-Up Unit, 2017).
51 Holley, E., (2019), 'Savannah gets green light for copper in Oman', *Mining Journal*, 9 August. Available at: <https://www.mining-journal.com/copper-news/news/1369114/savannah-gets-green-light-for-copper-in-oman> [accessed 12 March 2020].
52 Interview with a British trade representative in Oman (*Trade Representative B*), (Muscat, 11 March 2019).
53 Interview, Trade Representative A.
54 The largest non-British business representations being the Oman American Business Center and the Australian Business Group Oman.
55 Interview, Business Representative A.
56 Ibid.
57 See: Portland, *The Soft Power 30: A Global Ranking of Soft Power 2019'*. Available at: <https://softpower30.com/wp-content/uploads/2019/10/The-Soft-Power-30-Report-2019-1.pdf> [accessed 3 December 2020].
58 Interview Trade Representative A.
59 Department for International Trade, *Trade and Investment Core Statistics Book*, (London, DIT, June 2019), p.12.
60 Ibid., p.10.
61 See: <https://atlas.media.mit.edu/en/profile/country/omn/>.
62 Office for National Statistics, UK Trade experimental quarterly trade in goods and services: July to September 2018, (London, ONS, 2018).
63 Rose, A.K., *Like Me, Buy Me: The Effect of Soft Power on Exports* – Working Paper 21537, (Cambridge, MA, National Bureau of Economic Research, 2015), p.12.
64 Blanton, S.L. and Blanton, R.G., 'What Attracts Foreign Investors? An Examination of Human Rights and Foreign Direct Investment', *The Journal of Politics*, 69:1 (2007), p.143.
65 Oman, C.P., *Policy Competition for Foreign Direct Investment: A Study of Competition among Governments to Attract FDI*, (Paris, Development Centre of the Organisation for Economic Co-operation and Development, 2000), p.12.
66 What Attracts Foreign Investors?, p.148.

67 Dixit, A., 'International Trade, Foreign Direct Investment, and Security', *Annual Review of Economics*, 3 (2011), p.198.
68 See: UK Export Finance, *UK Export Finance Performance Highlights, 2016–17*, (London, UKEF, 2017), p.7.; Available at: <https://www.gov.uk/government/publications/category-a-project-supported-liwa-plastics-oman/liwa-plastics-oman> [accessed 14 January 2020].
69 'MENA Supplement: Oman Trade & Investment Forum promotes Oman/British business relations', *World Commerce Review*, 4:4 (2010), p.i.
70 HL Deb 11 July 2017 vol 783 c 1229.
71 Note: 1967 is the year that oil was first exported from Oman, so it is important to highlight how the industry has developed since then; data for years 1997–99 and 2001–04 could not be found.
   Data for the period 1967–96 was taken from: Al Yousef, M.b.M., *From Underdevelopment to Sustainable Development: The Role of State and Market in Oman, 1970–2010*, (London, Third Millennium Publishing, 2015), p.262.; Data for the years 2000 and 2005–17 is from several issues of the *Annual Statistics Year Book* (years 2005–17), (Muscat, National Centre for Statistics & Information).
72 National Centre for Statistics and Information, *Statistics Bulletin: Foreign Investment – 2012–2016 (12th issue)*, (Muscat, NCSI, 2018), p.27.

Bibliography

A BRIEF of The Ninth Five-Year Development Plan (2016–2020): A Plan Building on Achievements and Laying Foundations for the Future, (Muscat, Government of the Sultanate of Oman Supreme Council for Planning, 2016).

Aitchison, C.U., *A Collection of Treaties, Engagements and Sanads Relating to India and Neighbouring Countries, (5th ed.)*, (Calcutta, Government of India Central Publication Branch, 1933), vol. 11.

Allen Jr., C.H. and Rigsbee II, W.L., *Oman under Qaboos: From Coup to Constitution, 1970–1996*, (London, Frank Cass Publishers, 2000).

Al Yousef, M.b.M., *From Underdevelopment to Sustainable Development: The Role of State and Market in Oman, 1970–2010*, (London, Third Millennium Publishing, 2015).

Annual Statistics Year Book (Years 2005–2017), (Muscat, National Centre for Statistics & Information).

Baker, J.C., *Financing International Trade*, (Westport, CT, Praeger Publishers, 2003).

Blanton, S.L. and Blanton, R.G., 'What Attracts Foreign Investors? An Examination of Human Rights and Foreign Direct Investment', *The Journal of Politics*, 69:1 (2007), pp.143–155.

British and Foreign State Papers, 1890–1891, (London, HMSO, 1897), vol. 83.

Dempsey, N., *UK Defence Industry Exports*, House of Commons Library Briefing Paper: 8310, 18 May 2018.

Department for International Trade, *Trade and Investment Core Statistics Book*, (London, DIT, June 2019).

DIT Analysis – Statistics Brief: 'Trade and Investment between the United Kingdom and Oman (data reported by the UK)', (London, Department for International Trade, 2018).

DIT DSO, *Defence exports (based on orders/contracts signed): Estimated UK and competitor percentage market shares (2008 to 2017)*. Available at: <https://www.gov.uk/government/uploads/system/uploads/attachment_data/file/729935/Chart01.csv/preview>, [accessed 17 March 2019].

DIT DSO, *DIT DSO UK export statistics for 2017: tables*. Available at: <https://assets.publishing.service.gov.uk/government/uploads/system/uploads/attachment_data/file/732588/Tables_-_DSO_Statistics_2017_-_V2.xlsx>.

Dixit, A., 'International Trade, Foreign Direct Investment, and Security', *Annual Review of Economics*, 3 (2011), pp.191–214.

Fasano, U. and Iqbal, Z., *GCC Countries: From Oil Dependence to Diversification*, (Washington, DC, International Monetary Fund, 2003).

Gavin, J., (2012), 'Price could be right as BP targets Oman tight gas deal', *Interfax: Natural Gas*, Moscow, 13 September. Available at: <http://interfaxenergy.com/gasdaily/article/12095/price-could-be-right-as-bp-targets-oman-tight-gas-deal> [accessed 18 March 2019].

Hay, W.R., *The Persian Gulf States*, (Washington, DC, Middle East Institute, 1959).

HC Deb 17 September 2015 vol 599 cc389–390WH.

HC Deb 4 May 2016 vol 609 c 93WH.

HL Deb 11 July 2017 vol 783 c 1229.

HC Deb 16 May 2018 vol 641 c WS687.

HC Deb 19 September 2018 c 173554WA.

HC Deb 19 December 2018 c 202327W.

HC Deb 23 May 2019 vol 660 c854.

Holley, E., (2019), 'Savannah gets green light for copper in Oman', *Mining Journal*, 9 August. Available at: <https://www.mining-journal.com/copper-news/news/1369114/savannah-gets-green-light-for-copper-in-oman> [accessed 12 March 2020].

Implementation Support and Follow-Up Unit, *2017 Annual Report*, (Muscat, Implementation Support and Follow-Up Unit, 2017).

Interview with a British trade representative in Oman (*Trade Representative B*), (Muscat, 11 March 2019).

Interview with a former British diplomat, now an advisor on Gulf economics (Gulf economics advisor A), (London, 24 September 2018).

Interview with a senior executive at Royal Dutch Shell, Oman (*Shell Executive*), (Muscat, 25 November 2018).

Interview with a senior Gulf-focused diplomat at the UK FCO, (London, 10 September 2018).

Interview with a senior representative of the UK Department for International Trade (*Trade Representative A*), (Muscat, 11 March 2019).

Jabarkhyl, N. (2017), 'Oman counts on Chinese billions to build desert boom-town', *Reuters*, 5 September. Available at: <https://www.reuters.com/article/us-oman-china-investment/oman-counts-on-chinese-billions-to-build-desert-boomtown-idUSKCN1BG1WJ> [accessed 7 January 2020].

Jeffreys, A. (ed.), *The Report: Oman 2014*, (Dubai, Oxford Business Group, 2014).

Legatum Institute, *Global Index of Economic Openness 2019*, (London, Legatum Institute, 2019).

Malik, A., 'The Politics of Diversification in the Middle East', *Forum: A Quarterly Journal for Debating Energy Issues and Policies*, 118 (June 2019), pp.18–21.

Mason, R., *Foreign Policy in Iran and Saudi Arabia: Economics and Diplomacy in the Middle East*, (London, I.B.Tauris & Co Ltd, 2015).

Ministry of Defence, *Growing the Contribution of Defence to UK Prosperity: A Report for the Secretary of State for Defence*, (Ministry of Defence, Government Communication Service, 2018).

'MENA Supplement: Oman Trade & Investment Forum Promotes Oman/British Business Relations', *World Commerce Review*, 4:4 (2010), pp.i–iii.

'Muscat No.1 (1952), Cmd.8462.

National Centre for Statistics and Information, *Statistics Bulletin: Foreign Investment – 2012–2016 (12th issue)*, (Muscat, NCSI, 2018).

Nye, J., *Bound to Lead: The Changing Nature of American Power*, (London, Basic Books, 1990).

Oman, C.P., *Policy Competition for Foreign Direct Investment: A Study of Competition among Governments to Attract FDI*, (Paris, Development Centre of the Organisation for Economic Co-operation and Development, 2000).

Oman's General Budget for 2019, Times of Oman. Available at: <https://timesofoman.com/article/674400/Oman/Omans-General-Budget-for-2019> [accessed 7 March 2019].

Office for National Statistics, *UK Trade Experimental Quarterly Trade in Goods and Services: July to September 2018*, (London, ONS, 2018).

'Petronas buys stake in Khazzan field in Oman', *Oil & Gas Journal*, 22 October 2018. Available at: <https://www.ogj.com/articles/2018/10/petronas-buys-stake-in-khazzan-field-in-oman.html> [accessed 18 March 2019].

Portland, *The Soft Power 30: A Global Ranking of Soft Power 2019'*. Available at: <https://softpower30.com/wp-content/uploads/2019/10/The-Soft-Power-30-Report-2019-1.pdf> [accessed 3 December 2020].

Rose, A.K., *Like Me, Buy Me: The effect of soft power on exports* – Working Paper 21537, (Cambridge, MA, National Bureau of Economic Research, 2015).

Select Committee on Soft Power and the UK's Influence, *Persuasion and Power in the Modern World*, 11 March 2014, HL 2013–14, Ev 252. Oral and Written Evidence – Volume 2.

Smith, R. and Fontanel, J., 'Weapons procurement: Domestic production versus imports', in I. Bellany and T. Huxley (eds.), *Conventional Weapons and Western Defence*, (London, Frank Cass & Co. Ltd, 1987), pp.69–83.

UK Export Finance, *Export Credits Guarantee Department (UK Export Finance): Annual Report and Accounts 2016–17*, (London, HMSO, 2017).

UK Export Finance, *UK Export Finance Performance Highlights, 2016–17*, (London, UKEF, 2017). Available at: <https://www.gov.uk/government/publications/category-a-project-supported-liwa-plastics-oman/liwa-plastics-oman> [accessed 14 January 2020].

United Kingdom Treaty Series, No. 29 (1939), Cmd.6037.

Wilson, E.J. III, 'Hard Power, Soft Power, Smart Power', *The ANNALS of the American Academy of Political and Social Science*, 616:1 (2008), pp.110–124.

6 The development of UK–Bahraini economic influence since withdrawal

6.1 Introduction

Britain's economic relations with Bahrain are indelibly linked with the historic Political Residency, which chose Manama as its base in 1946 after relocating from Bushire directly across the waters of the Gulf. Prosperity was undoubtedly always a priority for decision makers in Britain, India, and the Gulf and was the underlying concern of policy makers involved with the decision to choose Bahrain over other Gulf states. As the new base of the Residency, complete with a large, educated expatriate community from across the British Empire, a need for banks, a functioning judiciary, shops, a taxation system, and a functioning free market, the Bahraini capital, Manama, was the first of the major cities in the Gulf to develop the economic tenets of a modern state. Bahrain was arguably an unlikely base of the Residency before the relocation was announced; relations with the rulers of Oman were seemingly closer than with the Al Khalifa family in Bahrain and Oman was located in a geostrategic location at the entrance to the Gulf. Nevertheless, the Residency was based in Manama for 25 years, and this historical background perhaps offers an explanation as to how and why Bahrain still remains an influential market for British goods and Bahrain still respects Britain as a partner in prosperity.

Representatives of the East India Company, who were the first Britons to show an interest in the Gulf, attempted to gain allies across the region to ensure that trade could pass through the waters of the Gulf to India as smoothly as possible, trade being the main impetus for much of their actions. Bahrain's ruler in November 1838, Shaikh 'Abd Allah bin Ahmad Al Khalifa, offered support for the Government of India's presence in the Gulf in return for occasional support from British gunboats. The request, put forward to the Government of India by Resident Captain Samuel Hennell, was initially rejected by lawmakers in Bombay and Calcutta.[1] It was only in 1880 and 1892, when Bahraini rulers signed treaties that handed British authorities sweeping powers over foreign and economic affairs, that the economy of Bahrain began to be developed on a British model. Although it was not officially acknowledged until 1907, the Bahraini protectorate increasingly

DOI: 10.4324/9781003302001-8

came under British economic influence. The early years of the Residency witnessed close cooperation between British and Bahraini nationals, but the relationship shifted towards British domination as the importance of Bahrain emerged.

As early as 1829, Bahraini officials were employed by the Residency to focus specifically on coordinating trade. In 1904, a British diplomat based in Manama was employed as Assistant Resident to focus specifically on attracting business from British companies, with the position being renamed Political Agent.[2] Bahraini customs and taxation also came fully under British control in 1904, with the Viceroy of India, Lord Curzon, determined to realise his desire that 'the Gulf represent[ed] one of India's imperial frontiers.'[3] To control the finances of Bahrain and to ensure that local spending could be determined by the Residency, Curzon ordered a restructuring of the customs agency, bringing it into line with the customs and excise departments in the Raj. To successfully achieve this, Bahraini customs were taken under the control of a trusted Indian firm of accountants, with all accounts kept in a north Indian language, thought to have been Sindhi. Bringing customs into the British economic sphere was arguably a less adversarial way to exert control over the most important domestic lever of the Bahraini state, money, without directly controlling the state as a colony.[4] The first Director of the customs agency, a British man named Claude de Grenier who stayed in post between 1924 and 1943, was responsible for restructuring the customs house and recruiting a number of clerks to work in the newly established state treasury.[5] Historically, British power was firmly coercive in nature.

6.2 British economic influence in the years after withdrawal

In March 1974, just three years after withdrawal, Lord Denman, the Chairman of the Committee for Middle East Trade, noticed on a visit to Bahrain that the bilateral economic relationship between Britain and Bahrain was under strain. He wrote in a report of his visit that

> political relations with Bahrain are extremely good at present. There is a strong tradition of close commercial relations, but these are showing signs of strain owing to the poor delivery times by most British firms. As a result, although Britain is still Bahrain's largest single supplier, its market share is declining.[6]

The fact that British companies were not delivering orders on time is not an issue that has been raised in any other reports, but if this was the case, it would undermine the trust that Bahraini officials had in their purchases from Britain and thus weaken the soft power influence that Britain had in the state. Senior UK government officials were aware that the bilateral economic relationship was facing challenges, including a recognition that the hegemonic market share that British companies historically took for granted in Bahrain was no longer secure. Aside from efforts to support defence trade with Bahrain, and smaller-scale initiatives in other areas of the economic relationship, the British Government has seemingly not responded to this loss of influence effectively, nor has the British position strengthened in a noticeable way since this report was produced in the years shortly after Britain's withdrawal from the economic affairs of the Kingdom. However, efforts have been made by both governments to build upon the foundations of the prosperity relationship, albeit now on a voluntary basis rather than as a result of treaties that were in force until 1971. Nye and others defined trust as one of the most important contributors to inter-state soft power, and on an economic level, it is necessary for a post-withdrawal Britain to meet its commitments to ensure that the attraction that drew Bahraini rulers to Britain is retained.

Since March 2013, the British–Bahraini relationship is being upheld at senior levels by biannual meetings of the *Joint Bahraini-British Working Group* (JBBWG), through the promotion of joint economic and cultural initiatives. After the first meeting, a joint statement was released by Alistair Burt, former Minister for the Middle East and North Africa, and Sheikh Khalid, Bahraini Minister of Foreign Affairs, to highlight the purpose of the six-monthly meetings; the first time that regular bilateral meetings between the two states had been held since withdrawal. The statement stated:

> Underlining the close and open relationship between Bahrain and the UK, Sheikh Khalid bin Ahmed bin Mohammed Al Khalifa and Mr Burt, together with ministers and senior officials from several Bahraini ministries, discussed a wide range of bilateral and regional issues, including cooperation on key trade and investment opportunities. ... Officials from both governments will work together, monitoring and evaluating areas of co-operation and assistance ...[7]

Meetings such as this were undoubtedly an attempt by the British Government to ensure that Britain remained relevant in Bahrain.

6.2.1 Bilateralism and a shift in the relationship

Although economics is only one issue of focus for the JBBWG, it is an important topic of discussion. The meetings are seemingly an attempt to diversify the relationship away from a reliance on the defence trade, which has proven to be the mainstay of British–Bahraini affairs. This working group is an influential method of power for the British Government. By holding bilateral meetings twice per year, Britain is demonstrating that Bahrain is still an important ally and a priority partner. These meetings also seemingly ensure that British Ministers continue to have a personal influence within Bahraini domestic affairs, albeit limited and not to the same extent as during the

Residency. The fact that these meetings are taking place at all is evidence of a historic shift in the bilateral relationship. Historically, there was no need for Britain to actively court Bahrain because the protectorate and exclusivity treaties ensured that Britain had an unrivalled influence in the country, but after withdrawal, Britain's unrivalled influence was quickly diminished. In contemporary times, Britain must put in the effort to secure its influence, and the working group is one tenet of this modern relationship.

Bahrain's willingness to host regular meetings with British representatives is evidence of British soft power in action. Bahrain is evidently still attracted to what Britain can offer and thus wants to retain a channel of communication so that they can access British guidance, trade and support. As the relationship has developed, however, Britain has become reliant on Bahrain as a destination country for trade as a result of the increased competition since 1971. The Bahraini–British Working Group is a high-level attempt to ensure that both parties are able to both develop and expand the relationship and as a roundtable to discuss issues that affect the strength of the relationship, such as alleged human rights infringements. A former senior British diplomat who served in the Gulf explained that

> the British influence in the Gulf has not necessarily declined, rather the American and French influence has increased. France's influence on defence sales has impacted the British influence because of their increased agility and effectiveness. Some Gulf states do not wish to appear beholden to the British.[8]

Charles Wright Mills, in *The Power Elite*, wrote that power and economics are inextricably linked, and decisions made by the three different levels of the power elite – government, military and corporate – ultimately define the strength of a state's influence.[9] Steven Lukes claimed that 'power can also be seen to be at work in shaping beliefs and preferences that can adversely affect people's interests.'[10] Lukes was referring to the hard power basis on which influence is traditionally associated; the basis on which British influence was first established in Bahrain. Building upon the theory of Bertrand Russell, who detailed economic power as the ability to control the materials for the cultivation of a state's resources, and to be able to meet market demands of others,[11] Lukes explained that power is not necessarily clearly defined as coercion. In the case of Britain in Bahrain, power can emerge as the result of unintended norms. He wrote that:

> Power is not only to be seen in the first dimension, where you have observable conflict, where the most obvious case is visible and observable coercion ... power need not involve intention; that the most effective forms of power can be the result of others complying without the powerful even knowing it or intending it; for example, by merely following the dictates of roles and norms with unintended consequences.[12]

154 *Trade and the power of money*

The economic legacy in Bahrain may be a consequence of hard power control over the financial levers, and research suggests that this legacy is still significant for determining the British influence over the domestic Bahraini economy, but withdrawal has had an impact and the British Government has had to try to secure the diminishing influence and build upon the remaining power leverage. There are, of course, numerous private sector partnerships between British and Bahraini companies which could be interpreted as a continuation of British power, most notably between Formula One and the Bahrain International Circuit and flag carrier Gulf Air and Chelsea Football Club. This research does not, however, intend to examine cultural partnerships such as these.

6.3 The arms trade since withdrawal

Defence exports are a key factor that has seemingly emerged as a bellwether to withdrawal and the diminishing British influence in other aspects of Bahraini affairs and cannot be considered from a solely strategic perspective. Arms sales are also an important economic factor and a significant convergence point between Britain's economic and strategic influence in Bahrain. The sale of weapons and defence-related equipment to Bahrain is to be considered an important method for preserving British influence in the Kingdom and the projection of power capabilities that both the British Government and British companies are able to utilise. A crucial point that becomes apparent when assessing the strength of bilateral defence trade relations, a relationship that is almost entirely weighted towards Britain, is that other states have gradually weakened the influence that Britain has on supplying arms to Bahrain as the years have progressed since withdrawal. There are many examples of trade discussions between senior British and Bahraini officials throughout the 1980s, most focusing on Bahrain's armament requirements for modernisation programmes. Between 1971 and 1982, trade discussions between Britain and Bahrain were sparse. This could be explained either as a result of Bahrain spending the 1970s establishing itself as an independent power in the Gulf and deciding how the Kingdom would develop and utilise its economic assets both domestically and internationally, or because of the rift that developed between the two governments as a result of Britain's rather hurried withdrawal from the Gulf and the resulting loss of British influence. The actual reason for the seeming lack of close economic cooperation was likely a combination of the two and Britain's position in relation to the development of future economic relations with the Gulf states being unclear until Margaret Thatcher secured her power as Prime Minister.

In the second half of the first Thatcher administration, around 1982, British Government ministries and private companies began to reopen and expand upon lines of communication with the Gulf states, with the Government of Bahrain being a major beneficiary of this attempt to re-establish Britain

Development of UK–Bahraini economic influence 155

as a trusted trade partner in the region. Senior Bahraini Government and military officials increasingly consulted British diplomats in the country on the defence trade, requesting presentations on weapons and equipment produced by British manufacturers and declaring their intention to purchase weapons from Britain.

In 1982, Roger Tomkys, the British Ambassador in Bahrain, was told by a British official close to the Bahraini Ministry of Defence that:

> on the equipment side they [Bahrain] made it plain they were delighted to be (about to be) in a financial position to consider equipment purchases from this country [Britain] again. They have evidently concluded that it is in the areas of armour and of air to ground, and perhaps air defence, missiles that UK material can best meet their new requirements.[13]

This re-engagement by the Government of Bahrain is a symbol that although Britain had withdrawn from all aspects of Bahraini affairs in 1971 and had allowed a hiatus in the relationship to develop since that time, Bahrain was still attracted to weapons produced by British companies and the relationship, even though the US had become the main supplier by this time. It could be argued, therefore, that a British soft power influence was retained as a result of the defence legacy present in the Kingdom. This soft power, as opposed to physical boots on the ground, can be attributed partly to the influence that arises from joint economic ties between the two states and the peace that has endured for more than a century. Norman Angell claimed that economic interdependence between states contributes to the prevention of war and this is worth considering in relation to defence trade between the two states. Contemporary industrialisation has resulted in the economies of some states becoming so inextricably linked that this relationship can be used by policymakers in one state to get the other state to do what they want – in the case of Britain's defence sales, this would be the purchase of weapons.

6.3.1 *The power dimension of arms sales*

Keohane and Nye, in reference to interdependent power, argued that state behaviour is dominated by the looming and constant threat of conflict.[14] This could offer an explanation as to why British defence manufacturers have been able to retain an amount of influence over Bahraini arms purchases. The Government of Bahrain undoubtedly understands its precarious situation between an increasingly interventionist Iran and a militarily powerful Saudi Arabia, so the perceived need to constantly modernise and expand its own defence capabilities has been offering British manufacturers avenues for indirect intervention since re-engagement in the 1980s. Although Bahrain can now choose to buy arms from companies around the world, there still exists a reliance on British companies within the small pool of

156 *Trade and the power of money*

arms suppliers approved by the Government of Bahrain. This reliance within Bahrain has given the British Government limited influence over Bahraini defence decisions.

The UK DIT, and its predecessors, have partnered with British Ambassadors and trade envoys in Bahrain to court the government there to ensure that they remain aware of Britain's abilities to supply the Bahraini security forces with weapons and equipment at times of modernisation. These British trade officials are one element of Britain's power assets in Bahrain, and the influence of the marketing efforts by these officials is significant. In 1983, the UK MoD arranged a showcase for British-manufactured military aircraft in Al Dhafra, in the UAE, and Bahraini military officials expressed interest in two different variations of Tornado aircraft:

> The presentation at Al Dhafra was well received. In closed discussion afterwards Captain Khalid (A and O) expressed the view that they were interested in Tornado F2 in the longer term, but of more immediate interest was the acquisition of 8 to 12 Tornado IDS for deep penetration missions against area and strategic targets. ... The objectives of our visit were therefore achieved; the value of the Tornado F2 in the Gulf was acknowledged ...[15]

6.3.2 *The impact of marketing British arms to Bahraini decision makers*

The British Government, via both trade and defence departments, has regularly arranged for Bahraini officials to see British equipment in operation in an attempt to sell this equipment in the face of increased competition from countries that were barred from selling to Bahrain until 1971. This is a process that is also used in Oman to attract orders, but in Oman, the marketing of equipment is via the large-scale *Saif Saarea* joint training exercises, whereas in Bahrain, it is on a more conventional ad hoc small-scale basis. Prior to the establishment of UKTI, later renamed DIT, much of the marketing of weapons and aircraft in Bahrain was undertaken directly by MoD officials, some based in London and others in the Gulf. Until the establishment of a semi-independent trade promotion department in May 1999, when British Trade International was founded, comprising Trade Partners UK to promote British exports, and Invest UK to attract investments into the UK, defence sales between Britain and Bahrain were on a government-to-government basis; this enabled the British Government to make use of the influence that had been retained after withdrawal. This bilateral governmental link was important for Britain's influence as no other country had the historic legacy of a 150-year presence in Bahrain. As more countries started to sell to Bahrain, this historic legacy was a launchpad from which Britain could promote sales to Bahraini decision makers. Ambassador Tomkys wrote in a telegram to the FCO in London that he was of the belief

Development of UK–Bahraini economic influence 157

that defence sales should not be considered solely as an economic matter, rather the arms trade should form part of the wider British political agenda for dealings with Bahrain. He wrote:

> Defence sales should be put in the context of Government-to-Government relations. I have suggested a Memorandum of Understanding or general letter of comfort to Shaikh Hamad from Mr Heseltine. The chances of selling the Vickers tank may depend directly on this. The climate for other sales would be improved considerably. DMAO has an important role to play in the same fashion, putting defence sales in the context of shared political interests rather than the commercial marketplace.[16]

The point raised by Tomkys, that defence sales are dependent on bilateral relations between the two governments, is an important factor to consider. On 3 April 1982, Brigadier Khalifa, Bahraini Chief of Staff, told Tomkys 'that the BDF wish to acquire a battalion of tanks and armoured personnel carriers ... The British tank of interest to Brigadier Khalifa was the Vickers Valiant ... The minimum BDF requirement was for 20 tanks and 40 APCs.'[17] It is not clear whether the Government of Bahrain directly approached the Ambassador to request his assistance with the purchase or the point was raised in a wider discussion, but what is clear is that the British Government was aware of its ability to exert some influence on decision-making by the Bahrainis. In the same year, manufacturer Vickers-Armstrongs approached ECGD to arrange credit financing for a Valiant bomber contract for Bahrain. 'Mr Bianco tells me Vickers have now had discussions with ECGD, Lazards and Williams and Glyns about the possibility of a supplier or buyer credit facility for a total order of £30–40m for Valiant.'[18]

Although the power debate generally focuses on Britain's power capabilities within the international system, by purchasing state of the art weapons from British companies, Bahrain attempted to enhance its own power through capability. The number and quality of the weapons that the Government of Bahrain has at its disposal contributes to its own power. This theory of power assumes that Bahraini decision makers have the independence to make their own decisions about which companies and countries to purchase from, but there are several high-profile examples where British manufacturers have still been chosen despite higher costs.

6.3.3 Competition to Britain's retained hegemony

Bahrain has also shifted its alliances and supplier partnerships since 1971, from a situation where the British Government was the only power able to dictate who Bahrain could purchase weapons from, to one where formerly barred states were quickly establishing a strong foothold in the Kingdom, led by the US. Bahrain was the most exclusive of the Residency states. The Exclusivity agreements in place ensured that defence sales to Bahrain could only come from Britain or states approved by the Residency. Of the countries that moved into the former British sphere in Bahrain, France and the US became the main British rivals. Throughout the first half of the 1980s, British diplomats and MoD officials in Bahrain reported back to Westminster that the once unrivalled British influence was no longer. Britain could no longer rely on Bahrain to buy from British companies, and diplomats had to actively sell British weapons. Post-withdrawal, Britain had to rely on its soft power strength in Bahrain to retain its presence as a major defence supplier during times of modernisation. This soft power influence was demonstrable in 1976 when the DSO reported that Prince Hamad, the son of former Emir Shaikh Isa and future King, wanted to buy arms from British manufacturers for the first major military modernisation since withdrawal. It was reported by a representative that:

> Dr Shehab told me that Prince Hamad remains keen to explore further the possibility of aircraft sales from the UK – one squadron plus full training, spares, and other support services. ... Dr Shehab went on to explain that Prince Hamad wished not only to consider the possibility of Jaguar but also the alternative of the Harrier, which has the advantage of being an all-British project.[19]

The strong British legacy as a trusted supplier to the Bahraini military cannot be underestimated as an important contributor to British influence, but situations such as this did not offer a true representation of the wider attitude amongst Bahraini decision makers. Other states had established their presence in Bahrain, and competitiveness for price and quality arguably became more influential than a longing to retain a British footprint. Tomkys highlighted in a telegram that the US and Saudi had established a position of influence in Bahraini defence affairs and were doing the work that was previously reserved for the British, and thus making it more likely that the Government of Bahrain would choose to buy weapons from non-British companies. Tomkys noted in 1983 that

> a US Army Corps of Engineers team had recently visited Bahrain ... This work would be paid for by the Saudis (cost, I think, Dollars 15 million) who would also arrange to wet lease the BDF a half-dozen F5E and F5F aircraft in about eighteen months. ... The BDF have 15–20 pilots who have trained or are training on F5s with RSAF in Dhahran.[20]

Providing free training to Bahraini pilots on American fighter aircraft and offering to lease rather than sell these aircraft to Bahrain is an important example of how the US can utilise smart power to achieve its commercial goals. The basic definition of smart power is a combination of soft power attraction to what a state can offer and hard power physical assets in the receiving state, so by offering free training on American aircraft, and eventually leasing these aircraft to the Bahrainis at favourable prices – and necessitating the secondment of American maintenance employees to Bahrain – the US Government has effectively manufactured an attraction to its aircraft and secured a new trading partnership. Ernest Wilson suggested that smart power is dependent on the dissemination of the knowledge of military technology by one state to another, which can then be sold to the weaker state by the more powerful state within the relationship. Teaching the Bahrainis on American aircraft could be interpreted as the sharing of knowledge and technology by the US Government.

6.3.4 The emergence of a competitive arms sales process

The US–Bahrain security relationship is as crucial for the projection of American power in the Middle East as the UK–Bahraini relationship is for projecting British power, but the main recipient of US military assistance and arms sales is the Bahrain Defence Force.

> Most U.S. military assistance to Bahrain is in the form of Foreign Military Financing (FMF), used to help Bahrain buy and maintain U.S.-origin weapons, to enhance interoperability with U.S. forces as well as with other GCC forces, to augment Bahrain's air defences, and to improve counterterrorism capabilities.[21]

The US has regularly sent 'excess defence articles' (EDA) – surplus military equipment that is no longer needed by the US military – to Bahrain since 1993. More than $400 million worth of EDA has been sent to Bahrain by various US Governments since 1993, including 50 M-60A3 tanks on a five-year no cost lease in 1995 and an FFG-7 Perry Class Subha frigate in 1997.[22] It is believed that around 85% of Bahraini arms purchases year-on-year are from US manufacturers, with a total since 1993 of between $4 and $5 billion according to open-source data.

In recent years, there has been an increase in potential contracts under consideration by the US State Department. In 2018 and 2019, contracts for the sale of 12 AH-1Z attack helicopters and related equipment and missiles worth $911.4 million,[23] the refurbishment of the Oliver Hazard Perry Class ship (formerly known as Robert G. Bradley) at a cost of $150 million in preparation for the sale to Bahrain,[24] and the sale of a Patriot Missile System worth $2.478 billion[25] were approved. The overt commitment that the US authorities demonstrate to Bahrain by providing their Bahraini counterparts with free or favourably priced arms arguably replaces the position that Britain held prior to 1971. The soft power that the US can exert upon Bahraini arms decisions does, however, take away a significant amount of influence from the British Government to do the same. The American strategic relationship with Bahrain is seemingly more rounded than the British one, with arms sales integrated into the wider relationship, and this is likely a major reason why the US has been able to establish such a strong influence in a relatively short amount of time. The US can assist the Government of Bahrain with its strategic modernisation in a way that Britain no longer can.

This challenge to Britain's defence sales in Bahrain was also evident in the French presence in the Kingdom in the early 1980s. In 1983, Tomkys wrote 'we have noted intense French activity with the Gulf states in the past month. The BDF's request for a firm offer on F1 aircraft looks ominously like a competitor for the possible Hawk purchases.'[26] In the same year, the Ambassador again raised the issue of the intensification of France's attempt to increase its own influence in the realm of defence economics when he told the MoD in London that

> the BDF have recently changed their tune, spoken well about their Panhards and implied that French armour may be an option for their own requirements. It is suggested that the French may also make a heavy play for Exocet and for their Puma helicopters.[27]

In an attempt to counter this increased competition, the MoD has used its presence in Bahrain to intensively market the weapons that it uses. In 1982, there was evidence that this tactic was starting to pay off, as reported in a letter sent by a representative of the MoD to the Embassy.

> The party seemed well impressed by both these vehicle types (Mark 4 Vickers Valiant tank and MCV 80 range of armoured carriers), and implied that what they had previously seen of French vehicles had been less satisfactory. ... I might add that that Col Ahmad made a point in private discussions we had, of stressing that he and his colleagues saw their visit as a stage in a welcome process of reinvolvement of this country in the defence and security of the Gulf area.[28]

A process of re-engagement in the 1980s by Britain in Bahraini defence affairs arguably marked a shift in the economic relationship. Prior to withdrawal, Britain was the only supplier of arms to Bahrain, between 1971 and the start of the 1980s, British companies lost much of their ability to sell to the Government of Bahrain because of the increased influence that competitors were having, and then from the start of the 1980s, British suppliers had to market their weapons to compete with non-British companies that had established a physical presence in the Kingdom. In 1987, it was announced that

> Bahrain have selected the British Aerospace Sea Skua Helicopters launched missile (£4 million) and at present are evaluating various platform options, including the Westland Lynx. ... Sea Skua (BAE) - £400m ... Rapier (BAE) - £49m ... Lynx (Westland Helicopters) - £26m.[29]

There is no evidence to support or contradict the argument that these orders were the result of increased marketing by the British Government to their Bahraini counterparts, but it is notable that BAE is the recipient of the largest orders for critical arms, just as in Oman.

Economic soft power is notable for the requirement of a presence to reinforce the sentiment held within the minds of decision makers. It is important to note that the increased presence of representatives from British manufacturers was enhanced from 1983, the year when Margaret Thatcher secured election victory for the second time; relations with Bahrain, and advances in arms sales to the Gulf states, are noticeably stronger during Conservative administrations. Domestic politics within Britain has an impact on the influence that British companies can exert in the Gulf.

6.3.5 British attempts to retain influence in Bahrain

Unlike in Oman, where there has been strong evidence within the senior ranks of the government for favouring British defence equipment since withdrawal, the situation in Bahrain is different. Bahrain is still a key export market for British defence manufacturers, but it could be argued that the British Government, in cooperation with private manufacturers, must actively market weapons and related defence equipment. There has been a strong British presence at the annual *Bahrain International Defence Exhibition and Conference* (BIDEC) since it was first held in October 2017. The purpose of BIDEC is to act as a marketplace for international companies to showcase their equipment to Bahraini decision makers, and the British contingent has consistently been one of the largest, with DIT offering financial support and advice to British companies looking to sell defence equipment to Bahrain. The most senior officials of the Government of Bahrain attend BIDEC each year, with the Commander-in-Chief of the Bahrain Defence Force, Sheikh Khalifa bin Ahmed Al Khalifa telling an audience at the opening ceremony in 2017 that BIDEC provides a forum for developing international military cooperation and to support the enhancement of Bahrain's military industry, which is important for Bahraini economic diversification.[30] The British presence at BIDEC 2019 was supported by DIT DSO, the British Government's defence trade body, which offers financial and practical assistance to British defence companies in the form of delegation management, VIP speaker recruitment, marketing, arranging meetings between companies and government representatives, and engagement with an export support team of serving military personnel who can offer practical advice and training.

BIDEC is organised by a British events company, Clarion Events, which also organises the biannual Defence and Security Equipment International (DSEI) arms fair in London. The Government of Bahrain's hiring of a British company to organise one of the most important events in the Kingdom's annual calendar is possibly demonstrable of Bahraini trust and respect for Britain and the historic relationship between the two states; it could also be purely because Clarion have experience in organising events of this nature, or it could be a combination of the two – the Government of Bahrain choosing to hire Clarion because they are experienced in organising defence events and because they have the support of the British Government and British manufacturers. Despite this strong British presence at the premier arms showcase, the October 2017 issue of the *Diplomatic Gazette*, distributed by the Bahraini Ministry of Foreign Affairs, stated that on the second day of BIDEC 2017, 'the Bahrain Defence Force (BDF) has announced the signing of a $3.8 billion-deal with Lockheed Martin to buy 16 upgraded F16- aircraft.'[31] Again, the physical presence of British manufacturers in Bahrain was the method chosen to secure the legacy of Britain's influence in the Kingdom, but the hold that the British Government once had in Bahrain was evidently no longer strong. The marketing of British arms to Bahraini decision makers was an attempt to utilise referent power to bolster Britain's influence over Bahrain's arms purchases, but it is not always successful.

6.3.6 Re-engagement and arms sales since withdrawal

The government-to-government ties and the resulting defence sales were ultimately accountable to the presence of a British soft power influence in Bahrain. It would be amiss to suggest that there are no arms sales to Bahrain in the contemporary era, because BAE Systems remains one of the preferred suppliers within the Government of Bahrain, but it would also be incorrect to claim that the hegemonic position enjoyed by British manufacturers from 1820 had not evolved in unison with other aspects of the relationship. The nature of arms sales makes it impossible to detach this aspect of the relationship from hard power, because there will always be elements of force required to uphold influence over the sale of weapons. However, the ability of British companies to retain their channels to sell arms to the Bahraini armed forces requires several forms of soft power – attraction by Bahraini decision makers to British-manufactured weapons and related defence equipment, trust in the reliability of these weapons, and a belief that they are being offered a financially appropriate deal, but also the power of officials within the Government of Bahrain to exert influence on their British counterparts to attract lower prices and better aftercare as competition has intensified since 1971.

Soft power through hard power arms sales sounds like a contradiction in concepts, but the marketing and sales of arms from Britain to Bahrain forms a branch of the new diplomacy introduced in the 1980s when Thatcher began to re-engage with the former Residency states after a hiatus of a decade. The post-1971 economic defence relationship between Britain and Bahrain represents the shift that has occurred. 'Prior to the 1970s, most arms supplied (especially to the developing countries) were the surplus and obsolete weapons of the major powers, which they wanted to eliminate from their inventories.'[32] Since 1971, the British arms industry has developed its competitiveness and openly markets its goods to the Bahraini authorities. Broad political considerations in both states, Bahrain's desire to continuously modernise its military and Britain's ambition to secure and expand on its commercial opportunities in Bahrain, secure bilateral power and replace physical military intervention with commercial processes are important factors. The US replaced Britain as the preferred arms supplier in 1971, and American companies quickly established their presence within the Bahraini royal court, but the likes of BAE have been able to utilise the historic legacy as the only supplier to the state to retain a footprint, regardless of how diminished it has become since withdrawal.

6.4 British power retention within Bahrain's economic diversification

The diversification of Bahraini economics is just as notable as defence relations. Bahrain was the first country to start its diversification away from oil because of limited supplies. The Bahraini oil industry was the first to be developed, with the Bahrain Petroleum Company (BAPCO) refinery being built in 1935 by Standard Oil Company of California (SoCal), who obtained the only concession in 1930. In 1936, half of the concession was sold to Texaco, and in 1980, the state-owned Bahrain National Oil Company purchased a controlling 60% stake in the oil refinery, with Caltex retaining the remaining 40%. It is significant that the Bahraini oil industry, one of the most important sectors in the Kingdom, was developed without the same British control that was present in Oman's PDO. Although Bahrain was historically at the centre of the Persian Gulf Residency and the first of the Gulf states to begin the process of economic development, the oil industry was always controlled by the Americans. This is an important factor, as the concession being awarded to SoCal was evidence of a loss of control and influence by the British authorities over the oil industry in its early stages, decades before withdrawal was even considered.

Although the Exclusivity Agreement, which restricted the Bahraini authorities from working solely with companies registered in the British Empire was technically still in force in 1935, the unrivalled British influence in Bahraini affairs at the time was arguably undermined by the methods used by SoCal to secure their investments. As SoCal was not registered in a country within the British Empire, it was ineligible to invest in Bahrain, so instead the company established a wholly owned Canadian subsidiary named BAPCO.[33] This subsidiary developed a dependency on American funding and expertise in what would become the largest contributor to domestic prosperity for almost a century. The indirect presence of large American energy companies in Bahraini economic affairs also established US soft power into the national infrastructure of the state, the opposite of the situation in Oman. When half of BAPCO shares were sold to Texaco in 1936, the new company Caltex was registered in the Bahamas, again to circumvent the British bias that was established within the Bahraini political system.[34] When the first barrels of oil were exported from Bahrain, they were in US ships, and according to Jeffrey Nugent, 'the US companies that came [to Bahrain] were not only oil companies, but also included numerous contractors and sub-contractors, law firms, oil drilling operators, and various service providers.'[35] This US presence in Bahrain's economics formed a backdrop to the development of the contemporary economy that would emerge after 1971.

The indirect involvement in domestic affairs by American companies in the emerging oil industry weakened Britain's influence whilst strengthening that of the US. Nye argued that economic soft power became more important in international politics after the First World War than military intervention; the active development of Bahrain's most important economic asset, the oil industry, granted the US Government an unrivalled amount of influence. The theory of power to influence is based on the ability of a state to influence or coerce other states, but the entry of American companies into the Bahraini oil industry both diminished the ability of Britain to influence the development of the burgeoning energy sector and proved that the Exclusivity Agreement that had established Britain as the hegemon in the Kingdom could no longer guarantee this influence. It also laid the foundations for the establishment of the US as one of the most important economic partners for the success of Bahraini diversification.

6.4.1 Britain and Bahrain's oil and gas industry

In what was further evidence of a loss of influence by the British Government and British companies in Bahrain, the Bahrain National Gas Company (BNGC) was established in 1985 as a joint venture between the Government of Bahrain, Kuwaiti petroleum companies, and Saudi Basic Industries Corporation. Again, British companies were not involved in the development of another important sector for Bahrain's economy. The gas industry began to be developed to diversify away from oil after withdrawal, and the lack of a British input could symbolise the lack of a retained British footprint after 1971, or the lack of soft power attractiveness in this area because of an absence of proven British expertise in Middle Eastern gas industries. The joint venture to develop a Bahraini gas industry between the three Gulf states is likely a result of economic initiatives within the GCC and financial agreements between Bahrain and Saudi Arabia. However, in early 2019, Bahrain discovered the largest reserves of tight oil, crude oil that can only be accessed via hydraulic fracturing, since 1932. Bahrain's Oil Minister at the time, Sheikh Mohammed bin Khalifa Al Khalifa, told reporters that he was actively talking to major American oil companies about granting them the rights to exploit the shale oil reserves, estimated to hold at least 80 billion barrels.[36] Italian oil company Eni was also awarded an oil contract by the

BNOGA in January 2019, which is yet more evidence of how little influence British energy companies have had in Bahrain since the first concession was allowed to be granted to a non-British company.

Control over Bahrain's most important economic resources, namely its oil and gas fields, is an influential hard power asset that Britain arguably lost in the 1930s and has been unable to regain since. The US–Saudi oil partnership is also undoubtedly the most influential soft power in Bahrain as far as energy production is concerned, with important Saudi collaboration with American energy corporations through the Saudi Arabian Oil Company. It is notable that senior government officials still court American companies when they discover new oil reserves. According to Nye, soft power is when 'a state can make its power seem legitimate in the eyes of others ... getting others to want what you want ...'[37] American oil companies want to expand their influence in Bahrain, build new oil fields and find new profit sources, and by offering Bahrain a good deal on the shared profits, they get Bahrain to do what they want – to sign future contracts with American companies. It could be argued that the US emerged as a stronger expert power in Bahrain than Britain when an American company was awarded the rights to exploit the oil resources.

6.4.2 Britain's contribution to Bahraini diversification

The hydrocarbon industry has remained the most important contributor to national GDP in Bahrain since the 1940s, unaffected by British withdrawal, and this is likely because of the lack of British involvement in the industry. However, since 1973, Bahrain has undertaken efforts to diversify its economy. A technical assistance brief produced by diplomats in Bahrain in 1973 detailed how the

> Government of Bahrain continues in its efforts to diversify its economy ... Our technical assistance programme, which concentrates on technical and vocational training and English language training is therefore in exactly the right areas and we need to maintain and increase our efforts.[38]

This assistance was an attempt to retain some influence in Bahraini domestic affairs and to ensure that Britain remained the preferred partner for necessary training to educate Bahraini nationals in sectoral skills in non-hydrocarbon industries.

As is the case in much of the Middle East, the British Government has offered its expertise in economic privatisation to the Government of Bahrain to assist with economic diversification and advancement of the *Economic Vision 2030* agenda. In 2017, the first *UK-GCC Public Private Partnership* conference was held in London, with a similar conference taking place each subsequent year. Dr Abdel Aziz bin Hamad Aluwaisheg, Assistant Secretary-General for Political Affairs and Negotiations at the Gulf Cooperation Council, said that 'the conference [was] focused on the implementation of the GCC-UK 2016 Summit and the Joint Action Plan agreed between the GCC and the United Kingdom on increasing opportunities for investment between the 2 sides.'[39] In Bahrain, British companies with experience in winning tenders to operate public services on behalf of the government are increasingly being asked to bid for contracts. One of the most notable privatisation contracts in Bahrain has been awarded to National Express Group, a multi-national public transport company headquartered in Birmingham, UK, to operate a new public bus system across the Kingdom for ten years. The contract, which began in 2015, is believed to be worth £170 million to the joint venture between National Express and the Bahraini conglomerate Ahmed Mansoor Al A'Ali, overseen by the Ministry of Transportation and Telecommunications.[40] Although this is only one contract, the fact that a large British company has been entrusted with developing and running an important public transport service in Bahrain is an influential method of soft power for Britain and a type of expert power – Britain has extensive experience in the privatisation of the transport sector and can share this with Bahrain. The London-headquartered consultancy firm PricewaterhouseCoopers and London-office of KPMG were shortlisted as favoured companies to provide financial, legal, and technical advice on the first four phases of the $2 billion Bahrain Metro Rail project. Again, major British private sector companies are being offered a tender to provide services to Bahrain's Ministry of Transportation and Telecommunications.[41] The recruitment of British companies to undertake projects for the Bahraini public sector is an important tenet of the economic diversification process in Bahrain.

The British Government has a strong team in Bahrain responsible for utilising its influence to secure bids for local projects.

> The British Embassy in Manama's trade department works across all economic sectors, everything from healthcare to construction, retail, creative, defence and security, and the DIT actively markets British companies to the government and potential partners in the private sector. British expats are an important leverage for British investments.[42]

The British University of Bahrain, established in 2018 as an international campus of the University of Salford, was promoted to the Government of Bahrain to fill gaps in local engineering and technology skills. Local industry will have the opportunity to directly cooperate with students and faculty.[43] It is this type of relevance that is contributing to the strengthening of Britain's economic and cultural influence in the Kingdom.

6.4.3 *Economic shifts in Bahrain*

Bahrain's process of economic diversification is an attempt to quickly shift the economy away from a reliance on oil rentierism. Although the British Government does not have a proven legacy of diversification in its own right, the corporatisation of Bahrain's diversification agenda since 1973 has arguably emerged as a channel through which British private sector companies are able to exert influence over the Bahraini process. The most obvious means of intervention by Britain into the diversification process is through consultancy contracts tendered to the London offices of large consulting agencies. This consulting on the privatisation of elements of the Bahraini economy, the education of Bahraini employees in British expertise, and the implementation of British standards into the working practices of Bahraini companies involved in the economic shift in the Kingdom ultimately offers Britain an amount of influence that few other countries enjoy. The corporatisation of government ministries in Bahrain, resulting from the move towards a more commercial-centric economy, includes a substantial amount of outsourcing to British companies and to British individuals.[44] The consultative aspect of diversification represents a continuation of the strong advisory position that British individuals held in Bahrain before withdrawal and, as the Government of Bahrain continues to request assistance from consultants with close links to British standards, the presence of soft power is evident. The private sector has increasingly emerged as an important determinant of British influence in Bahrain.

6.5 Why has Britain remained an influential partner in financial market cooperation with Bahrain?

The finance sector in Bahrain is one of the largest and most diverse in the Middle East, established in 1970 as the first banking sector in the Gulf. A significant economic diversifier, contributing 16.1% to national GDP in the first quarter of 2018,[45] the finance sector is also perhaps the most important non-defence sector contributing to British–Bahraini relations. The finance sectors in Manama and London share commonalities; both are considered to be well regulated by domestic authorities, both are central regional hubs for banking, and both are key contributors to GDP. A *Financial System Stability Assessment* of the economy of Bahrain, undertaken by the International Monetary Fund, concluded:

> Despite the small size of Bahrain's economy, the financial sector is well diversified and well developed. Bahrain plays host to over 360 financial institutions ... There are currently 28 Islamic financial institutions licensed and active in Bahrain, including 6 full commercial banks, 15 investment banks, and 3 offshore banking units. The financial sector is

open to foreign investors and there are no restrictions regarding foreign ownership of financial institutions.[46]

The Bahraini banking sector has its foundations in the final years of the Residency, with the first foreign banks listed in the dedicated finance sector being British owned. Eastern Bank Limited, which merged with Chartered Bank in 1957 and Standard Chartered Bank in 1971, was the first commercial bank to be established in Bahrain. The British Bank of the Middle East, established in Bahrain in 1944 and later amalgamated into HSBC, was another early bank in the Kingdom. These two large British banks were influential in the development of Bahrain's contemporary finance sector and were managed by influential Britons. The banks were also established at the peak of the British Empire, thus highlighting the connection between British banking expertise and the development of the Bahraini finance sector. Private finance, which is still a relatively new phenomenon in Bahrain, is inextricably linked to the privatisation agenda, a topic that the British Government is also familiar with – expert power.

The strength of British soft power in Bahrain, and power in general, is reliant on economic cooperation with the Bahraini authorities and a constant presence of British banks and investment companies in Bahrain. A report produced by the House of Lords Select Committee on International Relations entitled *The Middle East: Time for New Realism* inferred that there has been a loss of British influence in the Gulf, including in Bahrain in recent years, but that the British presence is highly visible in the area of banking and investment.[47] Britain's influence in the financial sphere could be categorised as an element of institutional power. Theorists of soft power, such as Nye, argue that if a state is able to make its presence appear legitimate to policy makers in other countries, then it is more likely that the state trying to enact change will encounter less resistance against its aims. Therefore, it could be argued that Britain does not have to rely on military power to achieve influence in Bahrain. The strong presence of British banks in the state, and the common financial system that is shared between the two economies, attracts Bahraini Government officials to cooperating with Britain, and British financial companies to investing in Bahrain.

6.5.1 Islamic finance cooperation

Since 2004, Britain has developed a multifaceted Islamic finance industry, with a strong regulatory framework in place, high-ranking universities offering degrees focusing specifically on Islamic finance, numerous British and international Islamic banks listed in Britain, and legal and professional services in place to sustain Britain's place as the hub of Islamic finance in Europe. This commitment to Islamic finance has attracted cooperation from Bahrain. By the end of 2014, the global Islamic finance industry 'was worth around US$1.3 trillion ... The UK is the leading western country and

Europe's premier centre for Islamic finance with US$19 billion of reported assets.[48] The reliance that British banks have developed on their Bahraini counterparts for expertise and best practice has created a level of influence that can be directed from Bahrain to Britain. There is, however, evidence that other Gulf states are more active within the UK Islamic finance industry than Bahrain. The economic relationship between the two states seemingly offered Bahrain an opportunity to expand its own influence in British economics that has not been fully utilised.

Norman Angell theorised that the influence of one state over another can arise from the power that comes from joint economic ties. It is notable that one of the first Sharia investment companies to establish a base in London was Bahraini. BFC Exchange Limited, owned by the Bahrain Financing Company which was established in 1917 in Manama as the first local financial institution permitted to trade bullion and foreign currencies, was launched in Britain in 2003. The contemporary relationship between Britain and Bahrain is based on a willingness to share best practices and expertise, which is a significant aspect of soft power. It appears, however, that the Bahraini authorities are not aware of their ability to exert influence on UK policy makers in this important area of finance. Economic influence, as opposed to military influence, is based on the confidence of decision makers in a state that they have skills and expertise that other states need. It could be contended that Bahraini financial institutions are rewarding Britain for its role in the establishment of Bahrain's finance sector by choosing to base their European operations in London. This undoubtedly grants Bahrain reward power and influences how Britain chooses to develop its Islamic finance industry.

British links with Islamic finance are wide-ranging, and in 2013, London hosted the 9th World Islamic Economic Forum, the first time that the conference has been held in a non-Islamic country. Former FCO Minister, Baroness Warsi, told Parliament that she had:

> discussed the forum meeting and broader Islamic finance issues with Ministers, senior officials and finance professionals across the region during my recent visit. In Dubai, Abu Dhabi, Doha, Manama and Kuwait City, the message was clear: the potential for Islamic finance is huge and growing. The interest in working with the UK is there. I am committed to ensuring that the UK benefits from this growing market.[49]

This recognition by Ministers in the world's leading Islamic finance centres of the importance of the UK's Islamic finance industry, including by Bahrain, which is considered to have been the first state to develop its modern Sharia finance sector, hosting the first Islamic banking conference in 1991, its Central Bank issuing the first Sukuk bonds in 2001, developing a Takaful insurance regulation system first, and launching short-term liquidity management processes first,[50] is a powerful soft power advantage for

Britain within the international system. If Islamic countries recognise the importance of London in Sharia finance, then it is likely that the British Government has been granted a significant amount of influence and trust. This seemingly grants Britain power through its capability as an Islamic finance centre and the ability to persuade other states to request assistance from British financial institutions to develop their own Islamic and dual Islamic-conventional financial systems.

The main competition to British economic influence in the Gulf tends to come from the US, France, and China, but the Islamic finance industry in these states is underdeveloped. The preservation of British economic influence is dependent on the UK remaining relevant to Bahrain, and the City of London's innovative regulations have ensured that an Islamic finance industry has developed relatively quickly, and UK policies have remained up to date. British financial power relations with Bahrain appear to be maintained through collaboration in the contemporary era, offering access to UK markets in return for knowledge and expertise sharing. Compared to competitors, the UK Islamic finance industry is robust and welcoming to Bahraini banks. This is certainly a win for British economic diplomacy.

6.5.2 British assistance with Bahrain's financial modernisation

Islamic finance is only one tenet of the international banking system utilised by Britain to increase its influence around the world. The British Government is also ensuring that British companies remain relevant in the modern Bahraini economy by assisting with the digitalisation of Bahrain's banking sector, a process that Britain has embraced in its own finance industry and has proven its capabilities to governments looking to introduce in their own systems. The British digital banking company, Banfico, signed a cooperation agreement with Bahraini company Gulf Business Machines (GBM), a digital infrastructure business, in March 2019. The agreement will enable Britain's sharing of best practice in banking digitalisation so that the Bahraini finance sector can meet the regulations laid out by the Central Bank of Bahrain to comply with open banking standards, thus further advancing Bahrain's position as the finance hub for the Gulf. The agreement with GBM will allow Banfico to consult on open banking and the transformation of digital banking, but more importantly for British influence in the region, this agreement will result in an indirect advancement of British digital finance across the Gulf as Bahrain expands its own influence in regional banking. As Bahraini capabilities expand, so will British expertise.

There is undoubtedly an underlying theory that could explain why British companies have been asked to assist with digital transformation, and that is the strength of British soft power in this important area of economics. As Nye argued, 'co-optive power is the ability of a country to structure a situation so that other countries develop preferences or define their interests in ways consistent with its own.'[51] By sharing expertise in digital finance,

Britain is using its expertise to co-opt Bahraini companies to develop preferences similar to those promoted by the British Government in finance companies operating in the City of London. The indirect influence that British companies like Banfico exert on Bahraini economics is arguably a continuation of the influence that British companies held throughout the Residency, most notably British banks that established the foundations of the contemporary Bahraini finance sector and secured the Kingdom's position as a banking hub for the region. This cooperation not only benefits Britain in the furthering of British influence of financial values in Bahrain, it also benefits Bahrain as the state utilises its close relations with and trust in Britain to assist with the modernisation and future proofing of its own economy.

The shared financial systems and values between Britain and Bahrain has also proven beneficial for the British economy: an example of the reliance that Britain has on both the Bahraini Government-owned sovereign wealth fund (SWF) and private investors for the success of the British economy as a destination for inward investment. Bahrain is also dependent on investments, although on a smaller scale, from private British companies. One method that countries use to expand their soft power influence is bilateral investments. Investments by Bahraini companies in the UK, primarily in London, and British companies in Bahrain, have defined the relationship for much of the five decades since withdrawal, with government policies and agreements ensuring that barriers to bilateral investments are reduced. In 2006, the British and Bahraini governments signed an agreement to protect and promote bilateral investments and to establish favourable conditions to increase investments by nationals and private sector companies of one state in another state.[52] London is a major investment market for Bahraini investments, and evidence suggests that since Britain voted to leave the European Union on 23 June 2016, Bahraini investments in London and Manchester's real estate markets have increased; this is despite Bahraini investors preferring to invest within the Middle East rather than elsewhere around the world.[53]

The Bahraini SWF, *Mumtalakat*, is quickly becoming a major investor in British businesses, acquiring 9.8% of the British investment company Cranemere Group Limited, 24% of Envirogen Group, an international environmental technology company, and a controlling 62.5% stake in the British car design and racing group, McLaren, in 2007.[54] The Bahraini-owned Phoenix 2021 Limited investment group also agreed to purchase Wigan Athletic Football Club on 15 March 2021.[55] These investments are supported by policies enacted by the British Government to make it easier for Bahraini companies to invest in the UK, including the *Avoidance of Double Taxation and the Prevention of Fiscal Evasion* treaty, which ensures that 'profits of an enterprise of a Contracting State shall be taxable only in that State'[56] and that 'dividends paid by a company which is a resident of a contracting state to a resident of the other contracting state may be taxed in that other state.'[57] The reliance that the British Government has on Gulf SWFs has been increasing each year, particularly during Conservative administrations who are more open to foreign purchases of British businesses and are committed to regional development across the UK. Bahraini SWFs, with offices in London, have become an integral part of the British infrastructure and provide funding for local development projects so that the British Government does not have to. Financial cooperation, by its very nature, tends to be two-sided, but in the case of Bahraini investments into Britain through its SWFs, Bahrain is able to exert soft power influence over domestic decision-making across the UK. According to an expert in UK–Gulf investments:

> London often acts as a base for wider operations by Gulf SWFs. The owners of Gulf SWFs are considerate investors and do not only invest in property and London. Managers of SWFs are increasingly interested in supporting tech projects and urban regeneration across the UK, establishing themselves as integral partners for regional development. The managers are conservative investors who respect the transparency and legal framework in place in Britain, but the ultimate aim is to make profits.[58]

6.5.3 *Financial education and the power of learning*

Without knowledge of the British financial system, it is unlikely that Bahrainis would consider investing in the UK. Educational ties are used by Britain to impart financial best practice into the domestic banking sector by initiating partnerships between British universities and the *Bahrain Institute of Banking and Finance* (BIBF), a governmental training body affiliated to the Central Bank of Bahrain. The BIBF is responsible for ensuring that employees within the finance sector across Bahrain are trained in leadership, management, Islamic and western finance, and executive development, and since its establishment in 1981, the number of applicants per year has expanded from 400 to 16,000. By partnering with the BIBF, British universities including the University of London, Coventry University and Bangor University are directly influencing the methods used within Bahraini finance when the students return home to work in Middle Eastern, American, and European banks and insurance companies operating in Bahrain. The training of students in finance at British universities contributes to the fulfilment of the *Economic Vision 2030 Bahrain* agenda, a significant part of which is the development of the banking sector.

It is not possible to collate statistics related to how many Bahraini students study financial subjects in the UK, but in 2013, 1,202 students from Bahrain (representing 26.8% of the total outbound student population from Bahrain) studied at British universities.[59] Significant numbers of Bahraini students also study English in language schools across the UK, as do medical students on secondment to British hospitals and pupils at British boarding schools. Soft power is the attractive output that a state can offer to another without having to resort to coercion or force. The Government of Bahrain pays to send students to study in the UK and demonstrates a sense of attraction to what British universities can offer to the Bahraini economy. If the theory of power is accepted as meaning the ability to get a state to replicate the behaviour of another, then by accepting cooperation with BIBF, Britain is able to capitalise on its ability to share expertise to further advance the indirect British footprint in Bahrain and the resulting influence. On financial education, British universities receive a larger number of funded students from Bahrain than any other country. The power dynamic is not wholly one-sided however, as British universities are increasingly reliant on international tuition fees, and the British banking sector requires other states, such as Bahrain, to adopt their policies to strengthen Britain's own financial sector.

Britain has one of the most attractive educational systems in the world, and, as a result, Britain is helping to teach conventional finance skills to Sharia scholars worldwide via the Islamic Finance Council UK (UKIFC), with the Central Bank of Bahrain providing significant funding to the Scholar Professional Development Programme. The aim of the programme, which is supported by the British Government, is to ensure that Britain's banking high standards are accepted around the world, and to indirectly expand British financial values in parts of the world, such as Bahrain, where banking values are at risk. As the finance industry in Bahrain was developed by British expatriates with British values, it is the optimal state in which to re-establish this influence. This policy of enlargement of British economic values is arguably an attempt to re-engage Bahrain in a new British sphere of influence, one that is built upon joint cooperation rather than imperial hegemony, as was the case prior to 1971. The Governor of the Central Bank of Bahrain, Rasheed Al Maraj, told UKIFC when discussing the benefits of cooperating with the Islamic Finance Council on its Scholar Professional Development Programme, that:

> This capacity building initiative with the UKIFC's aims to enhance Shariah scholars and Islamic banker's comparative understanding of conventional versus Islamic finance. This will go a long way in empowering the scholars and bankers.[60]

Education is an influential method that can be used to attract support for a particular policy aim or objective. By instilling the particular values of conventional banking and finance into the Bahraini system, based on the internationally respected system used in the City of London, UKIFC is arguably re-establishing Britain as the country of choice for non-Islamic finance. The theory of power as influence, as defined by Benjamin Cohen, is dependent on one state being more powerful than the other. As Bahrain requires training in non-Islamic finance, Britain has an innate power to actively achieve a change in the behaviour of practitioners within the domestic Bahraini economy. This could be interpreted as British expert power to influence Bahraini economic decision-making.

6.6 Bahraini financial reforms and the resulting British influence

Reforms within the Bahraini economy have dominated domestic politics since 1971, and this reform agenda has extended to Bahraini foreign policy. As the oldest economic partner of Bahrain, this reform programme has arguably had the greatest impact on Britain. The British Government has an export finance policy that is used to support trade with countries around the world, but by providing money to indirectly support projects that align with reforms in Bahrain, the British Government is able to enhance its soft power, albeit in competition with other states.

Since the end of the Second World War, the British Government has had an active export credit and international finance regime that is used with the intention of furthering British influence around the world and expanding the British footprint within the international economic system. The strength of the government-to-government economic support provided by Britain to Bahrain is an important indicator of the strength of the bilateral relationship; this financial support inevitably links back to defence sales and the programme of economic diversification being undertaken by Bahrain. Margaret Thatcher visited Bahrain and Kuwait in September 1981 in an attempt to rekindle the relationships with the two states and to market British public and private expertise in both economies. Upon Thatcher's return to London, a report on the opportunities for export credits was produced by the Department for Trade. The brief identified several development projects in Bahrain that could be open to assistance from British companies:

> Ammonia/Methanol Plant: Two British companies bidding, Davy McKee and another (with French) ... Hope for substantial British element in equipment. ... Arabian Gulf University: Hope British consultants you have chosen will work through to detailed design stage, perhaps including medical centre and British firms help with construction and supply too. ... Hope British companies will contribute: (a) Gulf Aluminium Rolling Mill; (b) extension of airport: Gibb have full HMG support; (c) next phase of aluminium smelter; traditional British involvement here.[61]

British companies demonstrated their interest in providing services to the Government of Bahrain to assist with the diversification of the Bahraini economy throughout the 1980s but investing substantial sums of money in

Development of UK–Bahraini economic influence

these infrastructure projects was risky for private companies. The same trade brief indicated that in 1980,

> UK exports £95m: imports £13m: UK is by far main supplier, with 28% of all OECD exports. But small population and exhaustion of oil have slowed Bahrain's development; now few big projects where pro-British sentiment can be exploited, and most jointly financed with neighbours, so Bahrainis cannot decide alone.[62]

The increased influence that non-British companies were having in Bahrain in the 1980s was evident in one of the largest infrastructure projects in modern Bahrain, the Bahraini/Saudi Causeway. The '$600m contract [was] recently awarded to [a] Saudi-Dutch consortium.'[63] This loss of influence led to the British Government offering financial support to British companies bidding to take on major infrastructure projects through export credits. The expansion of Bahrain International Airport, an important asset for economic diversification in the Kingdom, was deemed an important project for securing British influence and it was 'originally British built; British Airports International did extension plan. Sir Alexander Gibb bidding for the major consultancy against foreign competitors. Worth stressing that Gibb will have support of HMG and its agencies, BAA and BAI.' The expansion of Bahrain's largest aluminium smelter was also in the British Government's sights for export funding support.[64]

Major infrastructure projects related to chemical production, tourism, cross-border trade with Saudi Arabia, and the development of transport infrastructure correlate with the British Government's most recent foreign policy plan for the Gulf, first introduced during the 2010–15 Cameron administration. Funding British exports that support projects identified by the Government of Bahrain as integral to their diversification forms an aspect of the multidimensional relationship that Britain has with Bahrain. A senior British diplomat declared that:

> The UK Government prioritises prosperity in its relations with the Gulf states. As the Gulf states go down the road of national visions, the UK is able to share expertise and funded project guidance, through providing export finance to British companies operating in regional states, in the areas of health, education, privatisations, and security-critical projects.[65]

6.6.1 British governmental support for reforms

By openly supporting bids by British companies to contribute to infrastructure projects that would contribute to the development of the Bahraini economy, the British Government has been attempting to utilise its soft power capabilities, albeit diminished since the 1980s, in an attempt to persuade Bahrain to choose British expertise. In June 1981, ECGD had demonstrated its commitment to supporting Bahrain's economic development and diversification by offering substantially greater amounts of export support to British companies than competitor export departments. The table below (taken from Appendix C attached to the Department of Trade brief) demonstrates that the UK had *agreed* US$19.5 million more for firm short-term commitments to Bahrain than the closest rival Japan, US$77.8 million more than Japan in medium- and long-term commitments, but US$126.6 million less in *offers* of direct financial assistance than France, who *offered* the largest amount. Although diplomats claimed that pro-British sentiment had been diminished, these statistics suggest otherwise, and that there was still a willingness within Bahrain to accept financial support from the British Government to support cooperation with British companies.

It could be inferred that British smart power, a combination of soft power economic support and a hard power presence of British companies and contractors in Bahrain developing diversification-critical projects, was still available as a tool used to exert Britain's influence in this part of the Gulf. In his analysis, Ernest Wilson largely discounted soft power as a theory of power because he argued that it is hard to measure; the financial support secured for British projects in Bahrain contradicts this argument. In 1981 alone, which was the first year since withdrawal that ECGD extended loans to support Bahraini projects, Britain quickly re-established its presence, as demonstrated in an export finance report from the same year. It has been assumed that the US had quickly emerged as the main trade partner of Bahrain after withdrawal, but export credit reports suggest otherwise. Table 6.1 demonstrates that in 1981–82 alone, ECGD remained the major provider of *actual* economic support for projects in Bahrain, but France *offered* a larger sum that was not utilised:

Supporting the reform agenda of the Government of Bahrain has been a key tenet of the British Government's foreign policy interaction with

Table 6.1 International financial commitments made to Bahrain, 1981–82

	Short-term commitments (US$ millions)	Medium- and long-term commitments (US$ millions)	Offers of assistance (US$ millions)[77]
ECGD (UK)	34.5	103.8	39.6
COFACE (France)	2.3	24.7	166.2
SACE (Italy)	0.2	0	0
HERMES (West Germany)	0	0	74.0
OND (Belgium)	0.04	0	0
MITI (Japan)	15.0	26.0	0
EXIMBANK (USA)	1.2	22.1	0

the Gulf Kingdom since the Thatcher administration. Proponents of the various theories of power claim that intervention by one state in the affairs of another, whether by soft power covert means or hard power overt means, is a method primarily used by states to secure their own influence within the international system. This research does not intend to take an opinion on whether the international system is indeed inherently anarchic, from which the foundations of power theories are generally built, but it does focus on assessing the effect of economic interventions such as financially supporting export and investment opportunities for British companies in Bahrain and the resulting power. However, British governmental support for the exportation of goods and expertise to Bahrain, to assist the national government with its diversification programme, was restricted so that only certain British companies could rely on the support of the British Government to underwrite their interests in Bahrain.

The ECGD has historically prioritised larger and more prominent British companies, so the number of British companies operating in Bahrain is likely to be larger than government documents suggest, and the commitment that the British Government is providing to foster British private sector support to assist Bahrain is noticeably limited. The measurable types of power utilised by British companies in Bahrain are likely stronger than those that are overtly utilised by the British Government, but as commercial affairs are more secretive than between governments, it is difficult to measure.

6.6.2 Limitations of British assistance

An archival document from 1982 outlined a discussion within the Department of Trade that recommended 'the establishment of a formal Section 2 limit of £400 million. ... when agreeing to cover on a Davy McKee contract valued at £305 million. Other existing commitments amount to £42 million.'[66] Although £400m is a substantial amount of money for the British Government to commit to just one country, which was symbolic of the willingness of the Conservative administration's attempt to re-establish the diminished British economic influence in Bahrain, limiting the value of export support arguably suggests that this governmental support was not unconditional. In Bahrain, export credit guarantees are evidence of relational power in action. Providing financial assistance to other states to support the development of key infrastructure projects, and thus instilling British values in the design and development of new factories and airports that will ultimately aid with the transition away from a reliance on oil in Bahrain, is predicated on British companies utilising the leverage that this financial assistance and governmental support provides to achieve a degree of influence in the domestic affairs of states.

Relational power in action is dependent on one state within the bilateral relationship being more influential than the other and the degree of cooperation between the two states (the relations) to achieve domestic change within a state. It would be remiss to neglect the strength of the legacy that was present in the early 1980s, both in the actual presence of British companies in Bahrain and the impact that British individuals had on the development of infrastructure in the state prior to withdrawal. In a meeting in 1981 between the Chancellor of the Exchequer, Geoffrey Howe, and his Bahraini counterpart, Ibrahim Abdul Karim,

> Mr Karim ... said that it remained Bahraini policy to keep a special relationship with the UK. Over 160 British firms were operating in Bahrain. ... Mr Karim mentioned that he was impressed by the degree of professionalism of the British banks with whom he had dealings.[67]

This attractiveness to what Britain can offer to Bahrain, soft power, is an important asset that arguably granted British companies an advantage over companies from competing states. If Bahraini officials are confident that their cooperation with Britain will be hassle-free and that they can rely on their British counterparts, then the theory of soft power suggests that this cooperation should continue to evolve.

6.6.3 Public–private cooperation

Since the 1980s, it has become increasingly apparent that the economic relationship between Britain and Bahrain is dependent on private sector companies who are willing and able to assist the Bahraini authorities with their economic diversification programmes. This shift away from a government-to-government relationship, as was largely the case prior to withdrawal, may be a symbol of increased globalisation and the emergence of a Bahraini free market, but it could also be attributed to the rescinding of influence by the British Government in Bahraini affairs and a shift towards a commercial focus. In 1992, a ministerial delegation visited Bahrain to meet with their Bahraini counterparts, whilst simultaneously promoting British private companies to assist with the development of important infrastructure projects. An answer to a parliamentary question at the time reported that:

> the Minister of Health gave Mr Roberts the opportunity to promote Macksworth Medical, a Welsh firm of consultants, who may as a result obtain a contract to oversee the refurbishment of the existing hospital in Bahrain. As a result of this same meeting Welsh Health Development International may also benefit from a consultancy contract for the new $200 million hospital to be built in Bahrain.[68]

This ministerial promotion of experienced British companies in Bahrain, paired with the important support provided by ECGD to underpin any assistance offered, has continued since the 1980s and is an indicator of the importance of Bahrain to successive British administrations; the higher value of export credits from the ECGD and projects awarded to British companies by the Government of Bahrain is indicative of greater British influence in the Kingdom. Even in 2018, the British Government was actively working to support British investments in Bahrain through export finance. In a parliamentary debate relating to the British relationship with Bahrain, the former Secretary of State for International Trade, Liam Fox, told the HoC, 'I am pleased to announce that this morning UK Export Finance has provided a loan of £27.9 million, under its direct lending facility, to support UK water and waste specialists Bluewater Bio to upgrade water treatment in Bahrain.'[69] Again, the importance of private companies was evident as a key determinant of the strength of the British power to influence domestic affairs in Bahrain. Physical financial support is an important hard power asset by the British Government and the British Government is spending significant sums of money to assist with domestic Bahraini reforms through various technical assistance programmes. This is one of the integral topics of discussion at the Bahraini–British Working Group, with Britain committing to assist Bahrain with economic reforms. This continued economic support seemingly keeps a British foothold in Bahrain, and as Bahrain willingly accepts assistance from Britain, the soft power influence of the British Government is evidently strong.

As has previously been discussed, the presence of British companies working on important infrastructure projects in Bahrain is a constituent of the theory of power as influence. According to Benjamin Cohen, if there is intent by others, or 'agency,' to enact change in another state, then if the state trying to enact change achieves this, power arises from this influence. One of the most influential soft power assets that Britain has retained in Bahrain, despite withdrawal, is the presence of private companies ensuring that Britain retains its presence in the state. This is another tenet of the strength of British expert power in Bahrain.

6.6.4 Governmental funding for Bahraini development

Although export financing is an influential way to secure the presence of British companies in Bahrain, no private enterprise can exert more leverage in another state than the state itself. When considering the importance that the British Government puts on its ability to influence the reforms in the contemporary Bahraini state, it is necessary to discuss direct funding offered by the British authorities.

One of the most useful funds offered by the FCO is the *Magna Carta Fund*, which is

> the FCO's dedicated strategic fund for delivering human rights and democracy work. ... 65% went to human rights priority countries, a set of 30 countries in which the FCO concentrates its human rights activities (these include Bahrain, China and Iraq).[70]

Funding from the FCO was used in 2016 to

> encourage the development of effective and accountable institutions, strengthening the rule of law and justice reform. The UK continued to provide technical assistance to the National Institute of Human Rights (NIHR), the Ombudsman, the PDRC, and the SIU, amongst other institutions.[71]

This direct funding seemingly suggests that diversification is not just limited to economics but could also include political and judicial development initiatives in the Kingdom. This could be interpreted as an extension of the historic responsibility held by Britain to develop Bahraini society. In 2018, the Conservative administration acknowledged that development in Bahrain can only be achieved by offering technical assistance, largely through financial means via funds such as the Magna Carta Fund, and this would contribute to the preservation of British influence and power in a country that had become increasingly open to the international community since 1971. This funding seemingly blurs the lines between British hard and soft power capabilities in Bahrain, offering funding to support domestic development priorities but establishing a reliance within Bahrain on this funding and the continued willingness of the British Government to provide this money.

A government response to concerns raised by the HoC Foreign Affairs Committee regarding Global Britain's support for human rights projects stated that,

> in Bahrain, UK Technical Assistance supports Bahraini led reform programmes to support building effective and accountable public and judicial institutions. Only by working with Bahrain can we hope to achieve the changes we would like to see. All of our work is in line with international standards and aims to share UK expertise and experience.[72]

Key to this response was the confirmation that the British Government did have a number of changes that they wanted to bring about in Bahrain and that they were willing to fund activities that would enable British experts to share their expertise with the Bahraini authorities. This is a rare acknowledgement in the post-withdrawal context of the desire within the British Government to use economic expertise to achieve direct change. The British Government has several funds, most administered by the FCDO, that aim to instil British values into the developing Bahraini political system. Former Foreign Minister Alistair Burt responded to a written question stating that

> the Foreign and Commonwealth Office has funded programmes to support building effective and accountable public and judicial

institutions in Bahrain. In financial year 2016–17, £1.52 million was spent on UK expertise to support Bahraini-led reform through the Conflict Stability and Security Fund.[73]

Funding projects through programmes such as these illustrates how Britain's economic and strategic priorities in Bahrain converge, and also how influential British governmental power is when attempting to understand how the legacy affects the position of Britain in the Gulf.

A major aspect of the *Global Britain* agenda, introduced by the Conservative government in 2015, is the projection of UK's influence around the world. The *Global Britain* report defined the future work of the FCO as 'to strengthen democratic values and the rule of law globally [which] provides an important instrument for projecting the UK's influence overseas, driving trade and prosperity through the promotion of these values.'[74] Kenneth Waltz would categorise this ambition as 'power as capability.' Waltz argued that state power is determined by the extent to which a state is able to project its influence in the international system, and that weaker states need to choose to accept assistance from stronger states.[75] In the case of Bahrain, Britain has a legacy of building political, judicial, and economic structures that were based on the British system; this secured British power and hegemony in Bahrain until withdrawal. When financial support for economic reforms is put into the context of power politics, British soft power in Bahrain appears to be strong. Economic ties, including overt financial support from one state to another, which could encompass credit exports, are effective tools for getting states to do as policymakers in another state desire. As states become increasingly economically reliant on each other, they are more likely to contribute to peace within the international system and establish power for the states involved. The argument that the 'wealth, prosperity, and well-being of a nation depend in no way upon its political power'[76] does, however, contradict somewhat the hypothesis that Britain's ability to exert influence by economic means in Bahrain is dependent on the presence of power. This study has found that political power is a determinant of wealth, and Britain's power assets are important for the future viability of the British presence in Bahrain.

6.7 An economic legacy under strain?

The British economic legacy in Bahrain represents the continuation of a tradition that was first established in 1820, when representatives of the East India Company decided that they had to establish a presence in the state to secure their financial power. The policy of upholding this influence is now reliant on the will of both governments, whereas British hegemony and exclusivity was historically guaranteed. The power that Britain was able to wield over the domestic economic affairs of Bahrain was undoubtedly weakened when Standard Oil was permitted to develop the oil infrastructure of the state, with little oversight by the Residency or Agents on the ground. This loss of hard power over domestic economic affairs necessitated the gradual shift towards a softer power-centric approach by the British Government and an acceptance that British private sector companies no longer have a monopoly on advising and cooperation with the Government of Bahrain. Whilst the competition to British influence has increased exponentially since withdrawal, and the opportunities for British companies to sell their goods and services to Bahrain have decreased, there remains a limited number of fields in which the British presence remains strong as a result of diversification-critical expertise that British companies have and a historic trust that had been established with the Government of Bahrain.

The economic relationship has arguably been simplified since 1971, largely as a result of changes in British foreign policy and Gulf agendas pursued by successive Labour and Conservative administrations. The nature of the relationship has become significantly less complex than it was at the point of withdrawal. Any control that British officials had over the oil industry has been lost, the influence that British banks have on the development of the domestic finance industry has been diminished as home-grown banks and non-British finance companies have entered the market, and British arms manufacturers can no longer take for granted their ability to sell arms to the Bahraini armed forces. In an attempt to bolster the soft power influence that Britain has been able to retain since withdrawal, the British Government has emerged as the mainstay of the relationship. This attempt to develop relationships using soft power has largely fallen into two categories – partnerships between British organisations and their Bahraini counterparts, and the extension of substantial export credits. As the relationship started to develop from 1820, the power that Britain had was dependent on the government-to-government relations. This influence became more commercially focused as the relationship developed and the private sector, whether British or otherwise, emerged as the focus of the relationship and the government links weakened. It could be argued that after withdrawal, the bilateral government relations came to prominence once again, and policy actions are what determines the contemporary relationship. In the 1980s, when the Conservative government began to take an interest in improving relations with the Gulf states after the hiatus that had emerged since 1971, the value of export credits increased, correlating with an increase in economic activity between the two states.

It is important to consider the British legacy in Bahrain when trying to determine the power that Britain is able to wield in the contemporary Kingdom, but this bilateral relationship can only be fully understood when considered in context. Bahrain's domestic diversification agenda has dominated the relationship since withdrawal, when the independent Government of Bahrain realised that it could no longer rely solely on its oil income for public spending. Critical analysis suggests that British Government officials have only become aware of the impact that diversification has on their influence to impart change in Bahrain since the first Cameron administration in 2010. The finance sector, the oldest in the Gulf and initially developed by the Residency, has been identified as the main diversifier of the Bahraini economy by British officials. This is an area of economic affairs where Britain has expertise required by the government in Bahrain because of the international reputation of the City of London, resulting in soft power influence that Britain can apply to advance its position in Bahrain. Unlike the historic hegemonic situation, Bahrain's choice to cooperate with British universities and finance companies, and the reliance that Britain now has on the willingness of Bahraini decision makers to continue their collaboration with British counterparts, has developed Bahraini soft power within British policy decision-making.

6.7.1 The relevance of this research – UK–Bahraini economics

British influence over the economics of Bahrain is a complex picture, and this study has concluded that the British Government rarely prioritises this aspect of the bilateral relationship. Since 1971, the economic influence in the Kingdom has become irreversibly dependent on the private sector and consulting companies – the privatisation of influence. The findings within this research reflect the wider picture of Britain's relationship with Bahrain, a situation where the British influence is insecure and more at risk from intervention by other states. As a result, British power to influence economic decision-making in Bahrain is weak. To remedy this, future British policy needs to offer greater financial inducements to attract Bahrain and reformulate a British sphere of influence that has been lost. This study has concluded that, despite numerous requests from senior Bahraini royals since the 1980s, the British Government has not utilised its important export credit capabilities to bolster influence.

The lack of a permanent large-scale British military apparatus in Bahrain between 1971 and 2018, and the minor role held by British troops in joint training exercises, has meant that there have been few opportunities to market British arms and defence technology in action. Whilst the annual BIDEC showcase is an important platform to market British expertise, this research has found that expert power can only really be effective if the receiving party is convinced by their own experiences relating to what the sending party can offer. To utilise the limited economic advantage that Britain holds in Bahrain, the most prominent aspect of which is related to financial cooperation, the British Government must adopt policies that appeal to Bahraini decision makers. Although this chapter implies that the Britain's economic power in Bahrain has become weakened since withdrawal, banking and insurance expertise has seemingly survived withdrawal. When considering the British projection of power, opportunities to gain a more secure foothold in the Kingdom remain within the financial sphere. Bahraini banks and financial institutions require non-Sharia banking expertise, and as they have existing relations with British counterparts, supported by both governments, expert power remains constant within the bilateral relationship.

Notes

1. Onley, J., 'The Politics of Protection in the Gulf: The Arab Rulers and the British Residents in the Nineteenth Century', *New Arabian Studies*, 6 (2004), esp. pp.67–75.
2. Khuri, F.I., *Tribe and State in Bahrain: The Transformation of Social and Political Authority in an Arab State*, (Chicago, IL, University of Chicago Press, 1981), p.86.
3. Peterson, J.E., 'Britain and the Gulf: At the Periphery of Empire' in Lawrence G. Potter (ed.), *The Persian Gulf in History*, (New York, Palgrave Macmillan, 2009), p.279.
4. Busch, B.C., *Britain and the Persian Gulf: 1894–1914*, (Berkeley, University of California Press, 1967), p.138.
5. See: Fuccaro, N., *Histories of City and State in the Persian Gulf: Manama Since 1800*, (New York, Cambridge University Press, 2009), esp. p.114.
6. *Report of Lord Denman's visit to Bahrain (March 1974)*. OD 34/404 (1973-75), TNA.
7. UK Foreign & Commonwealth Office, (11 March 2013), *Joint Bahrain-UK Statement on Inaugural Meeting of Joint Working Group*. Available at: <https://www.gov.uk/government/news/joint-bahrain-uk-statement-on-inaugural-meeting-of-joint-working-group> [accessed 25 April 2019].
8. Interview with a former British Ambassador in the Gulf (*former British Ambassador C*), (Oxford, 9 November 2018).
9. Wright Mills, C., *The Power Elite*, (New York, Oxford University Press, 1956).
10. Lukes, S. and Hearn, J., 'Power and Economics', in R. Skidelsky and N. Craig, *Who Runs the Economy? The Role of Power in Economics*, (London, Palgrave Macmillan, 2016), p.20.
11. Russell, B., *Power: A New Social Analysis*, (London, Allen & Unwin, 1938), pp.97-101, 107.
12. Ibid., p.22.
13. Letter from A.G. Munro to Roger Tomkys, British Ambassador to Bahrain, 14 May 1982. FCO 8/4384 (1982), TNA.
14. Keohane, R.O. and Nye, J.S., *Power and Interdependence: World Politics in Transition*, (Harlow, Longman, 2001).
15. Telegram from R. Tomkys, British Ambassador to Bahrain, to MoD (UK) Head of Defence Sales, 26 May 1983. FCO 8/5030 (1983), TNA.
16. Diplomatic Telegram from W.R. Tomkys, British Ambassador to Bahrain to FCO and MoD (UK), 18 April 1983. FCO 8/5028 (1983), TNA.
17. Telegram from R. Tomkys, British Ambassador to Bahrain, to MoD (UK), 5 April 1982. FCO 8/4384 (1982), TNA.
18. Minute: Valiant for Bahrain (produced by A.G. Munro), 28 July 1983. FCO 8/5028 (1983), TNA.
19. Letter from J. Caines to H.R. Braden (Defence Sales Organisation, MoD UK): Bahrain – Aircraft Sales, 22 December 1976. FCO 8/2646 (1976), TNA.
20. Telegram from R. Tomkys, British Ambassador to Bahrain, to MoD (UK), 27 September 1983. FCO 8/5029 (1983), TNA.
21. Katzman, K., CRS Report: *Bahrain: Reform, Security and U.S. Policy*, Congressional Research Service (7 August 2017), p.21.
22. Ibid.

23 Defence Security Cooperation Agency, 'News Release: *Bahrain – AH-1Z Attack Helicopters'*. Transmittal No. 16-36 (Washington, DC, 27 April 2018), p.1.
24 Defence Security Cooperation Agency, 'News Release: *Bahrain – Refurbishment of the Oliver Hazard Perry Class Ship, Ex ROBERT G. BRADLEY (FFG 49)'*. Transmittal No. 19-61 (Washington, DC, 23 October 2019), p.1.
25 Defence Security Cooperation Agency, 'News Release: *Bahrain – Patriot Missile System and Related Support and Equipment'*. Transmittal No. 19-06 (Washington, DC, 3 May 2019), p.1.
26 Telegram from R. Tomkys (no. 127), British Ambassador to Bahrain, to MOD, DOT, Paris, Abu Dhabi, Doha, Kuwait, Jeddah and Muscat, 25 May 1983. FCO 8/5029 (1983), TNA.
27 DipTel from R. Tomkys, British Ambassador to Bahrain, to MoD (UK) – No. 182200Z, 18 May 1983. FCO 8/5028 (1983), TNA.
28 Letter from A.G. Munro to Roger Tomkys.
29 Minutes: Quarterly Report to the Prime Minister on Defence Sales and Prospects (produced by H.L. Myers), 11 June 1987. FCO 8/6532 (1987), TNA.
30 BizBahrain Magazine, *Grand Opening of the 1st Bahrain Tri Service Defence Expo and Conference*, (Manama, Stratford Publishing House, 2017).
31 Kingdom of Bahrain, Ministry of Foreign Affairs, (2017), *The Diplomatic Gazette – October 2017*, (ninth issue of the monthly newsletter), Manama, p.5.
32 Pierre, A.J., Arms Sales: The New Diplomacy, *Foreign Affairs*, 60:2 (1981), p.267.
33 See: Findley, A.M., *The Arab World*, (London, Routledge, 1994), esp. p.85.
34 See: Nugent, J.B., 'US-Bahrain relations', in Robert Looney (ed), *Handbook of US-Middle East Relations: Formative Factors and Regional Perspectives*, (Oxford, Routledge, 2014).
35 Ibid., p.436.
36 See: Barrington, L. and Barbuscia, D. (2019), '*Bahrain talking to U.S. oil companies about tight oil deal: minister*', Reuters. Available at: <https://www.reuters.com/article/us-bahrain-oil/bahrain-talking-to-u-s-oil-companies-about-tight-oil-deal-minister-idUSKCN1QF2CW> [accessed 26 April 2019].
37 Nye, J.S., 'Soft Power', *Foreign Policy*, 80 (1990), p.167.
38 *Note on Technical Assistance in Bahrain – Bahrain Technical Policy*. OD 34/404 (1973-75), TNA.
39 Department for International Trade, Press Release – '*Enhancing Economic Relationships between the UK-GCC through PPP*', (London, DIT, 2017).
40 Oxford Business Group, *The Report – Bahrain 2017*, (Dubai, Oxford Business Group, 2017), esp. p.116.
41 Consultancy-me, (2019), 'PwC and KPMG remain in hunt for Bahrain Metro Rail contract', *Consultancy Middle East* (24 July). Available at: <https://www.consultancy-me.com/news/2235/pwc-and-kpmg-remain-in-hunt-for-bahrain-metro-rail-contract> [accessed 1 February 2020].
42 Interview with a former Director in the DIT in the Gulf (*Former DIT Director*), (London, 25 September 2018).
43 See: Roue, L. (2018), 'New university to open in Gulf state after Salford partnership', *Manchester Evening News*, (Manchester, 13 February). Available at: <https://www.manchestereveningnews.co.uk/business/business-news/new-university-open-gulf-state-14283916> [accessed 5 March 2021].
44 Interview with the Director of a UK-Gulf business representation group (*Business Representative A*), (London, 24 September 2018).
45 *Economic and Banking Bulletin, First Quarter 2018*, (Manama, Bahrain Association of Banks, 2018), p.2.
46 Enoch, C. and Khan, M., *Kingdom of Bahrain: Financial System Stability Assessment, including Reports on the Observance of Standards and Codes on the following Topics, Banking Supervision, Insurance Supervision, Securities*

    Regulation, and Anti-Money Laundering and Combatting the Financing of Terrorism – IMF Country Report No. 06/91, (Washington, DC, International Monetary Fund, 2006), p.29.
47 House of Lords, Select Committee on International Relations, *The Middle East: Time for New Realism* (2nd Report, Session 2016–17), (London, House of Lords, 2017), HL Paper 159.
48 UK Trade and Investment, *UK Excellence in Islamic Finance*, (London, UKTI, 2014), p.3.
49 HL Deb 10 October 2013 vol 748 c70.
50 Bahrain Economic Development Board, Press release: '*Bahrain for Islamic Finance*', 2017, p.1. Available at: <https://bahrainedb.com/app/uploads/2017/06/IslamicFinance-254x179-Insert-Jun2017.pdf>.
51 Nye, J., 'Soft Power', *Foreign Policy*, 80, (1990), p.168.
52 See: Kasolowsky, B. and Miron, S., 'Can collective action clauses in sovereign bonds limit litigation risks for states?' in P.S. Kenadijian, K.-A. Bauer, A. Cahn and W. de Gruyter (eds.), *Collective Action Clauses and the Restructuring of Sovereign Debt*, (Berlin, Walter de Gruyter GmbH, 2013).
53 Wright, E., (2017), 'Brexit effect means Bahrain is buying British', *Estates Gazette* (8 May). Available at: <https://www.egi.co.uk/news/brexit-effect-means-bahrain-is-buying-british> [accessed 1 January 2018].
54 See: <http://www.mumtalakat.bh>.
55 Consultancy.uk. (2021), 'Administrators secure deal for Wigan Athletic', *Consultancy UK* (17 March). Available at: <https://www.consultancy.uk/news/27307/administrators-secure-deal-for-wigan-athletic> [accessed 17 March 2021].
56 *Agreement between the Government of the United Kingdom of Great Britain and Northern Ireland and the Government of the Kingdom of Bahrain for the Avoidance of Double Taxation and the Prevention of Fiscal Evasion with Respect to Taxes on Income and Capital Gains*, (2013), Treaty Series No.5, entered into force 19 December 2012, p.9.
57 Ibid., p.12.
58 Interview, *Business Representative A*.
59 Universities UK International, *State of the Relationship: UK Higher Education Engagement with the Cooperation Council for the Arab States of the Gulf*, (London, UUKI, 2015), p.6.
60 The Islamic Finance Council UK, Report – *Celebrating 10 Years, 2017/2018*, (London, UKIFC, 2018), p.14.
61 *Prime Minister's Visit to Bahrain and Kuwait (25–28 September 1981) – Brief by the Department of Trade*. T437/57 (1981–82), TNA, p.1.
62 Ibid., p.2.
63 Ibid., p.3.
64 Ibid., p.3.
65 Interview, *(FCO Diplomat A)*.
66 *Letter from Miss B M Anderson to Mr Adams (25 February 1982) – EG(82)5*, p.1. T437/57 (1981-82), TNA.
67 *Record of a conversation between the Chancellor of the Exchequer and the Finance Minister of Bahrain at 10AM on Tuesday 19 October in No.11 Downing Street*. T437/57 (1981-82), TNA.
68 *House of Commons Parliamentary Question: Minister of State's Visit to the Middle East* (27 January 1992). BD 41/395 (1992/93), TNA.
69 HC Deb 20 December 2018 vol 651 c971.
70 Foreign Affairs Select Committee, *Global Britain: Human Rights and the Rule of Law*, 11 September 2018, HC Standing Order No.134, chapter 2.

71 Foreign & Commonwealth Office, *Human Rights & Democracy: The 2016 Foreign & Commonwealth Office Report*, (London, FCO Communications Directorate, 2017), p.33.
72 House of Commons Foreign Affairs Committee, *Global Britain: Human Rights and the Rule of Law: Government Response to the Committee's Thirteenth Report*, (London, House of Commons, 2018), p.12.
73 HC Deb 3 July 2018 157713W.
74 House of Commons Foreign Affairs Committee, *Global Britain: Human Rights and the Rule of Law*, (London, House of Commons, 2018), p.15.
75 See: Waltz, K.N., 'The Emerging Structure of International Politics', *International Security*, 18:2 (1993), pp.61–70.
76 Angell, N., *Europe's Optical Illusion*, (London, Simpkin, Marshall, Hamilton, Kent & Co., 1909), pp.25-29.
77 Attitudes and commitments of other credit in*surers (at 30 June 1981) – Appendix C, p.7. T437/57 (1981-82), TNA*.

Bibliography

Agreement between the Government of the United Kingdom of Great Britain and Northern Ireland and the Government of the Kingdom of Bahrain for the Avoidance of Double Taxation and the Prevention of Fiscal Evasion with respect to Taxes on Income and Capital Gains, (2013), Treaty Series No.5, entered into force 19 December 2012.
Angell, N., *Europe's Optical Illusion*, (London, Simpkin, Marshall, Hamilton, Kent & Co., 1909).
Attitudes and Commitments of other credit insurers (at 30 June 1981) – Appendix C, p.7. T437/57 (1981–82), TNA.
Bahrain Economic Development Board, Press release: '*Bahrain for Islamic Finance*', 2017, p.1. Available at: <https://bahrainedb.com/app/uploads/2017/06/IslamicFinance-254x179-Insert-Jun2017.pdf>.
Barrington, L. and Barbuscia, D. (2019), 'Bahrain talking to U.S. oil companies about tight oil deal: minister', *Reuters*. Available at: <https://www.reuters.com/article/us-bahrain-oil/bahrain-talking-to-u-s-oil-companies-about-tight-oil-deal-minister-idUSKCN1QF2CW> [accessed 26 April 2019].
BizBahrain Magazine, *Grand Opening of the 1st Bahrain Tri Service Defence Expo and Conference*, (Manama, Stratford Publishing House, 2017).
Busch, B.C., *Britain and the Persian Gulf: 1894–1914*, (Berkeley, University of California Press, 1967).
Consultancy-me. (2019), 'PwC and KPMG remain in hunt for Bahrain Metro Rail contract', *Consultancy Middle East* (24 July). Available at: <https://www.consultancy-me.com/news/2235/pwc-and-kpmg-remain-in-hunt-for-bahrain-metro-rail-contract> [accessed 1 February 2020].
Consultancy.uk. (2021), 'Administrators secure deal for Wigan Athletic', *Consultancy UK* (17 March). Available at: <https://www.consultancy.uk/news/27307/administrators-secure-deal-for-wigan-athletic> [accessed 17 March 2021].
Defence Security Cooperation Agency, 'News Release: *Bahrain – AH-1Z Attack Helicopters*'. Transmittal No. 16–36 (Washington, DC, 27 April 2018).
Defence Security Cooperation Agency, 'News Release: *Bahrain – Patriot Missile System and Related Support and Equipment*'. Transmittal No. 19-06 (Washington, DC, 3 May 2019).

Defence Security Cooperation Agency, 'News Release: *Bahrain – Refurbishment of the Oliver Hazard Perry Class Ship, Ex ROBERT G. BRADLEY (FFG 49)'*. Transmittal No. 19–61 (Washington, DC, 23 October 2019).

Department for International Trade, Press Release – *'Enhancing Economic Relationships between the UK-GCC through PPP'*, (London, DIT, 2017).

Diplomatic Telegram from W.R. Tomkys, British Ambassador to Bahrain to FCO and MoD (UK), 18 April 1983. FCO 8/5028 (1983), TNA.

DipTel from R. Tomkys, British Ambassador to Bahrain, to MoD (UK) – No. 182200Z, 18 May 1983. FCO 8/5028 (1983), TNA.

Economic and Banking Bulletin, First Quarter 2018, (Manama, Bahrain Association of Banks, 2018).

Enoch, C. and Khan, M., *Kingdom of Bahrain: Financial System Stability Assessment, Including Reports on the Observance of Standards and Codes on the Following Topics, Banking Supervision, Insurance Supervision, Securities Regulation, and Anti-Money Laundering and Combatting the Financing of Terrorism – IMF Country Report No. 06/91*, (Washington, DC, International Monetary Fund, 2006).

Findley, A.M., *The Arab World*, (London, Routledge, 1994).

Foreign Affairs Select Committee, *Global Britain: Human rights and the rule of law*, 11 September 2018, HC Standing Order No.134, chapter 2.

Foreign & Commonwealth Office, Human Rights & Democracy: The 2016 Foreign & Commonwealth Office Report, (London, FCO Communications Directorate, 2017).

Fuccaro, N., *Histories of City and State in the Persian Gulf: Manama since 1800*, (New York, Cambridge University Press, 2009).

HC Deb 20 December 2018 vol 651 c971.

HC Deb 3 July 2018 157713W.

HL Deb 10 October 2013 vol 748 c70.

House of Commons Foreign Affairs Committee, *Global Britain: Human Rights and the Rule of Law: Government Response to the Committee's Thirteenth Report*, (London, House of Commons, 2018).

House of Commons Foreign Affairs Committee, *Global Britain: Human Rights and the Rule of Law*, (London, House of Commons, 2018).

House of Commons Parliamentary Question: Minister of State's Visit to the Middle East (27 January 1992). BD 41/395 (1992/93), TNA.

House of Lords, Select Committee on International Relations, *The Middle East: Time for New Realism* (2nd Report, Session 2016–17), (London, House of Lords, 2017), HL Paper 159.

Interview with the Director of a UK-Gulf business representation group (*Business Representative A*), (London, 24 September 2018).

Interview with a former British Ambassador in the Gulf (*former British Ambassador C*), (Oxford, 9 November 2018).

Interview with a former Director in the DIT in the Gulf (*Former DIT Director*), (London, 25 September 2018).

Interview with a senior diplomat in the FCOs Arabian Directorate (*FCO Diplomat A*), (London, 12 October 2018).

Kasolowsky, B. and Miron, S., 'Can Collective Action Clauses in Sovereign Bonds Limit Litigation Risks for States?' in P.S. Kenadijian, Bauer, K-A, Cahn, A. and W. de Gruyter (eds.), *Collective Action Clauses and the Restructuring of Sovereign Debt*, (Berlin, Walter de Gruyter GmbH, 2013).

Katzman, K., CRS Report: *Bahrain: Reform, Security and U.S. Policy*, Congressional Research Service (7 August 2017).

Keohane, R.O. and Nye, J.S., *Power and Interdependence: World Politics in Transition*, (Harlow, Longman, 2001).

Khuri, F.I., *Tribe and State in Bahrain: The Transformation of Social and Political Authority in an Arab State*, (Chicago, IL, University of Chicago Press, 1981).

Kingdom of Bahrain, Ministry of Foreign Affairs, (2017), *The Diplomatic Gazette – October 2017*, (ninth issue of the monthly newsletter), Manama.

Letter from A.G. Munro to Roger Tomkys, British Ambassador to Bahrain, 14 May 1982. FCO 8/4384 (1982), TNA.

Letter from J. Caines to H.R. Braden (Defence Sales Organisation, MoD UK): Bahrain – Aircraft Sales, 22 December 1976. FCO 8/2646 (1976), TNA.

Letter from Miss B M Anderson to Mr Adams (25 February 1982) – EG(82)5, p.1. T437/57 (1981–82), TNA.

Lukes, S. and Hearn, J., 'Power and economics', in R. Skidelsky and N. Craig (eds.), *Who Runs the Economy? The Role of Power in Economics*, (London, Palgrave Macmillan, 2016), pp.17–29.

Minute: Valiant for Bahrain (produced by A.G. Munro), 28 July 1983. FCO 8/5028 (1983), TNA.

Minutes: Quarterly Report to the Prime Minister on Defence Sales and Prospects (produced by H.L. Myers), 11 June 1987. FCO 8/6532 (1987), TNA.

Note on Technical Assistance in Bahrain – Bahrain Technical Policy. OD 34/404 (1973–75), TNA.

Nugent, J.B., 'US-Bahrain relations', in R. Looney (ed.), *Handbook of US-Middle East Relations: Formative Factors and Regional Perspectives*, (Oxford, Routledge, 2014).

Nye Jr., J.S., 'Soft Power', *Foreign Policy*, 80 (1990), pp.153–171.

Onley, J., 'The Politics of Protection in the Gulf: The Arab Rulers and the British Residents in the Nineteenth Century', *New Arabian Studies*, 6 (2004), pp.30–92.

Oxford Business Group, *The Report – Bahrain 2017*, (Dubai, Oxford Business Group, 2017).

Peterson, J.E., 'Britain and the Gulf: At the periphery of empire' in L.G. Potter (ed.), *The Persian Gulf in History*, (New York, Palgrave Macmillan, 2009), pp.277–293.

Pierre, A.J., 'Arms Sales: The New Diplomacy', *Foreign Affairs*, 60:2 (1981), pp.266–286.

Prime Minister's visit to Bahrain and Kuwait (25–28 September 1981) – Brief by the Department of Trade. T437/57 (1981–82), TNA.

Record of a conversation between the Chancellor of the Exchequer and the Finance Minister of Bahrain at 10AM on Tuesday 19 October in No.11 Downing Street. T437/57 (1981–82), TNA.

Report of Lord Denman's visit to Bahrain (March 1974). OD 34/404 (1973–75), TNA.

Roue, L. (2018), 'New university to open in Gulf state after Salford partnership', *Manchester Evening News*, (Manchester, 13 February). Available at: <https://www.manchestereveningnews.co.uk/business/business-news/new-university-open-gulf-state-14283916> [accessed 5 March 2021].

Russell, B., *Power: A New Social Analysis*, (London, Allen & Unwin, 1938).

Telegram from R. Tomkys (no. 127), British Ambassador to Bahrain, to MOD, DOT, Paris, Abu Dhabi, Doha, Kuwait, Jeddah and Muscat, 25 May 1983. FCO 8/5029 (1983), TNA.

Telegram from R. Tomkys, British Ambassador to Bahrain, to MoD (UK) Head of Defence Sales, 26 May 1983. FCO 8/5030 (1983), TNA.

Telegram from R. Tomkys, British Ambassador to Bahrain, to MoD (UK), 5 April 1982. FCO 8/4384 (1982), TNA.

Telegram from R. Tomkys, British Ambassador to Bahrain, to MoD (UK), 27 September 1983. FCO 8/5029 (1983), TNA.

The Islamic Finance Council UK, Report – *Celebrating 10 years, 2017/2018*, (London, UKIFC, 2018).

UK Foreign & Commonwealth Office, (11 March 2013), *Joint Bahrain-UK Statement on Inaugural Meeting of Joint Working Group*. Available at: <https://www.gov.uk/government/news/joint-bahrain-uk-statement-on-inaugural-meeting-of-joint-working-group> [accessed 25 April 2019].

UK Trade and Investment, *UK Excellence in Islamic Finance*, (London, UKTI, 2014).

Universities UK International, *State of the Relationship: UK Higher Education Engagement with the Cooperation Council for the Arab States of the Gulf*, (London, UUKI, 2015).

Waltz, K.N., 'The Emerging Structure of International Politics', *International Security*, 18:2 (1993), pp.61–70.

Wright, E., (2017), 'Brexit effect means Bahrain is buying British', *Estates Gazette* (8 May). Available at: <https://www.egi.co.uk/news/brexit-effect-means-bahrain-is-buying-british> [accessed 1 January 2018].

Wright Mills, C., *The Power Elite*, (New York, Oxford University Press, 1956).

7 British power in review

Applying an overarching theory to the study of one state's engagement with the most important tenets of another – namely, the economic and strategic affairs – is difficult, particularly in the period after long-term protectionist treaties have been withdrawn. Assessing the underlying reasons for this continued influence, whether as a result of the physical legacy of British assets in Oman and Bahrain, the mindset that was established amongst local decision makers over the preceding century, or the financial commitment that Britain had developed within the domestic economies has required an application of power analysis.

This study has demonstrated that traces of Britain's historic hard power remain visible in every aspect of relations with Oman and Bahrain, whether manifested as an overt continued military presence in Oman or in a more nuanced form via financial collaboration in Bahrain. Power softening transitions have taken place, but this is seemingly an attempt by British Government and commercial officials to remain relevant to the Gulf rulers and to retain influence in an increasingly competitive region. It can be concluded that the major reason for the divergence of Britain's relations with both Gulf states since 1971 is largely because of the developing needs of each state over five decades and the expertise and technology that Britain can offer in each individual case. It could be deduced from this research that Britain's contemporary Gulf diplomacy combines the legacy of historic British control with the most relevant knowledge and expertise when the Gulf states have economic and strategic deficits.

7.1 Historical foundations

Prior to 1971, Britain's political power was secured across the Arabian Gulf by protectionist treaties that were *directly* in place with Bahrain and *indirectly* with Oman. Similarly, exclusivity agreements secured the British economic foothold in domestic affairs. There are visible remnants of this legacy across various levels of the bilateral relationships. In the formative years following Britain's relatively hurried withdrawal from the Gulf – 1971 in Bahrain and 1975 in Oman because of the British involvement in the Dhofar War – the willingness of the local rulers to diversify their relationships away from Britain became apparent and has arguably dictated the post-withdrawal relationships that have come to define the types and breadth of British power in each of the Gulf states. At the point of withdrawal in Bahrain, local ruler Shaikh Isa had already established the right to choose his own political advisors independent of British control – which could be defined as the privatisation of advising – and the domestic economy had become dependent on rentier revenues provided by American oil companies and income generated from the large American naval presence in the state. British power had already weakened before withdrawal. Harold Wilson's decision to leave the Gulf seemingly hastened the dissolution of the British power hegemony and necessitated a shift from hard to soft power. Conversely, in Oman, Sultan Qaboos' accession to the throne in 1970 came at a time when the British presence had already started its contraction, but the new ruler decided to directly recruit Britons into senior government positions to retain the security and stability that the British presence guaranteed. In the early years of his reign, there were few notable changes to the strength of this influence except for the repeal of historic treaties that mandated the presence. In both cases, the British Government wanted the local rulers to become more self-sufficient to reduce the cost and responsibility to Britain. This ambition was notably more successful in Bahrain than in Oman and has remained as such, but a re-engagement in Gulf affairs by Conservative administrations has reinvigorated the power balance in the region.

This book has approached the continuation of a legacy in the Gulf, focusing on Oman and Bahrain in particular because of the differentiations in the relationships of these states with Britain, from a transitional power perspective. The Residency relocated its headquarters to the protectorate of Bahrain in 1946 whilst Oman never officially became a protectorate. It is difficult to generalise about the development of the strength of British influence in both states since withdrawal but approaching this research using the theory of power as a basis has found that Britain holds stronger soft power influence over Omani economic affairs than in Bahrain. The development of soft power in the realm of strategic affairs is similarly stronger in Oman than in Bahrain, but the nature of arms sales and joint security exercises inevitably leads to the further instilling of British hard power influence in domestic security affairs. By utilising soft power capabilities, both the British Government and private sector companies are modernising the influence that Britain has in the Gulf states, but smart power – a combination of soft and hard power tactics – inevitably has to be used because it is too reductive to use just one type of power over another. When studying the British relationship with the Gulf states, there are many obvious changes that have taken place since withdrawal, particularly on a strategic level, but to truly understand the development of the British power and influence in Oman and Bahrain, more attention in this study has focused on the continuities within the bilateral relationships than the differences.[1]

Prior to Wilson's announcement in 1968 informing the Gulf rulers that the Residency and protectorate system would be dismantled, and all British troops and government officials would be withdrawn by 1971, Britain enjoyed hegemonic influence over all aspects of the economic and strategic affairs of Oman and Bahrain. British companies had become the only organisations permitted to operate in Oman for over 150 years and had become responsible for developing the domestic oil industry, selling arms to the Omani armed forces to modernise the military, and building the limited infrastructure that was needed for the country to function. In Bahrain, British financial institutions and defence manufacturers were similarly unrivalled in the influence that they held over domestic economic affairs, but American and Canadian oil companies were permitted to develop the oil industry from the 1930s, reducing the influence that Britain had as the most important contributor to the Bahraini economy. In both states, however, the British hegemonic power over the defence and security infrastructure was indisputable. There were few opportunities for other world powers to challenge the British hegemony in the Gulf before 1971, largely as a result of the exclusivity agreements and political treaties that secured Britain as the protector and guarantor of peace in the region. On 16 December 1971, when the British protectorate system and military protection of the Gulf came to an end, the hegemonic British influence similarly weakened. In Bahrain, American private companies quickly entered the market and the former British naval base at Juffair was handed over to the US Navy and renamed *Administrative Support Unit Bahrain*. Conversely in Oman, the British armed forces retained their influence until 1975 because of the deployment to assist domestic troops quelling the Dhofar uprising. British companies also retained significant power because of the continued presence of British advisors to Sultan Qaboos. The relation between the British economic and strategic legacy, in that the security guaranteed by the British military presence and extent to which British advisors were in control of the security and economic apparatus of the state in the years following withdrawal, was considerably stronger in Oman than in Bahrain and similarly the British presence was more overt in Oman than in Bahrain. This power differentiation has continued as the relationships have developed throughout the 21st century.

7.2 Contributing factors to the power legacy

A majority of this study has been approached from the perspective of British activities and how these contribute to the development of an economic and strategic influence in the two Gulf states, but the importance of the national rulers and their personal ties to Britain cannot be underestimated. One fact that is obvious is that Oman retained one ruler between 1970 and

2020. Sultan Qaboos established the contemporary Omani state in his own image, recruited a coterie of British advisors with whom he was personally comfortable working and whom he trusted to develop the infrastructure of his state, and tended not to deviate from cooperating with individuals and companies that he was personally familiar with. Throughout Qaboos' reign until his death in January 2020, he developed close relations with British royalty and most Conservative Prime Ministers, permitted large British private companies including BAE and Shell to expand their interests in Oman, and gave permission for the British armed forces to train with and educate their Omani counterparts in British strategy. The stability brought about by Qaboos' long reign and the single point of contact that British officials could rely on is a crucial contributor to the development of influence in Oman that has not been present in Bahrain. Since 1971, Bahrain has had two rulers, Shaikh Isa bin Salman Al Khalifa and King Hamad bin Isa Al Khalifa, both using different ruling styles, and appointing various family members to key government departments. Shaikh Isa developed closer relations with the US authorities and Hamad with Saudi Arabia. The flux resulting from the transition of power and the relative instability caused by domestic issues in Bahrain since withdrawal has made it difficult for British decision makers to secure their power in the Kingdom, whether hard or soft in nature. Britain's access to decision makers within the Government of Bahrain has become more complex as the state has developed its international relationships since 1971.

This study has focused largely on the resulting effects of this legacy and the power influence that has arisen from this persisting legacy, but a number of observations have also been made in relation to how the unrivalled hegemony that Britain held in the Gulf states has diminished. Even though the formation of the militaries of both Oman and Bahrain was almost identical, with the systems and infrastructure imported from the Raj, 1970 marked the point of divergence between the two states. When Sultan Qaboos came to power in 1970, he wanted to bring to an end the Dhofar rebellion and to do this he had to put more trust in the British military officials who were based in Oman. British arms were the mainstay of the Sultan's Armed Forces, and as a result, British Aerospace and smaller British defence manufacturers secured their positions as the trusted suppliers to Oman. At this time, Oman had not yet permitted other powers to establish military bases in its territory, so the British strategic influence remained unchallenged. Conversely, when Wilson declared his intention to withdraw the military presence from East of the Suez, the Government of Bahrain – which was notably more independent than Oman – began courting the US which had sustained a limited naval presence in the state since the Second World War, albeit with the permission of the Residency.

The influence that British authorities gained from this continued military deployment to Oman, at the request of the Sultan, was multifaceted. Firstly, the divisive strategic withdrawal on which Wilson had based his foreign policy agenda was not wholly enacted by the succeeding Conservative administration, from where the most vocal opposition to withdrawal originated, and thus an important element of the presence was retained. Secondly, as British troops served in Oman at the request from Qaboos, and the weapons that were used in the Dhofar War were manufactured by British companies, Britons were required to maintain this equipment. The continued secondment of British troops to command and fight alongside their Omani counterparts could only persist after the accession of Qaboos if he had remained attracted to the tactics and capabilities of the British military; this attraction is manifested as soft power influence for Britain. It is important to note that the British military presence during the transition period between the pre- and post-withdrawal era in Oman shifted from a situation mandated by treaties to one where Qaboos willingly requested a continuation of assistance from Britain. This demonstrated an attraction by the new ruler of Oman at the most important time in the state's history, resulting in the British Government holding capability power and the future security of Oman in its hands.

The strategic aspect of the relationship between Britain and the two Gulf states and the differentiation between how Britain is able to influence the domestic security affairs of the states is symbolic of the strength of the continuation of British soft power. An essential feature of soft power that has been highlighted by theorists such as Joseph Nye is the attraction that one state has for what another can offer. The secondment and acceptance of trainee officers into British military academies arguably demonstrates the strength of the bilateral ties between Britain and the Gulf states. Annually, since the 1970s, Oman has seconded a noticeably larger number of trainee officers to British academies for all of the branches of the armed forces than Bahrain. Indeed, there has been a presence each year that data is available of Omani officer cadets but not their Bahraini counterparts.

The willingness of Oman to continue to permit the training of its future military leaders in Britain is an important indicator of the sentiment that Omani decision makers have for the skills and tactics that British troops demonstrated in Oman during the Dhofar conflict. This direct strategic legacy is not present in Bahrain, and since 1971, Bahrain has proven more willing to accept training in US military academies than British ones. The military training legacy with Oman has extended to the secondment of a British officer to an Omani academy in 2018, the first reverse secondment by the British Government and proof of the trust that Britain has for the skills that Oman can impart on British secondees, which Oman has ultimately learned from Britain over decades. The differentiation in the way that Britain engaged with the Gulf states on a practical training basis is symbolic of the strength of British soft power in Oman and not in Bahrain. Oman also seconds police officers to train with numerous regional police forces across the UK, but this is only replicated on a small scale in Bahrain with the direct recruitment by the Government of Bahrain of former Metropolitan police advisors to reorganise their domestic security apparatus; this comes with a stigma that is common with all cooperation with Bahrain. There were notable police training missions sent from Bahrain to West Yorkshire and Greater Manchester throughout the 1980s, and the first all-women programme for Bahraini officers in the UK, but these are not commonplace and heavily criticised by MPs.

It would not be amiss to argue that strong British soft power in Oman – the attraction that policy makers in the Sultanate have for British expertise and a willingness to continue accepting assistance from Britain without being forced to do so – has established a system of reliance that is not replicated elsewhere. Prior to withdrawal, Bahrain was also reliant on the Residency for training, but this hegemony was quickly lost to the US after 1971. Security training and the strength of Britain's influence on military training is inextricably linked to joint training exercises and arms sales.

7.3 Legacy of arms sales

Joint military exercises and arms sales from British manufacturers are arguably linked, and this marks the convergence point between strategic and economic interests in Britain's relations with the Gulf states. This area also demonstrates the differences in the strength of the British influence in both Gulf states. The quantitative value of the joint training exercises and the depth of this cooperation demonstrably leads to a larger number of arms sales from British manufacturers to partner states in the Gulf. The three *Saif Saarea* military training exercises that have taken place in November 1986, September–October 2001, and October–November 2018 between the British and Omani militaries have expanded the number of troops deployed to Oman each time. The willingness of the Government of Oman to commit to allowing the deployment of such a significant number of British troops to Oman, to train alongside their Omani counterparts, and share skills and techniques in military best-practice suggests that a legacy of trust exists within the minds of Omani decision makers for cooperation with Britain. This was undoubtedly established during the Residency era before 1971 when Britain was the only military power permitted to train the Omani forces. The third *Saif Saarea* exercise brought together 70,000 Omani and 5,500 British service personnel, making it one of the world's largest military exercises outside of war time.

These training exercises cannot be considered from a solely strategic perspective; the British Government, arms manufacturers across the UK and related service companies are fully aware of the positive effects that come from the practical use of weapons and technology in real-world environments. Throughout the joint exercises in Oman, the majority of fighter aircraft, tanks, and ships have been manufactured by BAE Systems, the largest defence manufacturer in Britain and one of the largest in the world. The presence of such a large private company in Oman, cooperating with the British military, gives the British Government significant leverage over Omani military affairs. The large British presence could be mistaken for a purely hard power tactic, but the exercises are dependent on requests from the SOAF and an attraction for continuing their cooperation with Britain. It could be argued, therefore, that British smart power is strong in Oman, a combination of hard power physical military training and soft power influence resulting from a desire within Oman to learn British tactics and impart these into the domestic security apparatus. There are joint training exercises with Bahrain, but these are on a much smaller scale and have a more specialised focus on special forces training in built-up environments. Unlike in Oman, the Bahraini exercises do not include every branch of the armed forces, nor do they include large numbers of personnel or require significant funding from the receiving state. British-manufactured weapons are only used alongside those produced by US companies in the Bahraini joint exercises. The influence that Britain gains from the exercises in Bahrain is negligible in comparison with Oman, but they both demonstrate that a strategic legacy is present, albeit to different extents, and that British soft power attraction is strong enough to warrant regular requests for joint training from both states.

The mindset element of the joint exercises is also a key factor to consider. The large presence of British military personnel in Oman, whether in tanks and personnel carriers on the streets, or in the shops and accommodation across the country, arguably demonstrates to the local population that the British are there to defend their interests and support Oman. The British presence in Bahrain cannot be interpreted on a similar level as the specialist British troops are in such a small number, and so heavily outnumbered by Americans, that they are largely unknown to the local population.

When Harold Wilson decided that he would withdraw the British presence from East of the Suez, he signalled that the local rulers needed to take over the responsibility for their own security. The main reason for this was to reduce the cost to the British Exchequer. Observers could conclude that this aim was unsuccessful as the British military presence has remained in an altered state in Oman, but when considered in greater detail, it could be argued that Oman's acceptance that it needs to pay many of the costs to host the British training missions is evidence of how the British presence has been able to avoid prolonged costs by remaining relevant as Oman's strategic priorities have developed since withdrawal. This relevance persuaded Oman's rulers to agree to subsidise the British secondment. This transfer of financial responsibility has not occurred because of a specific governmental agenda in London; instead Qaboos and his advisors arguably interpreted this as a way to retain the important British expertise in Oman, albeit on a more temporary basis, indirectly granting power to the British Government who is undoubtedly aware of the reliance that Oman still has on Britain for its military development. This also marked the growth of Oman's influence over British policy, as the British Government has to ensure that their armed forces remain skilled, equipped, and relevant to Oman to ensure that the Sultan's government remains willing to initiate bilateral exercises in the future. Oman gains power within their bilateral relationship with Britain because the British military needs to practice tactics in a desert environment with a partner state that shares common leadership styles and technology – no other country can offer both of these attributes to the British Government. This is in contrast to the situation in Bahrain since 1971, where strategic progress has become increasingly dependent on US training and financing, with power transferring from Britain to America immediately after withdrawal.

7.4 Convergence of Britain's strategic and economic priorities

The development of post-withdrawal deployment and joint training exercises with both Oman and Bahrain are, as has previously been discussed, inextricably linked to the economic aspect of strategic affairs and the capabilities of the British Government to increase arms sales from British manufacturers to the militaries of the two Gulf states. Arms sales has emerged as one of the most important tools for Britain's extension of influence in international affairs, largely because of the respect and trust that foreign governments have for BAE Systems, but British arms sales are dependent on actions of the British Government to market the weapons and equipment to the international community. As with the joint training exercises, arms sales can be considered as a hybrid form of power, defined as smart power by Joseph Nye. The fact that arms are hard power in nature – physical leverage that can be used as a bargaining chip by the British Government to support security priorities of the Gulf states – suggests that Britain has not wholly withdrawn from its hard power and coercive status in the region, but it has lost the hegemony that was enjoyed prior to withdrawal. As a result of the monetary nature of arms sales, and the ability for the governments of Oman and Bahrain to choose which states and companies to purchase arms from, attraction to the quality of British-manufactured arms and financial inducements offered by the British Government are important. As BAE remains one of the largest suppliers to the SOAF, and British manufacturers have become increasingly dependent on selling weapons to Oman since withdrawal as other markets outside of the Middle East have diversified their supplier base, a marked reversal in the Sultanate's power dynamics with Britain has taken place. Britain has become dependent on Omani contracts for profits and employee job security.

Direct requests by David Cameron to Sultan Qaboos to persuade him to opt for BAE Typhoon jets over US-manufactured alternatives, which would fit more easily into the existing Omani fleet, highlighted a shift in power. The British Government has developed a reliance on Omani purchasing decisions to sustain domestic employment in defence manufacturing, and although an element of soft power attraction is necessary to secure arms sales to Oman, the British Government has to put effort into ensuring that Britain does not lose its privileged position in the state. The DIT and FCDO are able to extend large sums of export credits to the Government of Oman to support significant arms contracts from British companies, the largest in British history have been for BAE contracts to supply fighter aircraft to modernise the RAFO. Significant numbers of associated contracts are also signed with companies to service these aircraft. Contrasted with the value of arms sales to Bahrain, those to Oman are integral for the projection of British power in the Middle East. In Bahrain, there has been a larger commercial presence for non-British arms manufacturers since the Second World War because of the US naval presence stationed there, and when the independent Bahraini authorities were modernising and consolidating their armed forces in 1971, American companies, such as Lockheed Martin and Boeing, had already established significant influence amongst decision makers. This can be linked back to the educational relations, with Bahraini decision makers learning their skills on American equipment in US academies. This physical presence, paired with the soft power influence imparted as senior Bahraini royals train in military academies in the US with American weapons, quickly diminished the British power to persuade Bahraini decision makers to buy British. There has been a notable lack of major arms contracts signed between the Government of Bahrain and British manufacturers since 1971. The presence of BAE, as the largest arms company in Britain, is much smaller in Bahrain than in Oman. As a result, the importance of Bahrain to BAE and other British arms manufacturers for commercial purposes is significantly less than Oman.

In 2006, BAE delivered six Hawk-100 aircraft to the Royal Bahraini Air Force, but most ventures for BAE are jointly operated with other companies from around the world. Most ventures for BAE in Oman are undertaken by the company alone, and the civic presence of BAE in Omani domestic affairs is more overt, funding scholarships to study in UK universities and providing money for Outbound Oman youth projects. As the meeting point between military and economic affairs, both Britain's priorities and post-withdrawal capabilities in both Gulf states can be defined by the volume and value of arms deals with British companies and the inducements offered by the British Government's trade department to enable these deals. The commitment that the UK Export Credits Guarantee Department puts into winning contracts from Oman, by offering the largest credit guarantees in British export history, arguably demonstrates an attempt by the British Government to ensuring that it retains its place as the main supplier to the Sultanate in light of increased competition from states that were historically barred. By offering financial support to Oman, the ECGD is boosting British influence by demonstrating how important Oman is for the projection of British power and the trust that the British Government has that Oman will repay the loans. Although there have been several smaller scale credit guarantees provided to Bahrain, these have not been for defence

200 *Trade and the power of money*

purposes. To effectively project power in the post-withdrawal Gulf, the British Government, in cooperation with the private sector, needs to utilise its strengths to increase its influence. Although export credits for arms sales are one of the most effective tools of economic soft power, there needs to be a willingness within the receiving state to accept the trade and increased British presence. The development of British trade relations with the Gulf states suggests therefore, that since withdrawal, Oman has been much more willing than Bahrain to accept increased arms sales from British companies and to inadvertently securing British power in Omani security affairs.

The convergence between Britain's economic and strategic priorities in Oman is evident in the appointment of Lord Astor of Hever as the Prime Minister's trade envoy to Oman in 2016. He was also appointed the Defence Secretary's Advisor for Military Cooperation with Oman. It is notable both that there are no equivalent representatives to Bahrain and that the official responsible for fostering trade with Oman is also an advisor on the advancement of bilateral military exercises with the Sultanate. This arguably suggests that the Conservative administration has recognised the inseparable correlation between defence cooperation and British trade with Oman, the influence that British companies gain over Omani affairs as a result of the close defence ties, and the realist value of arms sales to Oman. This is a strong example of how the British Government is attempting to utilise its smart power capabilities to advance influence in Oman in the contemporary era. Overt defence exercises are combined with the sale of goods to ensure that Britain retains its privileged position in Omani domestic affairs; Lord Astor's appointment epitomises this joint approach.

7.5 Economic priorities

Although arms sales are an important indicator of the continued strength of the British influence in the Gulf states, they cannot be considered wholly soft power in nature because of the force element that cannot be disconnected from this facet of the relationships. Developments within the energy sector represent the most striking example of how both the British Government and private sector companies are able to utilise the historic British position in both states to further develop the influence of Britain in Oman and Bahrain without a hard power basis. As with most aspects of the bilateral relationships, the British power to influence the energy affairs of the Gulf states has demonstrated a disparity between the states, much of which can be accounted to the legacy of how the domestic oil industries developed. The hydrocarbon industry in Bahrain was developed by Standard Oil of California, with a proportion sold to Texaco before part-nationalisation by the Government of Bahrain in 1975 and full nationalisation in 1980. From the beginning, Britain had little influence over the development of the oil industry in Bahrain and thus had few foundations on which to build its power. Bahrain has been more willing to cooperate closely with neighbouring

Saudi Arabia and imports much of its oil for refining from Saudi oil fields, and on Kuwait for the establishment of its domestic gas industry. Although British energy companies have had a presence in Bahrain since the 1930s, with the Anglo-Persian Oil Company establishing an exploratory office at the same time that oil was discovered, British soft power and investments in the sector have arguably never had the chance to become fully established. Contrasted with the situation in Oman, where Royal Dutch Shell, through the Iraq Petroleum Company, has had a presence since 1937 in all levels of exploration and refining, the British influence over domestic energy affairs in Bahrain is comparatively insignificant.

As Petroleum Development (Oman and Dhofar) Ltd was established, with British companies owning a combined 47.5% of shares, the British influence was secured as the industry developed. When the new Sultan Qaboos nationalised part of PDO in 1970, he allowed Shell to retain its significant influence as the largest private sector shareholder in the company. The respect that Qaboos had for Shell and the necessary expertise that British executives could share with their local counterparts granted Britain an amount of soft power influence over Omani oil affairs even after withdrawal. As Oman has become more dependent on income generated from oil exports, and as domestic oil use has increased on an almost annual basis since the 1980s, the influence that Britain enjoys has also expanded. This reliance on British energy companies continues to grow, with BP and Shell being awarded the majority of exploration licences for the burgeoning gas sector throughout the 2010s. This increased reliance also manifests itself as an increase in British influence, but with British private sector companies committed to the Omani energy industry to return profits from its investments, granting soft power influence to the Government of Oman and the power to impact upon these profits through the policies enacted. These multi-national energy corporations, headquartered (in the case of BP) or incorporated (in the case of Shell) in London, lost their ability to expand their operations in Oman without the approval of the local ruler and they have had to utilise their in-country presence to court the Sultan and senior officials since Qaboos' part-nationalisation of PDO. It has become necessary for these corporations to put effort into securing their position in Omani affairs and highlighted the importance of expert power to securing influence in the Sultanate.

The important influence that Shell has had on the development of PDO's skill base – PDO seconds officials to Shell's office in Oman to learn best-practice and Shell seconds its employees to PDO to share expertise – can be compared with the military secondments that take place between the two states. These types of skill-sharing exercises demonstrate the commitment that Britain had for the development of Oman's capabilities and the reliance that Oman continues to have on Britain for its economic and strategic success. Shell and BP retained their presence in Oman after Britain's declaration to withdraw, with their position in society arguably hardly changing as a result. The case could be made that the historic influence that had developed between Britain and Oman was a form of clientelist power, whereby political support in Oman for the continued presence of British energy companies was predicated on a quid-pro-quo supply of skills and investments provided to the Sultanate. This is a type of power that largely disappeared across the former British Empire as states gained independence, but it has remained important in the bilateral economic relationship with Oman. Expert relationships are one of Britain's greatest assets, as large British companies, as a result of their history and reputation, have the necessary expertise required by developing countries and thus can be used to gain leverage within the bilateral relationships.

On a wholly economic level, British soft power has undoubtedly secured the British Government and British companies as influential actors in the Gulf, but the power that is enjoyed is dependent on the overt commitment that is demonstrated to the local rulers. In Bahrain, export finance provided by the British Government's ECGD to support contracts from British companies trading with the state is largely linked to domestic economic development. Providing export funding to support the priorities of the Government of Bahrain is considered an important way to increase influence in the state, so by providing export finance from as early as 1981, the British Government had a limited impact upon Bahraini decision-making without resorting to force. In 1981, ECGD remained the largest funder of export financing, offering significantly more export credits to support Bahraini projects than any other state. From 1982, however, evidence suggests that export credits in support of Bahraini diversification were no longer unconditional and limits were placed on how much support could be offered for projects involving Bahrain.

The theory of relational power purports that one state within a bilateral relationship should be more powerful than another, and the more powerful state needs to retain its involvement in the secondary state to ensure that the influence does not become diminished. There have been countless examples of Bahraini officials praising the professionalism and respect for British companies, demonstrating the presence of an element of trust between the two partner states, but if the British Government has become reluctant to offer funding to remain relevant in the Kingdom, this necessary involvement is becoming diminished. The contemporary projects financed by the ECGD are on a much smaller scale than historic ones, but projects like the Bluewater Bio water treatment project are integral to the future of Bahraini infrastructure development. It could be argued that, as more competition has entered the Bahraini market since 1971, the opportunities for British private sector involvement, and resulting export financing, have reduced. Demonstrating a monetary commitment to assisting Bahrain with its development aims is the most constructive method to impart soft power influence on Bahraini decision makers, but as Britain has lost much of its privileged position within the Bahraini economy, the influence is diminishing. The export credit opportunities available to the British Government are more plentiful in Oman, and it seems that the Government of Oman has remained more receptive to accepting assistance from Britain; this also extends to foreign direct investments. Britain has remained the largest contributor of FDI into Oman each year since withdrawal, at as much as three times more than the second-largest contributor, the neighbouring state of the UAE.

There is a difference between export funding and FDI, but both concern the contribution of British money to support the economy of Oman. This has remained a common theme since the mid-1800s and has seemingly escaped the drawbacks of withdrawal. This could be explained as a result of the larger number of British interests in Oman than in Bahrain. British energy companies invest and require more investments from London in Oman, and the Government of Oman is committed to buying more defence equipment from British manufacturers than any other country. However, direct Malaysian involvement in the Omani diversification agenda and rapid Chinese investments in Duqm Port is reducing the economic power that Britain can rely on. Oman is a relatively rare example of a state in which British companies have remained the predominant investors after the ending of colonial-type treaties that guaranteed this hegemony, but the fact that powerful countries that have followed a similar economic path as Oman are being invited to cooperate with the Sultanate could imply that Britain is no longer as relevant as an economic partner as it once was. Economic relevance is an important contributor to the success of Britain's projection of power capabilities, and although this relevance is reducing in Oman, it is increasingly less diverse in Bahrain.

7.6 British re-engagement in the Gulf

In 1971, it was expected that the British withdrawal from the economic and strategic affairs of the Gulf states would result in an increased self-reliance by the local rulers and a less overt, divisive, or costly British presence East of the Suez. Harold Wilson and his cabinet paid little attention to the important benefits that a constant presence in the Gulf brought, particularly in Oman at the entrance to the region, and the projection of power capabilities that arose from this. The continued British presence in Gulf affairs since withdrawal cannot be solely attributed to the efforts of the British Government, although this undoubtedly plays an important part, rather it has been the willingness of the local rulers and their dependence on British expertise and investments that has dictated how much power and influence Britain has been able to retain in each state. The legacy that has remained in both Omani and Bahraini affairs is a direct descendant of the formal structures that were in place between 1820 and 1971 in both states. British companies enjoyed unrivalled influence over the development of the local economies and the largest energy and defence manufacturing companies have retained influence in Oman, British military advisors were secure in position in Oman and remained for the first two decades of Sultan Qaboos' rule, and bilateral governmental relations have remained strong.

An aspect of the relationship with Oman that is not present in Bahrain is the joint nature of the contemporary re-engagement. On the 218th anniversary of the signing of the first major treaty between British and Omani officials – the 'Unshook' Treaty – the *UK-Oman Comprehensive Agreement* was signed on 22 May 2019 between Foreign Secretary Jeremy Hunt and Omani Minister of Foreign Affairs Yousef bin Alawi. This followed the signing of the *Joint Defence Agreement* on 21 February and the *Joint Declaration on Enduring Friendship* in March of the same year. This commitment by both the British and Omani governments arguably demonstrates a joint economic and strategic priority by both partners and as a desire to ensure that the bilateral relationship continues to strengthen. This demonstrates that the relationship has survived withdrawal in a way that the relationship with Bahrain has not.

Re-engagement is manifested in various ways but is more prominent in the economic sphere in Bahrain and the strategic sphere in Oman. The financial cooperation between the Bahraini authorities and the City of London is demonstrable of an attempt by the British authorities and financial institutions to establish Britain as a reliable and necessary economic partner. Conversely in Oman, the British Government, in cooperation with the military and arms manufacturers based in Britain, has further strengthened the defence relationship. Although the strategic relationship with Oman never ceased after withdrawal, it became more temporary, so attempts by the British Government to open the permanent naval base at Duqm and ingrain the only bilateral secondment of officers between the militaries could be interpreted as visible re-engagement.

7.7 The commercialisation of influence and privatisation of bilateral affairs

A less obvious element of Britain's re-engagement efforts with the Gulf states that must be highlighted to understand the British legacy in the Gulf is the shift in who is responsible for developing these relationships. Since the British political and overt economic structures have been dismantled across the Gulf, both the British Government and private sector companies have had to devise methods suitable for the contemporary era. This reformulation of methods to secure influence in both Oman and Bahrain has become manifested in a number of ways that can be seen as a direct legacy of the Residency framework. The development of Britain's influence since withdrawal has increasingly relied on the private sector, whether through the continued presence of these companies in key economic sectors within the Gulf states or as trusted suppliers to regional militaries. The transition to a more commercial projection of power process can be identified throughout analysis of the bilateral relationships since 1971. It cannot be claimed that private British companies did not hold influence over decision-making within the Residency, as the likes of Shell and BP, British Aerospace, HSBC, and Cobham have had a presence in both Bahrain and Oman for more than a century and were influential investors in the domestic economies at times of development and modernisation throughout the 19th and first half of the 20th centuries. Since withdrawal, however, these major private companies are increasingly taking over the responsibility to uphold the British presence in the Gulf, working directly with local government officials and establishing domestic subsidiaries to bypass the bureaucracy of the political relationships. In the contemporary era,

> the most significant change is that they [private companies] no longer interact with the rest of the world via their respective states, but partly establish their own external relations, both with their counterparts in other countries and with other types of actors.[2]

The commercialisation of diplomacy since withdrawal has redefined how Britain interacts with the Gulf states.

Historically, diplomacy was divided between 'high politics,' usually restricted to direct relations between governments, and 'low politics,' or the less official level of relations. What has happened since 1971 is the blurring of these boundaries.

> Not only have non-state, i.e. private actors thus intruded into what was formerly the exclusive domain of the state, i.e. diplomacy in general, but they have also ventured into what used to be considered the 'hard' and 'high-politics' segments thereof.[3]

This shift to a more commercial form of diplomacy lends itself to the softening of British power in the Gulf states. This shift has been replicated in both Oman and Bahrain, with less focus on overt military domination and more on British private arms manufacturers and energy companies competing with rival companies from other countries on the quality of service, price, and after-service offered to secure the wide-ranging British presence. Although the legacy plays a part, the ability of British companies to adapt to the modernisation of relations and willingness of the British Government to support the private sector (through export credits and political support) to expand its influence abroad, has further ingrained private companies into bilateral political affairs.

The shift to a more commercial relationship has arguably established Britain as a more flexible partner, but evidence has also proven that the commercial focus could be a disadvantage for British power and influence. During economic downturns, including during the Covid-19 outbreak in the first-half of 2020, the Gulf governments announced significant curbs on governmental spending because of decreased oil and tourism revenues.

As Britain's commercial exposure in Oman is significantly larger than in Bahrain, budget cuts in the Sultanate have the potential to negatively affect British power more than that in Bahrain. A circular sent from the Finance Ministry of the Sultanate of Oman to government departments on 12 March 2020 stated that the central government intended to

> reduce the approved budgets of civil, military and security agencies for the year 2020 by 5%, the Ministry of Finance would like to inform all government agencies that the aforementioned percentage has been deducted from the approved budget for each agency.[4]

These budget restrictions will ultimately have an impact on Oman's ability to purchase arms, equipment, or services from British companies. The closure of Oman's airspace and limitations on non-GCC nationals travelling to the Sultanate will also affect which Britons will be able to visit Oman to market their goods and services to decision makers there, and potentially how many Britons opt to return to work in Oman in the months and years after the restrictions are lifted. The increased reliance on private companies to secure trade deals, and thus extend Britain's influence in Oman, is dependent on Oman's spending capabilities. Fewer Britons are employed in Bahrain and the presence of many British private companies operating in Bahrain is more temporary than in Oman. This differentiation highlights how exposed British influence is to domestic Omani politics.

This study has concluded that British-manufactured arms are rarely the cheapest available to Oman, so DIT in Oman has focused more on marketing by quality rather than price. If domestic budgets are cut but the SOAF continues to require weapons and services, then Oman is likely to prioritise cheaper products in the short term rather than purchase from British manufacturers, even if a strong legacy is present. On 1 January 2020, the Government of Oman announced that its total budget for the year was OMR 13.2 billion, of which 3.45 billion was for defence and security, 2.23 billion for oil and gas production, and 1.3 billion for civil development projects[5] – British companies are most exposed to these sectors. It could be deduced that the total budget was cut to OMR 12.5 billion, and this would result in cuts within all departments, and cuts to money that could be spent on orders from British companies. Reduced oil revenues have also resulted in ratings agencies Moody's and Fitch cutting the country's credit rating to junk status, thus reducing the credit trustworthiness of the government there. There is less direct exposure to the Bahraini economy, and the exposure that does exist is largely based on long-term contracts. Although the Government of Bahrain has not publicly announced budget cuts, the small number of British commercial contracts are usually paid in advance and thus able to withstand any short-term economic disruption.

The commercialisation of Britain's influence in the Gulf has both positive and negative effects. The direct costs and reliance on the British

Government to attract orders that ultimately expand Britain's influence in the Gulf states is reduced as the private sector increases its physical presence across the region. However, the increased reliance on an increasingly competitive commercial system leaves Britain's influence open to fluctuations in the markets and spending capabilities of the governments involved. This issue of governmental support for British exports to the Gulf states, through export finance, does continue to expose the British public to events in the Gulf; something that has not changed since the initial engagement in the Gulf in 1820.

It could be argued that the early responsibility for establishing British diplomacy in the Gulf was reliant on activities by the private East India Company, transitioned to British Government officials until withdrawal, and the responsibility for upholding this influence is once again shifting back to the private sector.

7.8 What effect will the death of Sultan Qaboos have on British influence in Oman?

When the death of Sultan Qaboos on 10 January 2020 was announced by Omani state media the following day, a long-standing British ally and a reliable constant for British access to the Sultanate was lost. As in many other countries around the world where leaders sympathetic to upholding strong relations with their former protector have died or been overthrown, the successor to Qaboos could eventually shift his allegiances or become closer to the US, like many other Middle Eastern states. The actual name written in the infamous letters of succession left by Qaboos that were opened by the family council on 11 January were considered of little importance for the British Government, what was more imperative for Britain at this time of change is that soft power capabilities are used to their full potential. Arguably the most important method of soft power projection is to uphold the visible presence of senior British officials in Oman, and the arrival of Prince Charles, Boris Johnson, Defence Secretary Ben Wallace, and Chief of the Defence Staff General Sir Nicholas Carter to attend a condolence event for Qaboos and to hold meetings with the new Sultan, Haitham bin Tariq Al Said, on 12 January demonstrated Britain's commitment to Oman in the most visible way. The members of the British contingent were the first non-Arab officials to visit the new Sultan, demonstrating the British Government's desire to remain relevant within the state, and ensuring that this commitment by Britain remains at the forefront of decision-making by Sultan Haitham. This mirrors the time of Qaboos' accession, when the first officials that he met were British, but the backdrop in 2020 is significantly different to 1970.

Although Sultan Haitham was educated at the University of Oxford and was a Foreign Minister who met with British Government officials numerous times, he does not have the military or cultural connections that Qaboos had to Britain, and Oman has become an important regional player in its own right since 1970. When Qaboos came to power, he was reliant on British military support to end the Dhofar War and to uphold Omani foreign policy, with Britons holding most senior economic and political positions. The unrivalled power held by the Residency when Qaboos acceded to the throne was not present when Haitham took over. British defence manufacturers are also no longer the only supplier permitted to sell arms to the SOAF, nor are the British armed forces the only military with a presence in Oman. Britain cannot take its influence in Oman for granted, so the strength of its power to influence, both soft and smart in nature, will be tested within the first few years of Haitham's rule as he makes significant infrastructure and economic diversification decisions, including the expansion of Duqm Port, the implementation of the *Vision 2040* agenda, and the future of military cooperation with allies – all of which could potentially have an impact on Britain's influence in the Sultanate. In this sense, Bahrain could be considered a more stable country in the short-term for British influence until Haitham's priorities become clearer.

7.9 Policy implications of this research and future research opportunities

The common misunderstanding within both academic and non-academic audiences is that the British Government applies a universal policy to the GCC and its effects are universal across the region. This study has found that this is, in fact, not the case. This research has concluded that significantly more British political and economic capital has been dedicated to developing the diplomatic relationship with Oman than that with Bahrain since 1971. This does not directly correlate with the historical economic foundations on which the bilateral relationships were built, as Manama was chosen to host the Residency after it moved from Persia, and development efforts were more prominent in Bahrain than in Oman. On a strategic level, however, Britain's dedication to Oman has been more overt in its commitment than to Bahrain, with British troops openly fighting in support of the Sultan during the Dhofar War and in the joint military exercises that have taken place since.

The research findings in this study could be interpreted by policy makers in Britain and the Gulf states as evidence of a diminished legacy in Bahrain. As the British Government has re-focused its development of economic relationships with states outside of the European Union since 2020, when the UK officially withdrew from the EU, the existing relational foundations that exist with Bahrain could be utilised to gain greater access to the domestic Bahraini market. Strong partnerships are present between domestic banks in Bahrain and Islamic banks in Britain, with the educational relations between them defining Britain's contemporary soft power in the Kingdom, as are links between both stock markets. It is this influence that

British policymakers can use to develop future influence throughout the Bahraini economic sphere, as banking is the mainstay of economic affairs. This research has demonstrated that there are fewer evident strategic partnerships between Britain and Bahrain, so British policy has to focus on attracting orders from the Bahraini armed forces for British manufacturers through the extension of more consistent and higher-value export credit guarantees, like those offered to Oman. In Oman, Sultan Qaboos requested that the three *Saif Saarea* military exercises take place, but Bahrain has only offered small-scale exercises. Even the new Bahraini-funded HMS Juffair base cannot be fully utilised by the Royal Navy because it is not a deep-water port. British defence policy in relation to Bahrain should, therefore, follow the same theme of the relationship with Oman, and to secure British military power in Bahrain and the wider Gulf, the British Government should offer Bahrain cost-effective joint training and loans for arms to utilise British smart power – the provision of hard power assets to achieve soft power attraction and stronger future cooperation. In the case of Oman, bilateral cooperation is almost as strong as it was since withdrawal as a result of the unrestricted value of export credits offered to Oman and the prominent presence of British banks, energy companies and large-scale military exercises with the Sultanate. Britain has remained committed to Oman. However, the resulting influence has become dependent on the continued attraction of Omani decision makers to British expertise and technology. To develop this influence further, British policy practitioners need to be educated in the importance of British smart power and how to utilise it to secure influence across the Gulf.

7.9.1 Implications of cross-governmental working on the British position in the Gulf

The findings within this study further highlight how departmental priorities in London are increasingly taking on power traits when officials decide how to interact with their Gulf counterparts. The British Government uses the banner of 'Global Britain' to achieve shared policy goals between departments. The close cooperation between the Ministry of Defence and the Foreign Office to sustain joint military training with Gulf partners and establish future defence partnerships, and between the Department for International Trade (and its predecessors) and the Foreign Office to enhance British trade access to the markets of Oman and Bahrain and target trade financing demonstrates this joint policy approach. These integrated policy priorities align with 'the fusion doctrine' outlined in the 2015 *National Security Capability Review* (NSCR), which aimed to align British trade, security, and developmental priorities in international partnerships. The three mutually reinforcing priorities – economic, security, and influence – can be seen in action across the Gulf. The NSCR concluded that 'building a culture of common purpose across departments requires improved accountability to shift incentives and behaviours towards a more genuinely whole-of-government approach.'[6]

A major conclusion that can be made from this study is that a British whole-of-government approach has increasingly been implemented in Oman since 1975, but in Bahrain, the approach remains largely disconnected. Oman also benefits from the interrelationship between the Foreign Office, the MoD, the Home Office, the Department for International Development, and the devolved Northern Ireland Assembly. Financing for Command and Control and youth justice projects is provided to the Northern Ireland Assembly to train their Omani counterparts from the *Conflict, Stability and Security Fund*, a cross-governmental aid budget – worth around £900,000 in 2017.[7] On 16 June 2020, Boris Johnson announced that the FCO and DFID departments and budgets were to be merged. This joined up approach for aid policy has already proven successful for the projection of British power and influence in Oman. Opportunities in Bahrain are fewer, but this new approach could prove beneficial for the projection of influence.

This newfound cross-governmental approach, and a recognition that the Gulf is important to British prosperity and the projection of power resulted in Boris Johnson appointing his former Chief of Staff and Chief Strategic Advisor, Lord Edward Udny-Lister, as the new special envoy for the Gulf on 12 February 2021. Johnson recognised at the point of this appointment that the Gulf is key to British security and economic sustainability after withdrawal from the European Union. Although Lord Lister left this role two months later, the new envoy position offers a direct channel between key decision makers in the UK and Gulf Governments, akin to the role of historic Persian Gulf Residents prior to 1971.

Notes

1 Stansfield, G. and Kelly, S., 'A Return to East of Suez: UK Deployment to the Gulf', *RUSI Briefing Paper* (April 2013).
2 Møller, B., 'Privatisation of Conflict, Security and War', *DIIS Working Paper*, 2 (2005), p.5.
3 Ibid., p.7.
4 Barbuscia, D. and Barrington, L. (2020), 'UPDATE 2 – Oman finance ministry cuts 2020 budget for govt agencies by 5%', *Reuters*, 17 March. Available at: <https://www.reuters.com/article/oman-economy-budget/update-2-oman-finance-ministry-cuts-2020-budget-for-govt-agencies-by-5-idUSL8N2BA0SV> [accessed 1 April 2020].
5 KPMG, *Oman Budget 2020: KPMG Insights* (no. 2616), (Muscat, KPMG Lower Gulf, 2020), p.3.
6 Cabinet Office, 'National Security Capability Review', (London, Cabinet Office, 2018), p.11.
7 FOI0471/17, 28 July 2017.

Bibliography

Barbuscia, D. and Barrington, L. (2020), 'UPDATE 2 – Oman finance ministry cuts 2020 budget for govt agencies by 5%', *Reuters*, 17 March. Available at: <https://www.reuters.com/article/oman-economy-budget/update-2-oman-finance-ministry-cuts-2020-budget-for-govt-agencies-by-5-idUSL8N2BA0SV> [accessed 1 April 2020].

Cabinet Office, 'National Security Capability Review', (London, Cabinet Office, 2018).

FOI 0471-17 (FCO), 28 July 2017. Available at: <https://assets.publishing.service.gov.uk/government/uploads/system/uploads/attachment_data/file/638782/FOI_0471-17_response.pdf>.

KPMG, *Oman Budget 2020: KPMG Insights* (no. 2616), (Muscat, KPMG Lower Gulf, 2020).

Møller, B., 'Privatisation of Conflict, Security and War', *DIIS Working Paper*, 2 (2005), pp.3–41.

Stansfield, G. and Kelly, S., 'A Return to East of Suez: UK Deployment to the Gulf', *RUSI Briefing Paper* (April 2013), pp.1–16.

Index

accountability 7, 36, 210
advisors 5–6, 55, 59, 88, 97, 99, 141, 146, 148, 197, 200
alliances 7, 13, 157
allies 12–13, 19, 21, 34–35, 43, 76, 87, 90–91, 95, 103, 119
American oil companies 165, 192
American Power 145, 149, 159
American PR companies 99
Americans 2, 6, 103, 153, 163, 172, 197
American strategic relationship 159
American weapons 199
Anglo-Omani Society 64, 68, 133
Annual Defence Review 65–66
Annual Report 64–67, 146, 148
Arabian Frontier 7, 14, 16
Arabian Gulf 1, 19, 31, 61, 191
Arab Spring 7, 14, 16, 24–27, 40
Arab State 5, 14–15, 20, 104, 108, 184, 186, 189–190
armaments 12–13, 56, 95
arms exports 115–116, 120
arms manufacturers 104, 196, 204
arms sales 61, 63, 92, 94–96, 116, 118–119, 154–155, 159, 161–162, 185, 192, 196, 198–200
arms trade 106–107, 154, 157
attraction 9–10, 35, 39, 45, 47, 83, 85, 87, 116, 132–133, 159, 162, 195–198

BAE 53–54, 96, 117–119, 160–161, 194, 198–199
BAE Systems 2, 53, 62, 65–66, 96, 117–118, 135, 162, 196, 198
Bahrain 1–2, 7–8, 31, 33, 36, 38, 53–54, 58–59, 63–64, 67, 70–109, 150–206, 208–210
Bahrain Defence Force *see* BDF
Bahrain Economic Development Board 186–187

Bahraini affairs 70, 72, 76, 90–91, 97, 152, 154–155, 163, 178, 203
Bahraini authorities 78, 84, 88, 90–91, 96, 102–103, 163, 168–169, 178, 180, 204
Bahraini banks 170, 183
Bahraini companies 154, 167, 171
Bahraini decision makers 77, 80–83, 90–91, 156–158, 161–162, 183, 199, 202
Bahraini defence 71, 74
Bahraini defence affairs 75, 103, 158, 160
Bahraini development 99, 179
Bahraini diversification 164–165, 202
Bahraini economic influence 151–189
Bahraini economy 97, 167, 173–175, 183, 193, 202, 206
Bahraini finance sector 168, 170
Bahraini governments 76, 87, 92, 168, 171
Bahraini investments in London 171
Bahraini military 91, 158
Bahraini oil industry 163–164
Bahraini police force 72, 76, 91
Bahraini police officers 76, 80
Bahraini relationship 71, 97, 152, 159
Bahrainis 77–83, 85, 87–88, 92, 94, 98–99, 150, 152–153, 156–157, 161–166, 169, 171–172, 174–175, 178–180, 209
Bahraini security 71, 82–83, 90, 92, 100, 102
Bahraini security affairs 71, 82, 103
Bahraini security relationship 8, 70
Bahrainis seconded 79
Bahrain National Gas Company (BNGC) 164
Bahrain Petroleum Company (BAPCO) 163
Bahrain's diversification agenda 167

Bahrain's economy 164, 167
Bahrain's police force 78, 80
Bahrain's rulers 70–71, 82, 91, 150
Bahrain's security 7, 100
Bahrain Technical Assistance 104, 109
banking 63, 119, 132, 167–168, 172, 183, 209
banking and investment 168
banking sectors 138, 144, 172
banks 62, 117, 150, 168, 185, 188
BAPCO (Bahrain Petroleum Company) 163
barriers 132, 171
BBF 134–135
BDF (Bahrain Defence Force) 74–76, 78, 82, 92, 104, 108, 157–162
BIDEC 161–162
bilateral cooperation 81, 88, 209
bilateral defence relationships 50, 60
bilateralism 62, 152
bilateral military committee 105, 108
bilateral relations 1, 36, 157
bilateral relationship 1, 3, 10–11, 62–63, 81, 118, 133–134, 142, 182–184, 191, 193, 198, 200, 202, 204
BNGC (Bahrain National Gas Company) 164
Bombay Marine 32, 70–71, 113
BP 62, 115, 117, 127–128, 130, 143, 201, 205
Britain & Oman 3, 13, 15
Britain's commitment 58, 136, 207
Britain's defence capabilities 100, 102
Britain's defence sales 92, 155, 160
Britain's influence 6, 71–72, 91, 95, 114–115, 117, 119, 123, 127–128, 136, 142, 204, 206–208
Britain's military relations 31, 59
Britain's power 34, 62, 97, 143
Britain's shifting strategic power in Bahrain 71–109
Britain's sphere 44, 71, 87, 120
Britain's withdrawal 6, 52, 132, 152
Britannia Royal Naval College 36–37, 64, 67, 79, 107
British academies 41, 78, 195
British activities 63, 193
British administrations 25, 178
British advisors 5, 20, 25, 40, 46, 55–56, 84, 98, 122, 130, 193–194
British Aerospace 48, 135, 194, 205
British Agents 7, 31, 57, 77, 97
British Ambassador 63, 65–69, 184–185, 188–190

British Ambassador in Oman 54, 57
British Ambassador to Bahrain 184–185, 188–190
British armed forces 34, 52, 60, 66, 69, 77, 119, 193–194, 208
British arms 95, 117, 121, 162, 194
British arms manufacturers 43, 50, 53, 99, 182, 199
British arms sales 50, 91, 198
British Army 21, 23, 26–27, 35, 43, 61, 78
British assets 99, 191
British assistance 82, 142, 170, 177
British authorities 25, 76, 84, 150, 163, 179, 194, 204
British banking sector 173
British banks 117, 135, 168–169, 171, 178, 182, 209
British businesses 133, 135, 171–172
British Business Forum 133–134
British commitment 75, 117
British companies 51, 55–56, 118–120, 126–127, 129–130, 132–135, 137–144, 151–152, 154–155, 157–158, 160–161, 164, 166–167, 170–171, 174–177, 179, 193, 199–200, 202–203, 206
British companies in Bahrain 171, 177–179
British contributions 142, 144
British control 124, 151, 163, 192
British Counterinsurgency 26–27
British counterparts 52, 162, 178, 183–184
British decision makers 18, 194
British defence companies 50, 53–55, 161
British defence equipment 120–121, 161
British defence manufacturers 33, 50, 53, 56, 60, 94, 155, 161, 194, 208
British defence policy 58–59, 90, 209
British diplomats 7–8, 35, 64, 68, 83, 87, 91, 100, 151, 153, 158
British Domination 3, 15, 151
British economic influence 151, 170
British economic legacy 141, 181
British economic sphere 151
British economic values 173
British economy 94, 123, 171
British Embassy 32, 48, 74, 105, 107, 120, 134
British Empire 71, 150, 163, 168
British energy companies 128, 165, 201–203
British engineers 50–51
British equipment 56, 92, 156
British expatriates 4–6, 33, 53, 58, 122–123, 134, 141, 173

Index 215

British expats 126, 166
British expertise 47, 83, 167, 170, 176, 183, 196, 209
British expert power 38, 78, 174, 179
British exports 118, 137, 156, 207
British FDI 122, 136, 143
British financial institutions 170, 193
British footprint 1, 131, 158, 174
British forces 18, 39, 72, 77, 89, 91
British foreign policy 2, 95
British Government 18–22, 32–35, 44, 46–50, 57–63, 71–78, 80–83, 85–90, 92–98, 103–104, 116–124, 126–131, 134–136, 139–141, 156–157, 170–180, 182–183, 195–200, 202–205, 207–209
British hard power 23, 42, 86, 99
British hegemony 1, 114, 181, 193
British individuals 8, 81, 135, 167, 178
British interests 25, 44, 88, 93, 100, 123, 135, 203
British investments 134, 166, 179
British involvement 4, 8, 18, 32, 104, 136, 165, 191
British legacy 32, 36, 40, 58, 61, 72, 126, 182, 204
British Loan Service Personnel 45, 49
British long-term military support 60
British LSPs 46–48, 50, 52
British-manufactured weapons 39, 60, 120, 162, 197
British manufacturers 50–51, 91, 94, 96, 116–117, 120, 142, 155, 157–158, 161–162, 196, 198–199, 203, 206, 209
British military 42, 45, 48, 52, 57, 59, 81, 88–89, 100, 102, 193, 195, 197–198
British military academies 34, 36, 61, 72, 78, 195
British military activities 23, 31
British military advisors 203
British Military Assistance 48, 65, 68
British military officials 39, 49, 194
British military personnel 32, 34, 50, 78, 197
British military procedures 34, 81
British military strategy in Bahrain 89
British military withdrawal 48, 73
British money 129, 141, 203
British officers 5, 39, 50, 60, 81, 195
British officials 2, 18, 24, 62, 71, 75, 85, 93, 96–97, 136, 182–183
British organisations 133, 182
British policy 63, 71, 95, 183, 197, 209
British policy makers 60, 116
British policymakers 25, 42, 84, 209

British policymaking 94, 102
British power 1–3, 19–27, 90–91, 95, 97, 101, 114, 116, 141–142, 144, 151, 154, 191–211
British power dimension 113–149
British PR companies 97–98, 104
British private companies 2, 10, 206
British private sector companies 62, 167, 182, 201
British private sector involvement 131, 202
British protection 32, 41, 70, 101
British relationship 70, 179, 192
British representatives 71, 77, 153
British role 72, 126
British security 57, 82, 90
British service personnel 46, 196
British smart power 58, 176, 197, 209
British soft power 47, 50, 78, 80–81, 85, 118, 126, 168, 170, 195, 202
British soft power attraction 197
British soft power tools 9
British sphere 70, 140, 142, 183
British strategic capabilities 61
British strategic influence 62, 194
British suppliers 56, 92, 95, 140, 160
British support 7, 21, 60, 122, 139
British tactics 45, 50, 77–78, 81–82, 197
British tanks 51, 157
British technology 52, 92
British trade 3, 119, 139, 146, 148, 200, 209
British training 36, 73, 78
British troops 32–34, 39, 42–43, 47, 52, 59, 62, 72, 76, 81, 86, 193, 195–197
British universities 38, 172–173
British values 42, 138, 173, 177, 180
British weapons 55, 116, 120, 158
British withdrawal 4–6, 53, 141, 165, 203

Cabinet Office 14–15, 210–211
cadets 38, 72, 78
capabilities 2, 10–12, 23, 36, 41, 43–44, 99, 170, 176, 195, 198
capacity 12, 78, 93, 102
capacity building initiative 173
China 19, 22, 26, 45, 100, 132, 140, 143, 170, 179
Chinese 58, 145, 148
City of London 53, 171, 173, 183, 204
close cooperation 33, 39, 85, 100, 209
coerce 42, 47, 164
coercion 9, 11, 153, 173
collaboration 21, 23, 63, 86, 98, 170, 183

216 *Index*

Colonel Dennison 5
Colonel Ian Henderson 8, 72
Colonel Tim Landon 6
Combined Maritime Forces 101, 103
commercialisation 62, 204–206
commercial relationships 117, 205
commercial treaties 113–114
commitments 34, 41, 43, 59, 62–63, 71, 74–75, 81, 103, 117, 119, 176–177, 187, 199, 207–208
competition 12–13, 96, 99, 127–128, 132, 146, 149, 157, 162, 174, 182
competitors 95, 119, 144, 147, 160, 170
concerted effort 74–75, 132
conflict 10, 40, 43, 64, 66, 70, 76, 80, 155, 210–211
Conflict, Stability and Security Fund *see* CSSF
Conservative administrations 52, 56, 58, 161, 172, 177, 180, 182, 192, 195, 200
Conservative governments 41, 181–182
consultants 97, 131, 167, 178
contemporary influence 5, 76, 89, 103, 114
contemporary relationship 93, 99, 102, 169, 182
contractors 51, 164, 176
convergence 95, 142, 198, 200
cooperation 43, 45, 77, 80–82, 85–86, 89–91, 98, 100, 171, 173, 177–178, 196–197, 200; covert 44; financial 11, 172, 183, 204; formal 135; historic 87; joint 173; strategic 91; voluntary 32, 58
cooperation agreement 170
Cooperation Council 186, 190
coterie 39, 143, 194
counter-insurgency 20, 26–27
coup 6, 14–15, 39, 64, 66, 145, 147
covert 20, 44, 57, 98, 119
credit 86, 118, 187
Cross-Government Approach 64, 66
CSSF (Conflict, Stability and Security Fund) 40, 64, 66, 80–81, 210

decision makers 9–10, 93, 95–96, 100, 120, 133, 135, 137, 139, 142, 156, 161, 194
decisions 12, 21, 54, 56, 58–59, 81, 119, 150, 153, 157, 198
DEFE 26–27, 65, 67–68
defence 33–34, 42–43, 52, 54–55, 61, 65–69, 92–93, 99, 101–102, 104–105, 107–108, 119–120, 132, 143–144, 148

defence agreements 85, 100
Defence and Security Equipment International (DSEI) 161
defence capabilities 115, 155
defence cooperation 11, 66, 200
defence economics 93–95, 97, 160
defence equipment 39, 50, 52, 54, 57, 61, 91, 121, 161–162, 203
Defence exports 96, 137, 144, 147, 154
defence infrastructure 82, 122
defence legacy 155
defence manufacturers 81, 193
defence manufacturing 117, 198
defence partnerships 62, 209
defence policy 32, 61, 63, 65, 68, 71, 93
defence procurement 51, 81
defence prosperity 93
defence relations 120, 163
defence relationship 60, 73, 86, 204
defence sales 50, 54, 66, 68, 92–94, 116, 153, 156–157, 174, 184–185, 189–190
Defence Secretary 62, 66, 93, 207
Defence Security Cooperation Agency 185, 187–188
defence trade 114, 116–117, 120, 152, 155
defender 59, 75, 103
Department for International Trade 121, 145–147, 185, 188, 209
Department of Trade 135, 176–177, 186, 189
dependence 90, 94, 115, 203
deployment 62, 75, 101, 193, 196
development 4–5, 7–8, 14–15, 17, 20–21, 38–39, 58–61, 82–84, 86, 103–104, 114–115, 122–123, 126, 131–132, 138–139, 149–151, 153–189, 192–194, 200–201, 203–205
Dhofar 18–24, 49, 123–124, 201
Dhofar Campaign 26–27
Dhofar conflict 104, 195
Dhofar Liberation Front *see* DLF
Dhofar Rebellion 18, 26–27, 72, 194
Dhofar War 23, 26–27, 39, 41–42, 46–47, 49–50, 57, 59, 116, 118–119, 192, 195, 208
diplomacy 3, 13, 15–16, 90, 145, 148, 205
divergence 39, 191, 194
diversification 87, 114, 129–131, 146, 148, 163, 167, 174, 176, 180, 182
diversification agenda 126, 129, 143
diversify 6, 85, 95, 126, 128–132, 142, 152, 164–165, 192
DLF (Dhofar Liberation Front) 18–19

Index   217

DSEI (Defence and Security Equipment International) 161
DSO 120–121, 144–145, 147–148, 158, 161
Duqm 25, 58–59, 122, 204
Duqm Port 33, 58–59, 62, 122, 203, 208

ECGD (Export Credits Guarantee Department) 106, 109, 117, 119, 145, 149, 157, 176–179, 199, 202
economic affairs 114–115, 128, 142, 150, 152, 163, 183, 192, 199, 209
economic developments 18, 127–128, 140, 163, 176
economic diversification 124–125, 131, 143, 161, 163, 165, 167, 174–175
Economic diversification in Oman 114–115
economic influence 102, 129, 133, 135–136, 139–140, 142, 144, 150, 169, 183
economic legacy 133, 141, 154, 181
Economic Openness 115, 144, 148
economic partner 136, 174, 203–204
economic power 45, 142, 144, 183, 203
economic priorities 54, 95, 115, 198, 200
economic relations 113, 116, 128, 134, 150, 154
economic relationship 116, 133, 152, 160, 169, 178, 182, 208
economic support 23, 174, 176, 179
education 35–36, 39, 60, 76, 78, 132, 167, 173, 175
energy 132, 138, 143
energy companies 205, 209
energy sector 63, 115, 122–123, 128–130, 139–140, 164, 200
engagement 57, 161
equipment 48, 50, 54–56, 91–92, 94, 96–97, 120, 155–156, 159, 161, 185, 187, 195, 198
exclusivity agreements 91, 93, 136, 157, 163–164, 191, 193
expansion 13, 45, 86, 95, 175, 208
experience 23, 48, 87, 162, 166, 180
expert 10, 20, 57–58, 172
expertise 8, 10, 126–128, 130, 132, 135, 163, 165, 169–171, 177, 180, 183, 191, 201–202
expert power 2, 10, 35, 40, 47, 72, 74, 80, 165–166, 168, 183–184
export credits 174–175, 177, 182, 199–200, 202, 205, 209
Export Credits Guarantee Department *see* ECGD

export finance 121, 129, 179, 202, 207
export financing 3, 115–116, 119, 122, 179, 202
exports 9, 12, 93, 96, 115, 118, 120, 138, 146, 149, 177

FCDO 63, 114, 180, 199
FCO 40, 63–69, 73, 80–81, 92, 104–109, 136, 156, 179–181, 184–185, 188–190
FDI 132, 137–139, 143, 203
finance 130–131, 139, 151, 169, 172–173, 186, 206
finance sector 167, 172, 183
financial market cooperation 167
First Gulf War 32, 43
Foreign & Commonwealth Office 63, 69, 106–107, 187–188
Foreign Affairs 15–16, 64, 68, 152, 162, 185, 189
Foreign Direct Investment 137, 146–149, 203
foreign investment 141, 147, 149
foreign policy 4, 9–10, 13, 60–61, 65–68, 88, 106, 108–109, 174, 185–186, 189
formalisation 20, 75
formation 4, 48, 136, 194
France 3–4, 6, 44, 50, 91, 96, 100, 106, 108, 158, 160, 170, 176
French influence 153
Friendship 8, 31, 71, 73

gas industry 115, 127–128, 130, 164
GCC 33, 88, 140, 166, 208
Global Britain 61, 66–67, 181, 186–188, 209
goods 136–137, 139–140, 146, 149, 163, 177, 182, 200, 206
goods and services 136–137, 139, 146, 182, 206
Government Communication Service 144, 148
growth 71, 137, 197
Gulf rulers 34, 75, 191, 193
Gulf Security Policy 7, 14, 16
Gulf Shaikhdoms 63, 68, 104, 108
Gulf states 1–2, 10, 31, 33, 35, 83–84, 101–104, 153–154, 160–161, 163–164, 175, 191–196, 198–200, 203–205, 207–208

hard power assets 50, 92, 122, 126, 209
hard power characteristics 89
Hawk Aircraft 92, 96, 118
hegemon 12, 83, 103, 164

218 Index

hegemonic influence 119, 193
hegemony 3, 12, 43, 54, 70, 181, 196, 198, 203
historic position 6, 83, 98, 122
HM Government 64, 66–67, 105, 108
HMS Jufair 87, 91, 93, 100
human rights projection 138

implementation 19–20, 98, 130–131, 141, 166–167, 208
Implementation Support 131, 146, 148
imports 115, 138, 145, 149, 175, 201
India 7, 45, 70–71, 132, 137, 140, 142–144, 147, 150–151
individuals 10, 39, 50, 61, 82, 98, 100, 121–122, 134, 194
inducements 9, 199; financial 119, 183, 198; monetary 117
industry 127–128, 132, 147, 165, 201
infrastructure 129, 178, 194
infrastructure projects 119, 175
instability 64, 66, 129, 139
institutions, financial 167–169, 183, 204
intelligence 5, 7, 44–45, 60, 80, 82–83
intelligence cooperation 45, 83
interconnectedness 90
interconnectivity 133
interdependence 38, 184, 189
interests 9, 12, 92, 100, 102, 106–107, 156–157, 169–170, 174, 177, 182, 194, 197
internationalisation 95, 100
International Trade 106–107, 114, 121, 136, 145–148, 179, 185, 188, 209
intervention 88, 96, 98, 167, 177, 183
investments 62, 66, 131–132, 134–135, 139, 141, 143, 145, 147, 163, 166, 168, 171, 201–203
ISS 44–45

jobs 114, 119, 122, 129, 131
joint exercises 44, 52, 89, 196–197
joint training exercises 42, 61–63, 142, 156, 183, 196–198
joint venture 164, 166
Juffair 58, 99, 102, 193
justice reform 40, 80, 180

key contributors 57, 114, 167

labour 74, 95, 131, 182
legacy 1, 33, 35, 120–121, 162, 178, 181, 191–192, 194, 196, 200, 203, 205

leverage 35, 95, 177, 179
limitations 76, 88, 92, 98, 177, 206
loaning 52, 60, 65, 68
loans 117–118, 179, 199, 209
loan service personnel 32, 48, 50
LSPs 45–47, 49–50, 52, 60–61, 65, 68

Magna Carta Fund 98, 179–180
military academies 38, 45, 199
military affairs 4, 31, 35, 39, 46–47, 75, 90
military assets 12, 100, 103
military assistance 4, 159
military bases 194
military equipment 51, 53, 120
military exercises 43, 63, 88, 209; joint 42, 81, 208
military influence 13, 47, 169
military interventions 9, 164
military officials 19, 81, 155
Military partnerships 72, 82
military personnel 21, 49–50, 91
military protection 70–71, 89, 193
military sphere 81, 90
military strategies 12, 88
military strength 9, 137
military structures 57
military support 23, 47
military tactics 34, 43, 56, 77
military technology 10, 159
military training 11, 34–36, 39, 44, 56, 61, 74, 196
mindset 18, 39, 57, 78, 82, 90, 113, 116, 126, 143, 191
Ministry of Defence 66, 105, 107–108, 144, 148, 209
Ministry of Overseas Development 104, 109
missiles 94, 155, 159–160
modernising 192, 199
multidimensional relationship 35, 175
Mumtalakat 171
Muscat 3–4, 13, 15, 20, 24, 31, 63–68, 120–121, 131, 134, 142, 144–149, 210–211

National Centre for Statistics and Information (NCSI) 136, 147, 149
National Security Capability Review 209–211
natural gas 139, 146, 148
naval base 58, 100, 102, 122
NCSI (National Centre for Statistics and Information) 136, 147, 149

Index 219

Ninth Five-Year Development Plan 124, 146–147
Northern Ireland 13, 40–41, 80, 104, 108, 186–187

OBFA (Omani British Friendship Association) 133–134
offering financial support 161, 175, 199
officers, seconded 36, 64, 67, 107
officer training 37, 79
oil companies 123, 164, 185, 187
oil dependence 130, 146, 148
oil exports 117, 122, 124–125, 201
oil revenues 4, 124, 132
oil sector 124, 129
Oman 1–7, 11, 13–27, 31–70, 72–73, 80–81, 84, 86, 88, 113–150, 156, 161, 163, 191–210
Oman Drydock Company 122, 136
Omani affairs 3, 18, 23, 32, 66, 200–201
Omani authorities 41, 45, 59, 140
Omani British Friendship Association *see* OBFA
Omani business community 134
Omani businesses 133–134
Omani cadets 38, 51
Omani diversification agenda 129–130, 203
Omani economy 114–115, 127–128, 131, 136, 141–142
Omani exports 118, 137
Omani governments 25, 33, 40, 44, 46–48, 51, 56–57, 121, 136, 141, 204
Omani militaries 2, 22, 34–35, 38, 41, 43, 45, 48–50, 52, 60, 63
Omani prosperity 113–149
Omani relationship 3, 31, 41, 44–45, 47, 50
Omanis 24, 32, 35–39, 42–43, 45–48, 50–52, 54–55, 57–58, 60–61, 64–67, 114, 116–117, 124, 127–129, 134, 192–193, 198–200
Omanisation 48, 141
Omanisation policies 49–50, 65, 141
Omani security 62, 119
Omani security affairs 41, 200
Omani Sultans 3, 66, 142
Omani troops 20, 33, 46, 48, 52, 59–60
Oman's Air Force 53
Oman's Armed Forces 18
Oman's defence 49
Oman's defence spending 117
Oman's diversification policies 139
Oman's GDP 115, 124

Oman's intelligence cooperation 44
Oman's officer training academy 39
Oman's oil 122, 128
Oman's oil industry 123
Oman Trade & Investment Forum 147, 149
Outward Bound Oman 53
Overseas Development 104, 109

partnerships 13, 33–34, 45, 82, 120, 126, 131, 182
PDO (Petroleum Development Oman) 122–124, 126–128, 201
Persian Gulf 7, 14, 16, 22, 31, 63, 68, 70, 73, 184, 187–189
Persian Gulf States 7, 145, 148
personnel, loaned 33, 46, 48
persuasion 39, 105, 109, 145, 149
Persuasion and Power 105, 109, 145, 149
Petroleum Development Oman *see* PDO
police training 40, 80
police training missions 80
policy implications 144, 208
Political Authority 104, 108, 184, 189
political power 14, 16, 181, 191
Political Resident 31, 63, 68, 70, 123
power 1–2, 4–18, 23–24, 39–41, 70, 86–88, 90, 101–105, 109, 115–116, 128–129, 141–145, 152–154, 157, 173, 179–184, 189, 194, 197–198, 200–203; capability 195; clientelist 202; coercive 10, 70; colonial 121; co-optive 170; covert 11; defined 11; direct 122; hard 10, 12–13, 15, 17, 32, 34, 85, 92, 94, 96, 103–104, 139, 142, 176–177, 197–198; referent 9, 52–53, 92–93, 116, 162
power base 10
power capabilities 2, 62, 73, 89, 154, 203
power differentiation 193
power dimension 121
Power Elite 153, 184, 190
power in Oman 1, 18, 35, 142–143
power legacy 1, 71, 119, 193
power of money 114–210
power politics 181
power projection 62, 90, 103, 210; soft 207
PR companies 97, 106
private companies 95, 99, 124, 127, 136, 154, 175, 179, 205–206
private sector 58, 63, 100, 119, 124, 130–131, 166–167, 182–183, 200, 204–205, 207

private sector assistance 117
private sector companies 1, 171, 178, 192, 200, 204
privatisation 131, 166–167, 175, 183, 192, 204, 210–211
privileged position 18, 52, 72, 74, 136, 199–200, 202
programmes 131, 143, 173–174, 181
promotions 131, 135, 152, 181
prosperity 93, 114–115, 123, 150, 181
protection 59, 63, 68, 70, 88, 93, 99, 102, 104, 108, 113, 184, 189
protector 34, 91, 193
protectorate 71, 153, 192
PSNI 64, 67, 80
PSNI Training Assistance 64, 67
purchase weapons 155, 157

Qaboos 3–6, 14–15, 20–21, 23–24, 35, 39, 41, 45–48, 54, 56–57, 59, 61, 114, 117–119, 123–124, 126–127, 143, 194–195, 207–208
Qaboos' accession 23, 34–35, 117–118, 120, 122, 207

RAF 19, 21, 42
RAF College Cranwell 36–37, 64, 67, 107
RAF Cranwell 36, 38, 64, 67, 78–79
recognition 61, 74, 99, 129, 144, 151, 169, 210
re-engagement 75, 88, 90, 101, 155, 160, 192, 204
reform agenda 98, 174, 176
reform programmes 174, 180
reforms 40, 174–175, 179, 181, 184, 189; economic 24, 179, 181; political 20, 138
regulations 132, 170, 186
relational power 11, 115, 123, 177, 202
relationship: historic 45, 57, 161; special 42, 44, 178
relationship shift 52, 87
relevance 39, 166, 183, 197, 203
reliance 4–5, 31–32, 47, 130, 132, 152, 155–156, 167, 169, 171–172, 177, 180, 183, 196–198, 201
reliance on oil 130, 177
reliant 1, 3–4, 36, 101–102, 124, 130, 132, 168, 173, 181, 207–208
re-pivot 58, 90, 104
representation 10, 135, 158
representatives 2, 92, 129, 150, 161, 181, 200
reputation 97, 202

request assistance 167, 170
Residency states 157
Residency system 62, 123
responsibility 62, 84, 93, 99, 136, 192, 197, 205, 207
restrictions 86, 141, 168, 206
retained hegemony 157
RMA Sandhurst 35–38, 64, 67, 78, 104, 108
RMTT (Royal Marines Training Team) 75–76, 87, 104, 108
RNC Britannia 38, 64, 67
ROP (Royal Oman Police) 39–41, 64, 68
Royal Dutch Shell 122, 124, 145, 148, 201
Royal Marines 22, 86
Royal Marines Training Team *see* RMTT
Royal Navy 71, 87, 89, 101–104, 209
Royal Oman Police *see* ROP

SAF 19, 23, 43, 46–47, 50, 53
Saif Saarea 38, 41–44, 52, 58, 63, 86, 88, 120, 156, 196, 209
sale of arms 86, 142
sale of arms to Oman 142
Sandhurst 21, 35–39, 51, 64, 78–79
Sandhurst Connection 35, 64, 67
SAS 20–23, 72–74
SAS Group 104, 107
SAS training exercise 74
SAS training team 75
SAS troops 20, 72
Saudi Arabia 87–88, 117, 120, 145, 148, 155, 164, 175, 194, 201
secondment 6, 45–46, 61, 130, 159, 173, 195
Secretary of State for International Trade 106–107, 136
security 4, 6, 11–13, 29, 32–69, 71–72, 74–109, 147–148, 189, 192–193, 195, 197, 206, 209–211; domestic 18, 45, 72, 80; national 12, 15–16, 93, 95, 123
security cooperation 45, 83, 86
security infrastructure 56, 193
security relations 74, 87–88
security relationship 58, 60, 70, 83
Security Review 89, 93, 105–106, 108–109
security sphere 81, 85
security training 39, 41, 72, 80, 196
sentiment 35, 46, 57, 113–114, 116, 142, 161, 195
Shell 62, 117, 122–124, 126–128, 130, 134, 143, 194, 201, 205
Shell's PDO operations 126

shift 32, 34, 40, 47–49, 113–114, 129–130, 133, 160, 162, 167, 178, 204–205, 207
ships 42, 58–59, 70, 101, 103, 106, 108, 120, 196
signatory states 113
smart power 13, 15–17, 85, 94, 100, 142, 146, 149, 158–159, 192, 198
SOAF 22, 47–51, 53–55, 60, 118–119, 142, 197–198, 206, 208
soft power 9, 13–17, 42, 58–59, 75, 85–86, 92, 94–95, 98–100, 104–106, 108–109, 121–122, 128–129, 135–136, 138, 145–146, 149, 162–163, 165–169, 173–176; economic 161, 164, 200
soft power attraction 121, 139, 158, 198, 209
soft power influence 75, 77–78, 84, 90, 92, 95, 171–172, 179, 182–183, 192, 195, 197, 199, 201–202
soft power strength 114, 117, 135, 158
Soviet Union 19, 22
stability 33, 88, 192, 194
Strategic Defence and Security Review 89, 93, 105–106, 108–109
strategic engagement 31–69
strategic influence 1, 57, 61–62, 76, 115, 154, 193
strategic legacy 193, 197
strategic priorities 95, 100, 181, 197, 200, 204
strategic relationship 54, 99, 120, 204
strategic withdrawal 104
Suez 32, 34, 57–59, 63, 67, 72, 99, 106, 109, 194, 197, 203, 210–211
Sultan Haitham 39, 45, 57, 207
Sultan of Oman's Air Force 53
Sultan of Oman's Armed Forces 18
Sultan Qaboos 2, 4–6, 23–25, 32, 34–35, 42, 44, 49, 51, 53–54, 56, 140–142, 192–194, 207, 209
Sultan Sa'id 4, 18–19, 41
Sultan's Armed Forces 5, 45–46, 64, 68, 194
Sultan's government 20, 115, 126, 129, 131, 198
supplier 55, 60, 91, 95, 157, 160, 163, 208
support for arms sales 119
support projects 174–175

tactics 19–20, 35, 72, 160, 195
technical assistance 76, 95, 165, 180, 185, 189
technical assistance programmes 77, 165, 179

terrorism 60, 186, 188
theory of power 11, 13, 141, 157, 173, 176, 192
threats 10, 18, 40, 44, 59, 87, 90, 95, 100, 139
TNA 26–27, 63, 65–69, 104–105, 107–109, 184–190
tourism 126, 131, 175
trade 2, 13, 44, 57, 101, 111–148, 150–154, 156–210
trade hegemony 33
trade policy 96
training and development 76, 104, 108
training exercises 42–44, 86, 196
transition 1–2, 41, 48, 58, 60, 177, 184, 189, 194, 204
treaties 1, 31, 34, 45, 47, 71, 73, 113, 144, 147, 152
Trucial Oman Scouts 18, 46, 50–51, 64, 67, 116
trust 34, 44, 56, 59, 82, 89, 162, 170–171, 194–196, 198–199, 202
Typhoons 118–119

UAE 44, 64, 67, 84, 105, 107, 134, 137, 143, 156, 203
UKEF 118–119, 147, 149
UK Export Finance 106, 145, 147, 149
UK Government 40, 53, 94, 118–119
UKIFC 173, 186, 190
UK Joint Logistics Support Base 25, 58
UK MoD 36, 43, 46, 72, 76, 83, 114, 156
United Kingdom Maritime Component Command 100
United States Fifth Fleet 88
unrivalled influence 99, 102, 153, 203
US companies 54, 164, 197
US Government 159, 164
US military academies 195
US military assistance 159
US Naval Forces Central Command 88, 91
US Navy 87, 193
US training 198

Valiant 157, 184, 189

weapons 18, 21, 50–51, 53–54, 56, 91–94, 96–97, 99, 117, 142, 154–158, 160, 162, 195–196, 198
withdrawal 1–6, 33–35, 40–41, 45–47, 49–50, 54–56, 59–60, 71–78, 82–89, 91, 93, 96–97, 99–100, 141–142, 150–154, 160–164, 178–179, 181–183, 192–198, 203–205

Printed in the United States
by Baker & Taylor Publisher Services